# *PRETTY RIBBONS*

# *Contents*

Hans-Michael Herzog

# *Serious Play: Donigan Cumming Photographs Nettie Harris*

# *PRETTY*

**Donigan Cumming**

# *RIBBONS*

*Edited by Hans-Michael Herzog*

EDITION STEMMLE

Only rarely does Nettie look at the photographer, and even then her gazes pass through or beyond him. Her eyes are closed most of the time in an expression of mute devotion that has nothing to do with submissiveness. She seems fully collected, concentrated, totally at one with herself and content to accept her own existence. Nettie has no message to proclaim. Surely she knows that her body commands a more eloquent language than her tongue could ever speak.

Nettie carried the touchingly innocent, natural grace of a young girl with her into old age. Nevertheless, her posture, gestures and facial expressions remind us again and again how well aware she is of her staged self-depiction. After all, it was Nettie herself who struck the poses within the situations created by Donigan Cumming in his photographs. "As a film actress, her mannerisms and dramatic expressions can be disruptive. I have never tried to curb Nettie's urge to improvise since I discovered the compelling images in the spaces between her gestures and moods." (Cumming, 1990) "Pretty Ribbons" is concerned with her self-portrayal on her own stage, with her life itself. While she does act in these scenes, she does not play the part of an actress; instead she takes up in great earnest the various roles that make up her own person, remaining fully aware of the serious nature of her play. Conscious of the reality of her existence, she does not attempt to flee from it but rather to depict it. At the same time her staged playing counteracts the gravity of the situation, the serious side of her life.

The artist became acquainted with Nettie Harris in 1982. In the following years, she became his most important model. Her husband having died, her children grown, the former journalist sought work as a film actress. The two began to work together. Gradually, a sense of mutual respect took form and eventually grew to become a relationship of trust which provided the foundation for "Pretty Ribbons", the photo series presented here. The "pretty ribbons" are not to be taken literally; the viewer of these photographs will search for them in vain. Yet they may perhaps be found in the slowly developing ties of tenderness between the photographer and his model.

Nettie's physical and psychic presence is breathtaking. Her desolate corporeality nevertheless evokes hope. Desperation and comforting security are united in one; vulnerability and triumphant strength stand side by side. Nettie's repertoire ranges from slapstick comedy and amusing irony to scurrilous and absurd situations and even to black humor and crude shock effects. There are only a very few pictures in the history of photography capable of etching themselves in the viewer's memory so deeply as that of Nettie standing with her panty hose hanging from mid-thigh in front of her open, full refrigerator (Page 31). Her laughter in this photo-

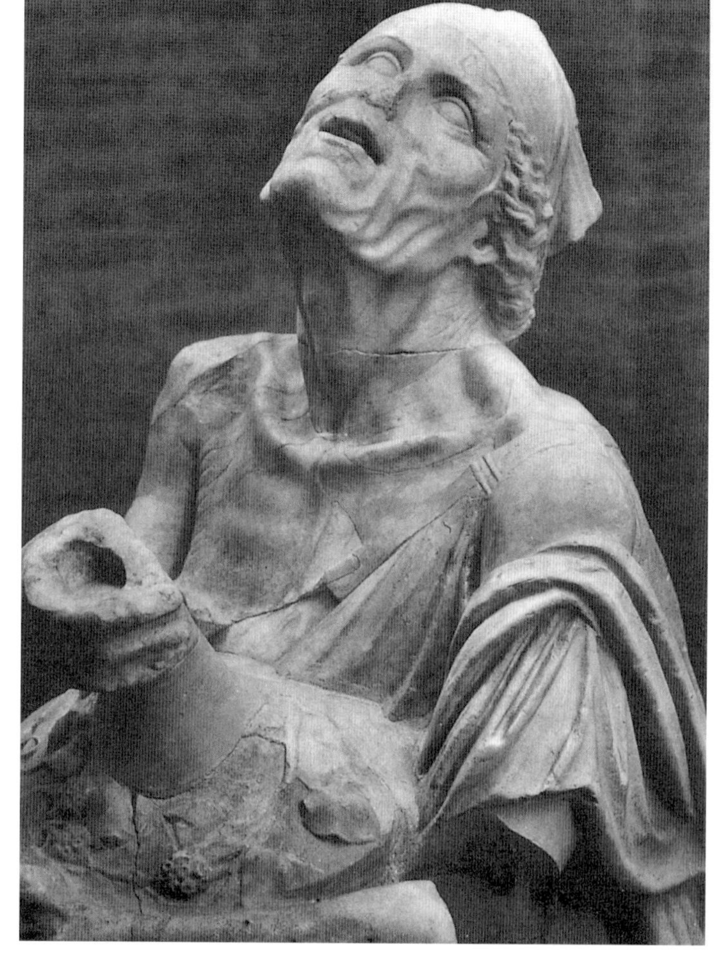

**Ill. 1:** Drunken Old Woman
Roman copy based on an original dated circa 190 B. C.
Paros marble, height: 92 cm, Glyptothek, Munich

graph is demoniacal, a grotesque grimace of exaltation. She plays out the aspect of crassness in the situation to the hilt. The tawdriness of ageing flesh, a senseless consumerist sellout and grinning, naked death form a united front that no viewer can possibly ignore. In contrast, relief is provided by a photo showing Nettie leaning, cheerful and relaxed – as if during a break in shooting – on the shoulder of a male model and smoking a cigarette in an attitude of apparent amusement with a hint of overconfidence, much like a young girl in the mood for fun (Page 59).

Again and again, the images of Nettie Harris speak of the grey areas of life, of severe exhaustion, of sleep, of weariness of life and of death. Some of the horizontal positions she assumes suggest both the comfort and security of the embryo and the soft approach of death at the same time. Nettie's body shown reclining in a fetal posture alludes to both a prenatal coming-to-life and prehistoric burial rites. Lying in the grass, her limbs extended (Page 85), her body converses privately with death, just as in the photograph showing her in the bathtub (Page 54) with a face reminiscent of a death mask. Nettie was aware of her latent proximity to death, and she never excluded it from her serious play. While the images of Nettie associated with death are dramatic and highly expressive, they are totally devoid of pathos. Their sheer immediacy prevents them from turning to kitsch.

Nettie's sexuality is a matter of interest as well, most notably in the photographs showing her together with male models who are usually nude. Not without a certain amount of vanity and coquettishness, Nettie's body signals that she is aware of its sensual qualities and quite capable of putting them to use. These pictures are disturbing and shocking in a society which encloses sex in old age firmly in taboo and which is only now beginning to examine this issue, truly an everyday concern, in all of its social ramifications. Nettie's intense involvement with her own physical nature is a major theme in "Pretty Ribbons". Her spectrum extends from desperate attempts at humor to tragi-comical, clownish distortions and on to images of grace, beauty and tenderness. Again and again we are reminded of the close intimacy that underlay the relationship between Nettie Harris and Donigan Cumming and must certainly be regarded as a necessary precondition for the model's ability to open herself without reservation to her photographer. Much more intimate and subject to even stronger taboos than the exposure of her ageing, naked body, for example, is the scene showing Nettie holding her false teeth in front of her mouth, in a sense the ultimate proof of her trust in her male documentarian (Pages 40/41).

Merciless realism is also evident in the photograph showing both a spotlight that illuminates

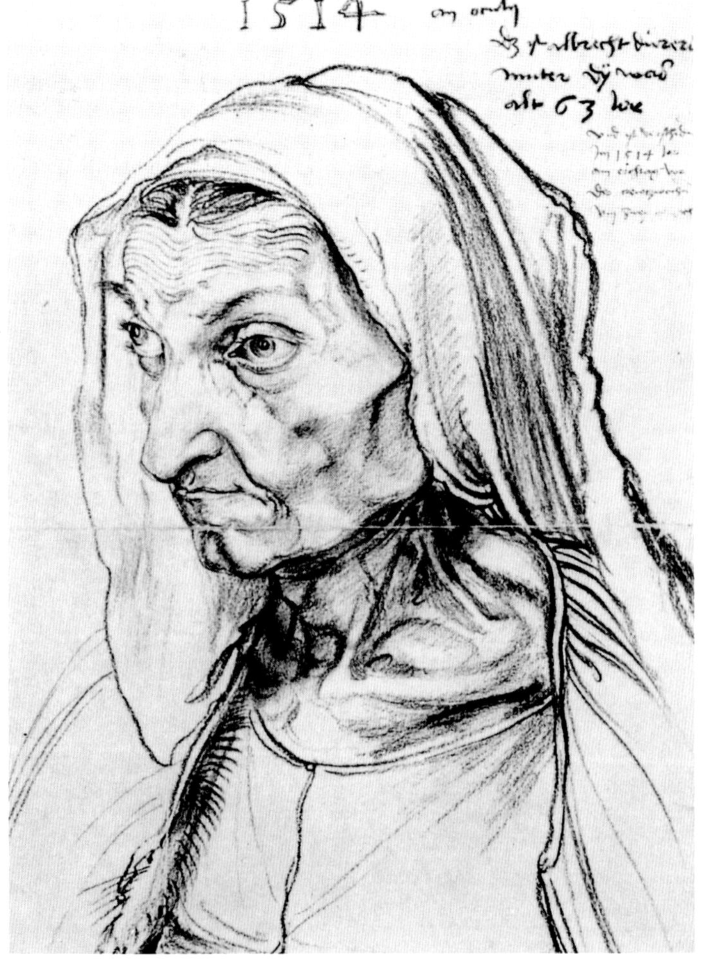


**Ill. 2:** Albrecht Dürer, Die Mutter des Künstlers (The Artist's Mother), 1514
Charcoal, 42,3 x 30,5 cm, Kupferstichkabinett, SMPK, Berlin

the scene and Nettie, cavorting like a spirit through the room (Page 26). Not only does this picture allude to the technical process of producing the photographs, it also emphasizes in an impressive manner the numerous trials and tribulations that process entails. The photographer's loving concern for his model is revealed in pictures such as that showing Nettie's head inclined to one side as if in sleep (Page 37). In another photo, where Nettie is seen putting her hair up, one has the impression that Donigan Cumming is (photographically) caressing the back of her neck (Page 46). The strong emotional bond is clearly evident in the color photograph showing the severely wrinkled area around Nettie's eyes, with its rays of wrinkles bursting forth triumphantly in every direction (Page 93). Here, Nettie's countless wrinkles and folds, features generally seen as ugly in the conventional view, are transformed effortlessly into an image full of inner beauty and *joie de vivre.*

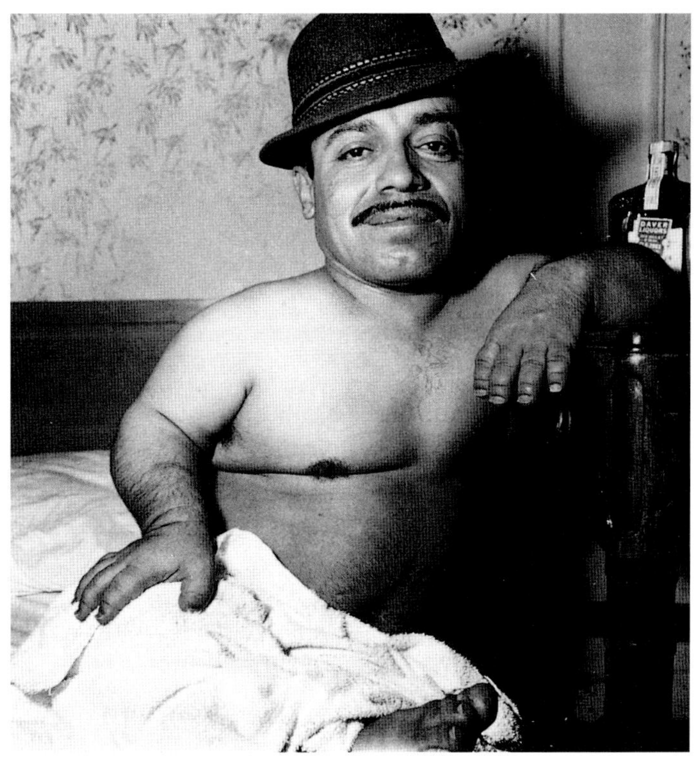

**Ill. 3:** Diane Arbus, Mexican dwarf in his hotel room in N.Y. C., 1970
Photograph

Thus the image of Nettie Harris is reflected in a countless variety of facets, all of which are captured in the abundant subtleties and nuances of "Pretty Ribbons". Nevertheless, the viewer gains an overall impression of Nettie Harris's psycho-physical condition, as one image above all – her own image – begins to crystallize in our minds, an image that, despite its many contradictions and its open-endedness, reveals this particular woman's being in an incredibly open, intense and immediate manner. It is an image full of inner, living beauty that is also experienced by the photographer, an image whose verisimilitude emphatically evokes consternation. False modesty, illusions and fictions cease to exist, having given way to a clarity of vision rarely found in the history of photography or elsewhere (Ills. 1 and 2).

As important as the ambience of Nettie's home, her countless accessories and the male models may be to the individual pictorial creations, they appear secondary in themselves. Ultimately, these things fade from view in Nettie's presence, even though they play a major role in defining the circumstances of her life for us; her surroundings seem almost interchangeable with any others. She herself gives the impression that she has nothing at all to do with her familiar environment. In many of the photos she appears as if cut out and inserted as in a collage. Her strong personality seems to extrapolate on itself. It makes no difference at all whether she is lying amidst the chaos of countless distributed objects on her sofa at home or standing in a landscape. Wherever she is, she seems to have arrived there accidentally and only for a moment. She is

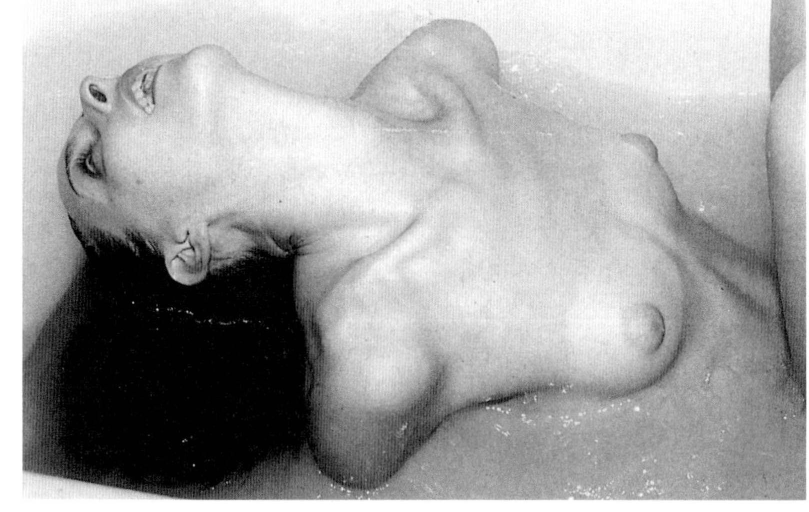

**Ill. 4:** Nan Goldin, Greer in her Bathtub, New York, 1983
Photograph

and remains alone – with her photographer.

The photographer, on the other hand, remains largely in the background. Like a good film director he develops his dramatic sequences, which occupy the viewer in such a way that he hardly takes notice of the author of the images as he contemplates the numerous impressions that present themselves. But despite their apparent spontaneity, Donigan Cumming's ingenious, aesthetically sophisticated pictorial compositions and his keen eye for material-tactile, sensual qualities, masterfully rendered through photography, are irresistibly captivating. A prime example is his treatment of skin, a material of central importance in "Pretty Ribbons". Images of extreme tautness and great symbolic power bear witness to the fact that it is he who knows how first to capture Nettie Harris's psychic being in pictures expressive of general truths and then to condense and intensify them. It is he who unites form and content, appearance and being (Pages 99 and 116). He did not disrupt Nettie's behavior with his photographic intervention in her life; instead he supported and encouraged her serious play, whose playfulness could switch to gravity at any given

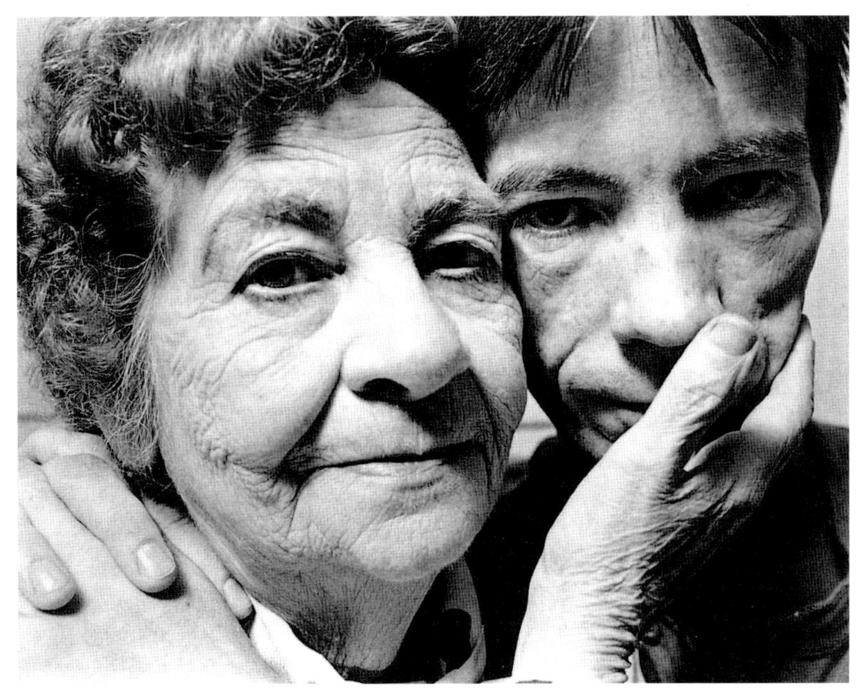

**Ill. 5:** Nicholas Nixon, Catherine and Tom Moran, East Braintree, Massachusetts, 1987
Photograph

moment – much as it does in the absurd theater of Samuel Beckett. In none of these photographs does Donigan Cumming permit himself any judgment of Nettie Harris. This strengthens the documentary character of "Pretty Ribbons", which exists on an equal footing with the artistic quality of the series. Donigan Cumming set out in the early 1980s to counteract the decline and corruption of documentary photography and concerned himself programmatically with the issue in "Reality and Motive in Documentary Photography", one of his most important series of works. He has now accomplished a work of documentary representation in its purest sense.

Such a fascinated and fascinating depiction of grotesque, scurrilous and absurd situations may also be found in the work of Diane Arbus (Ill. 3). Donigan Cumming's photography, however, is less devoted to the exotic appeal of the freakish, which is in fact only one of the many aspects of his work. Nor is there any implication of an exploitive attitude in his work with Nettie; after all, "Pretty Ribbons" is the result of a gradual, sensitive approach towards intimacy with his model over a period of several years. Similar in their immediacy are Nan Goldin's emphatically journalistic photographs, which in comparison to Cumming's works seem much more situation-bound and snapshot-like (Ill. 4). Goldin does not stage her photographs. Her gaze remains more superficial and voyeuristic; only occasionally does she open her view to reveal existential abysses. Nicholas Nixon, in his series entitled "People with Aids", approaches his models in a very quiet, thoughtful, respectful and dignified manner (Ill. 5). While his work has a documentary quality, he does not seek to penetrate his subject to such depths. Closely related in intensity to “Pretty Ribbons” are Ferdinand Hodler’s drawings depicting the suffering and death of his lover Valentine Godé-Darel (Ill. 6). In these we find both intimacy and the incorruptible gaze of an objective chronicler. Much like Hodler in his drawings, Donigan Cumming brings art and documentary together to form an indivisible unity.

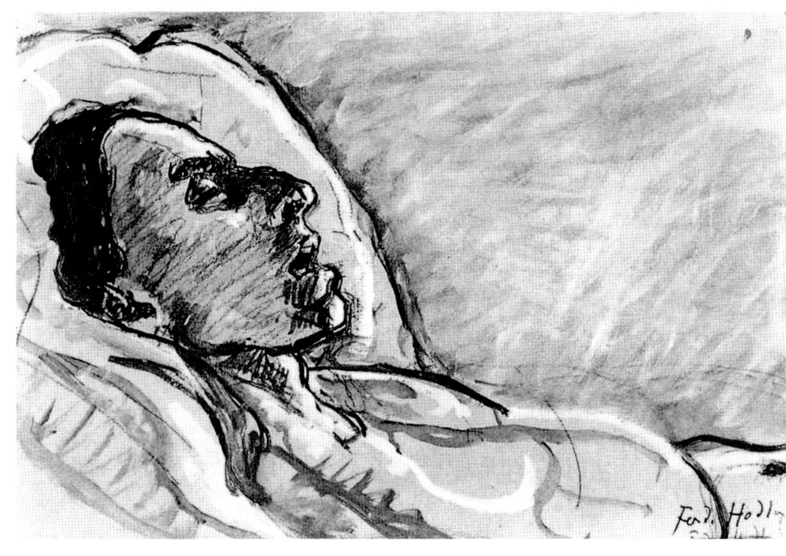

**Ill. 6:** Ferdinand Hodler, Die sterbende Valentine Godé-Darel (Valentine Godé-Darel Approaching Death), right profile, 1915
Gouache, oil and charcoal on paper, 37 x 52 cm, Musée d’Art et d’Histoire, Geneva

# *Plates*

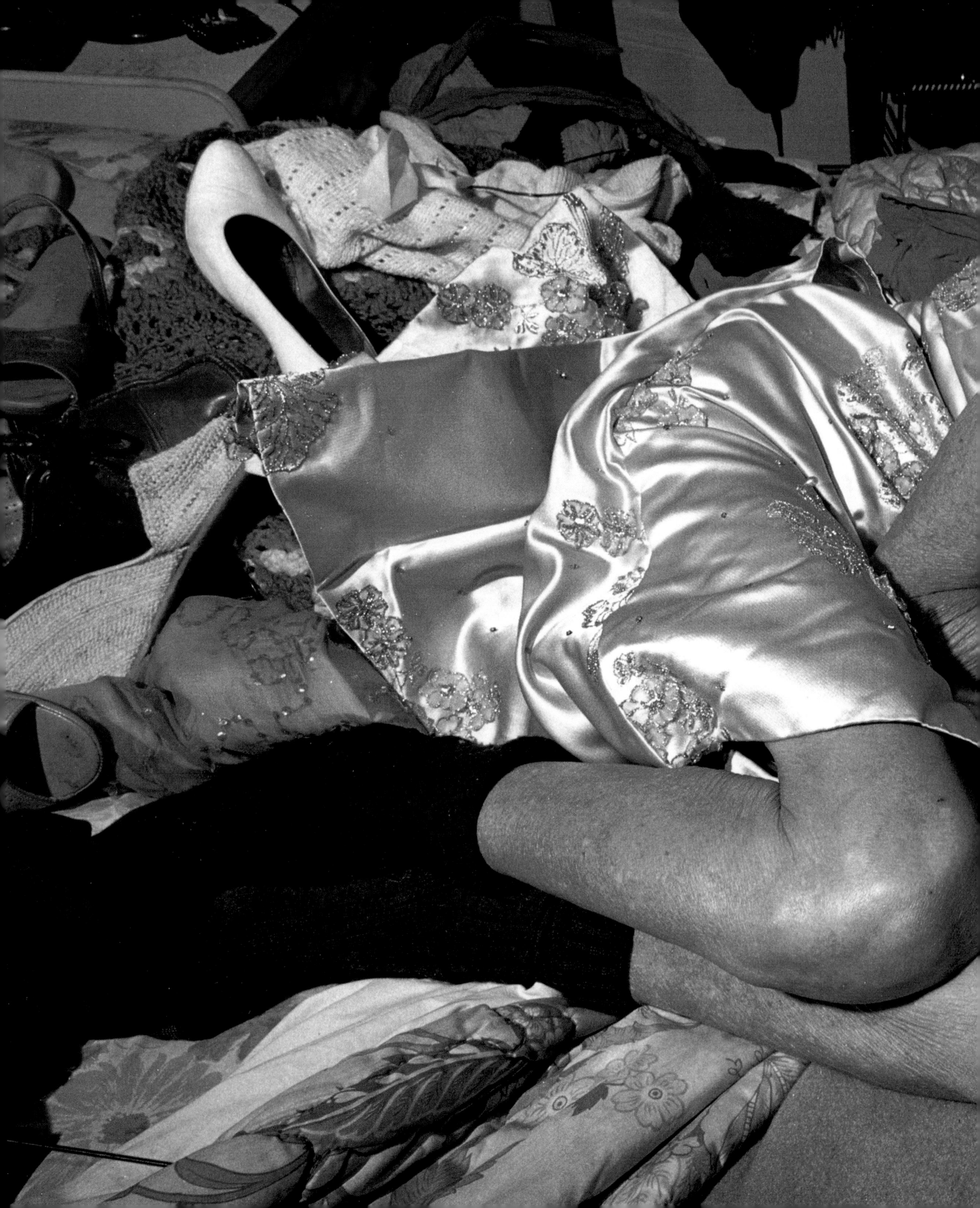

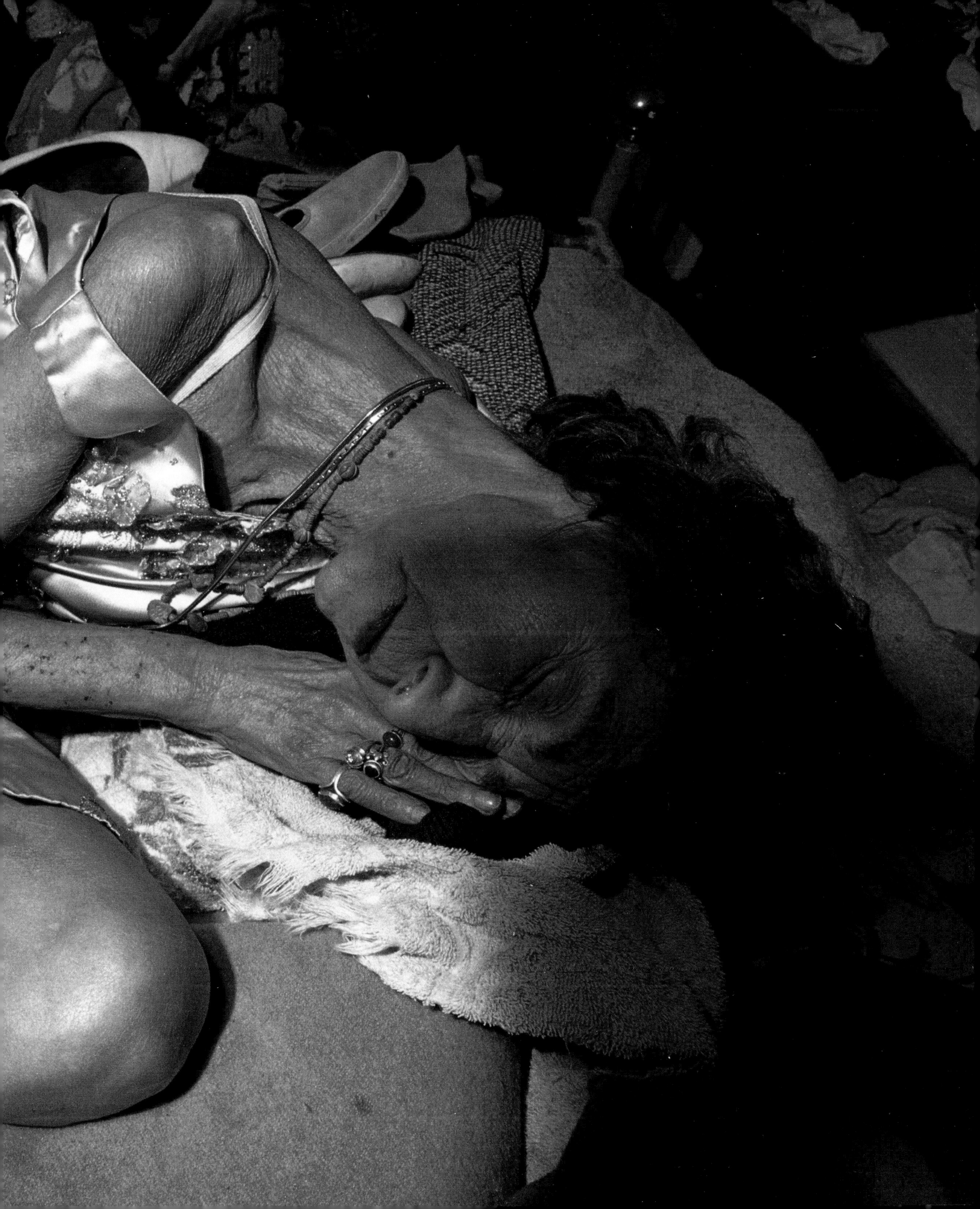

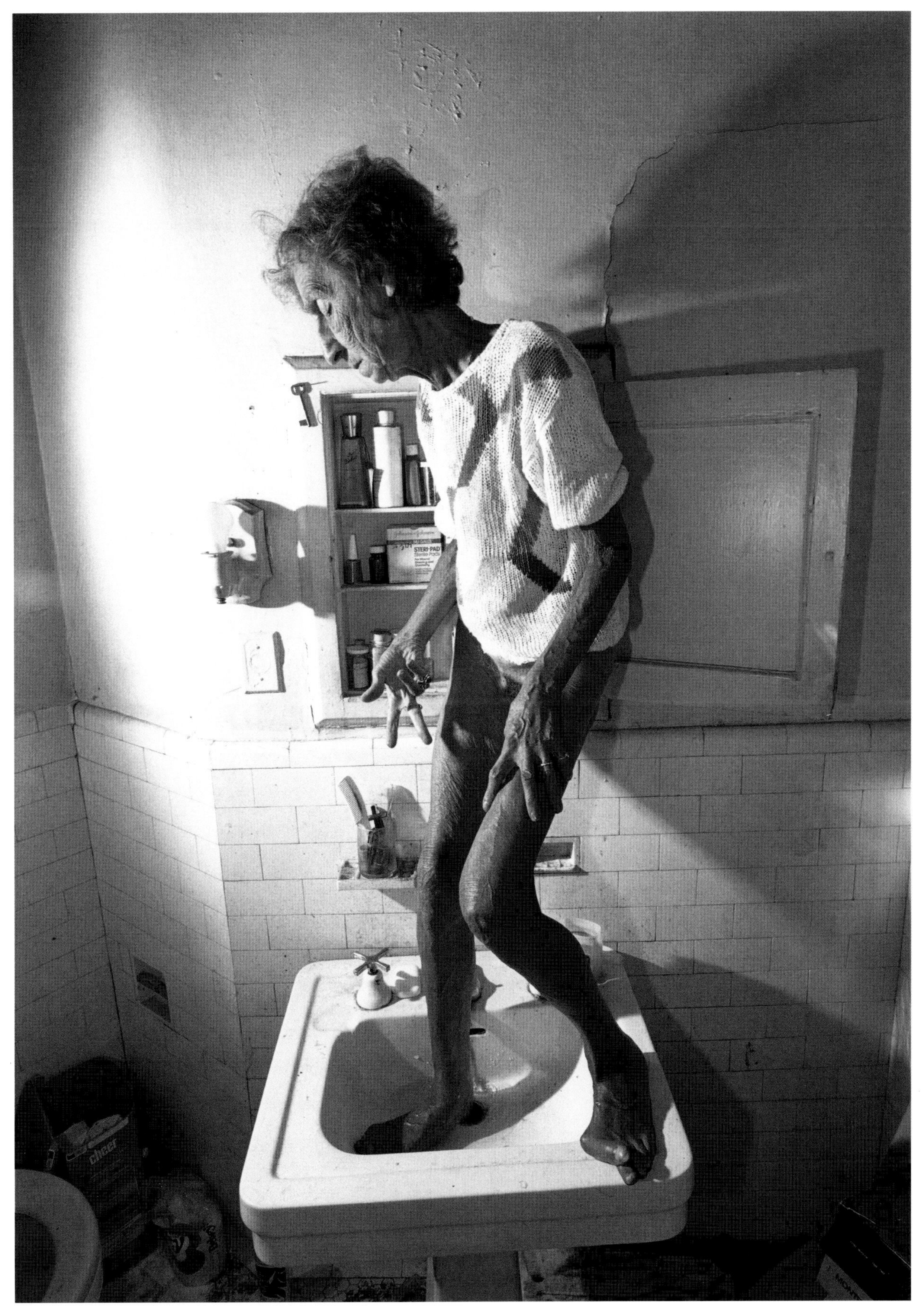




August 30, 1989

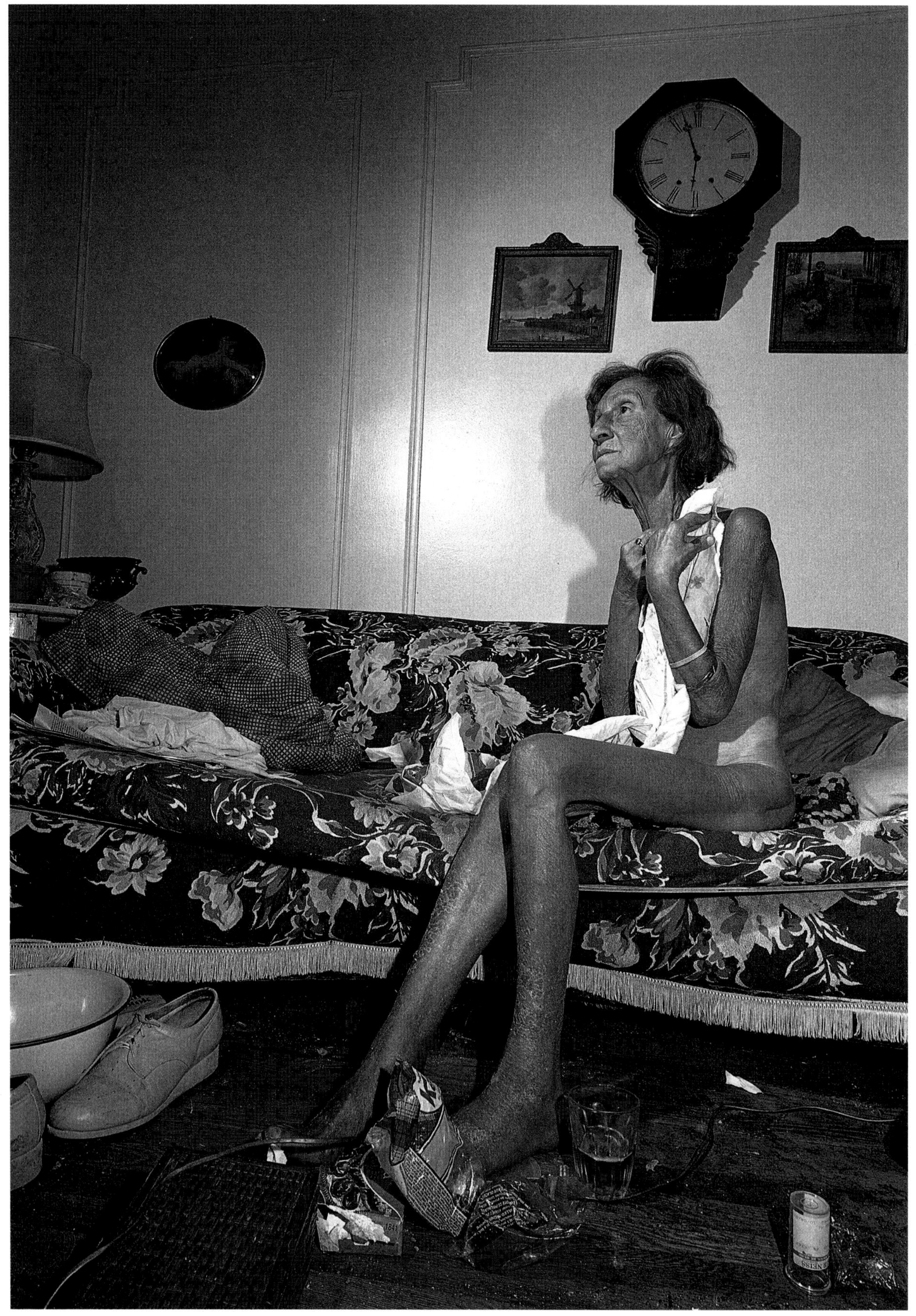



April 24, 1989

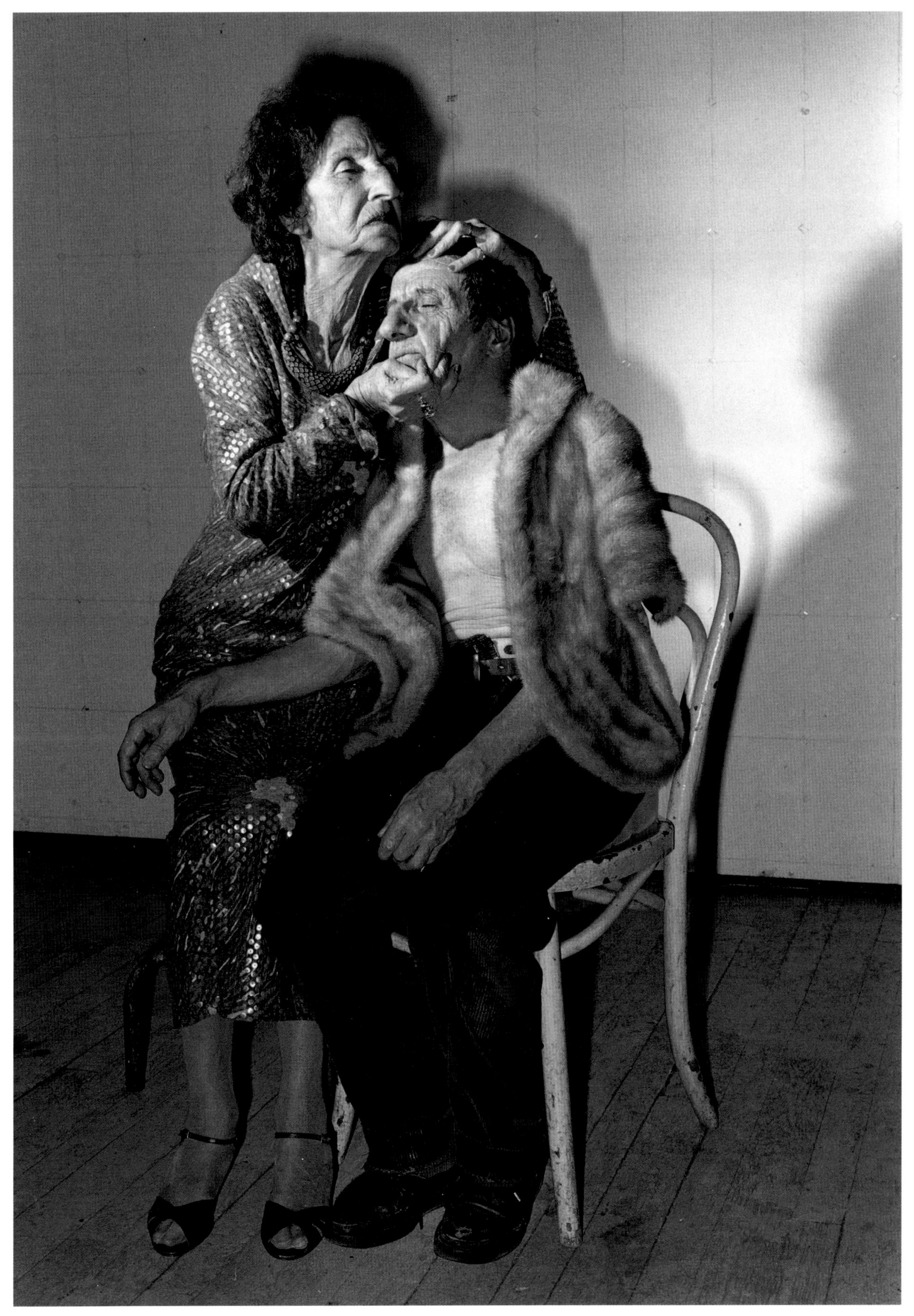



November 21, 1991

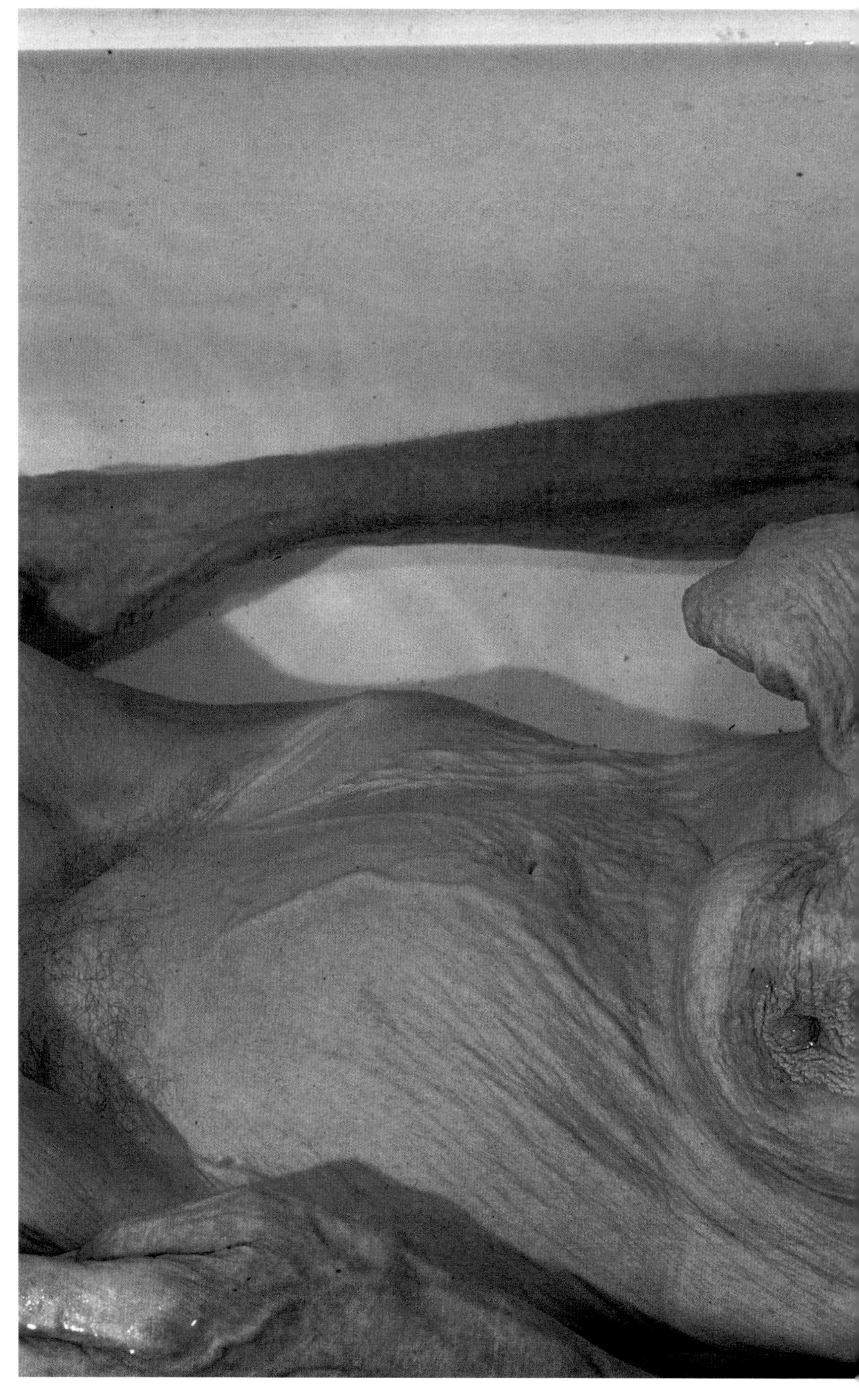

May 24, 1989

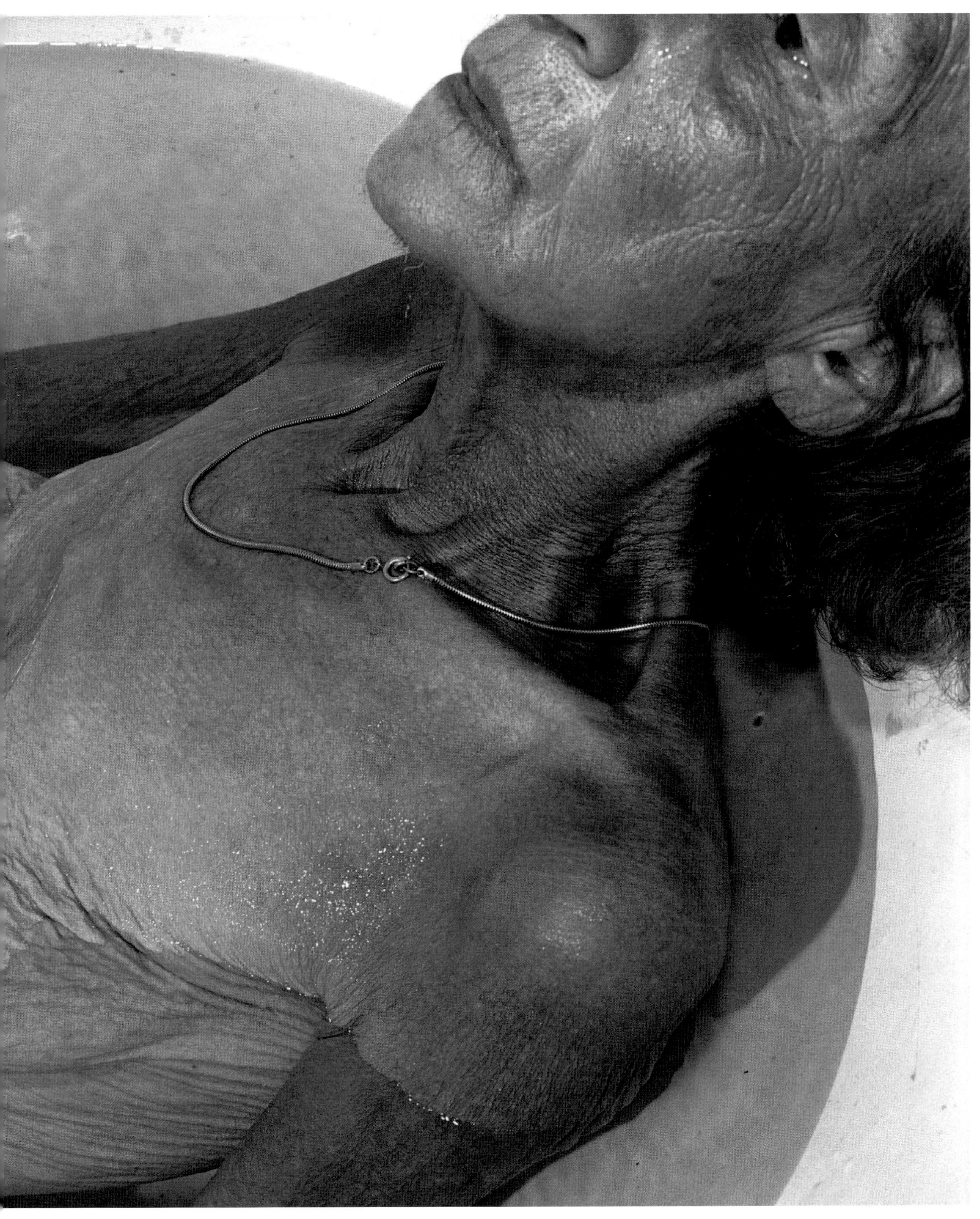

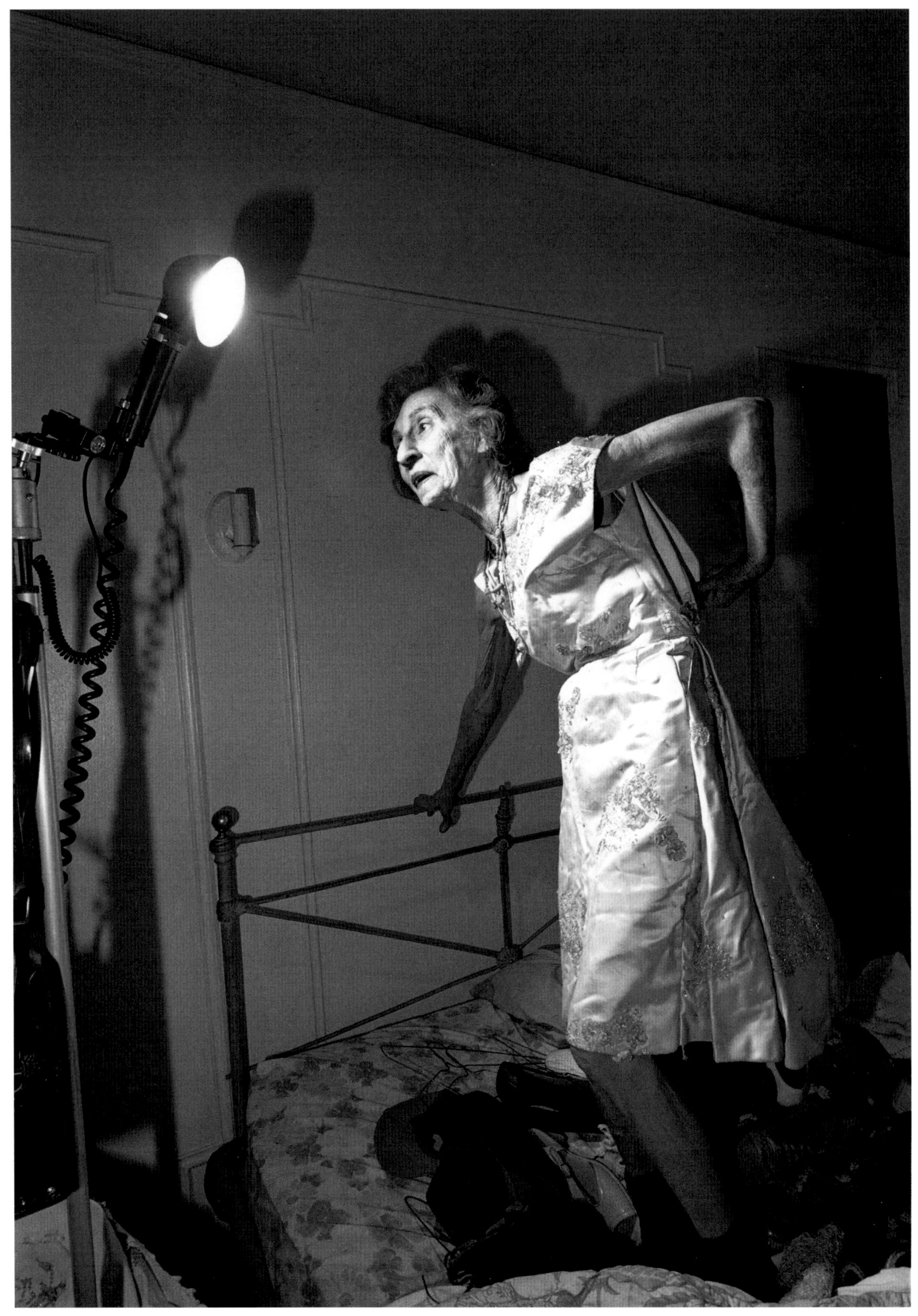

January 28, 1990

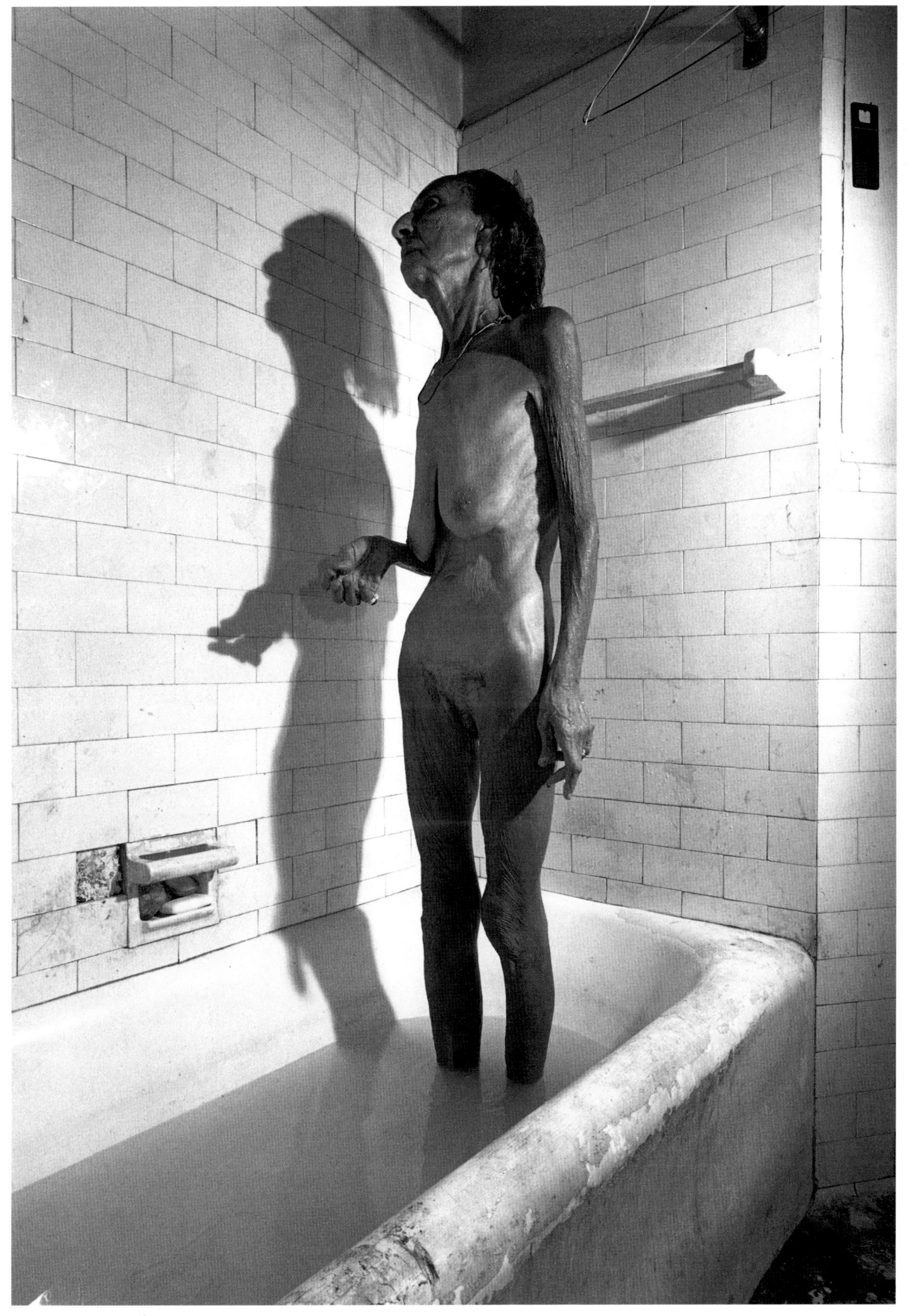



May 31, 1989

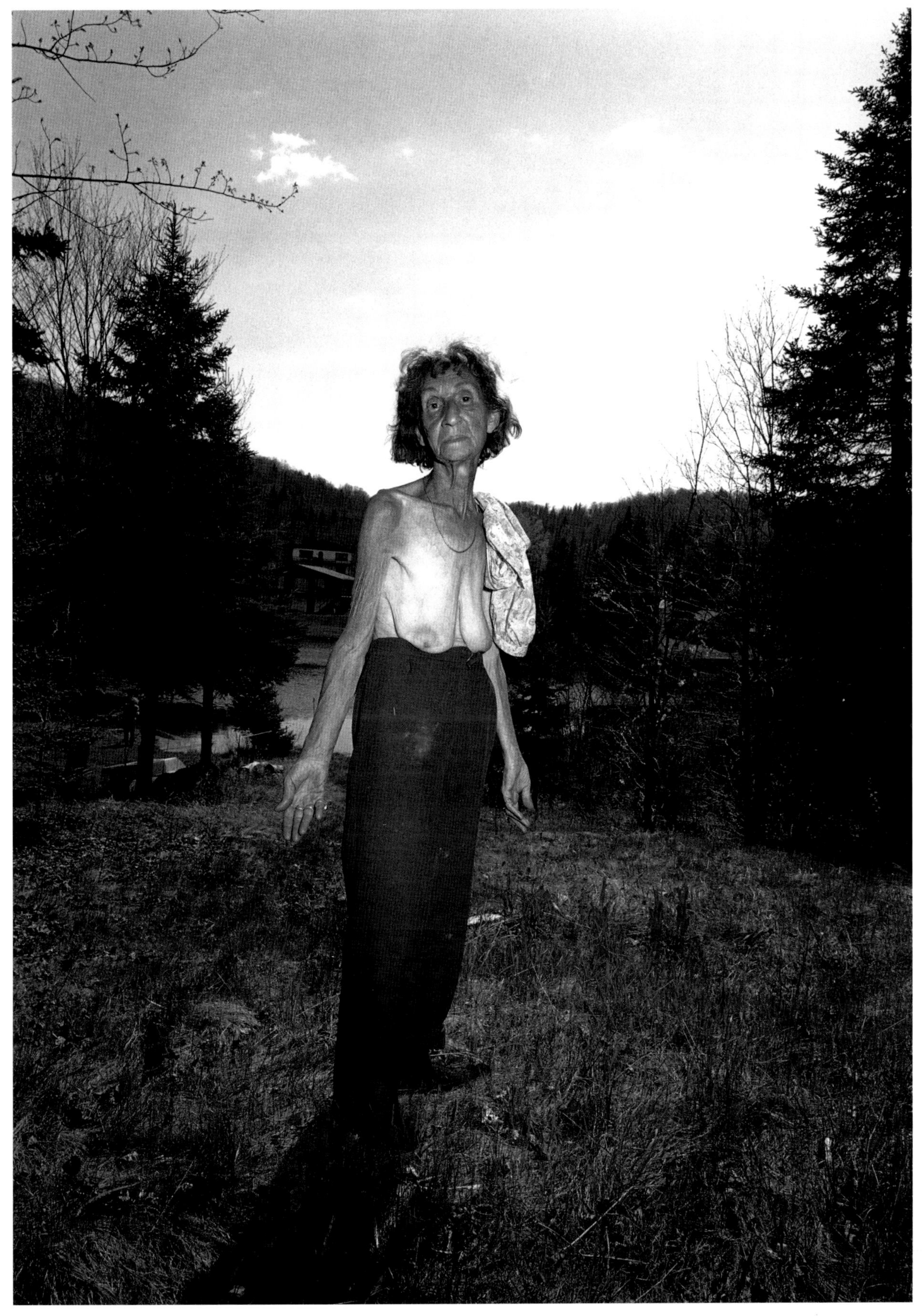



May 17, 1989

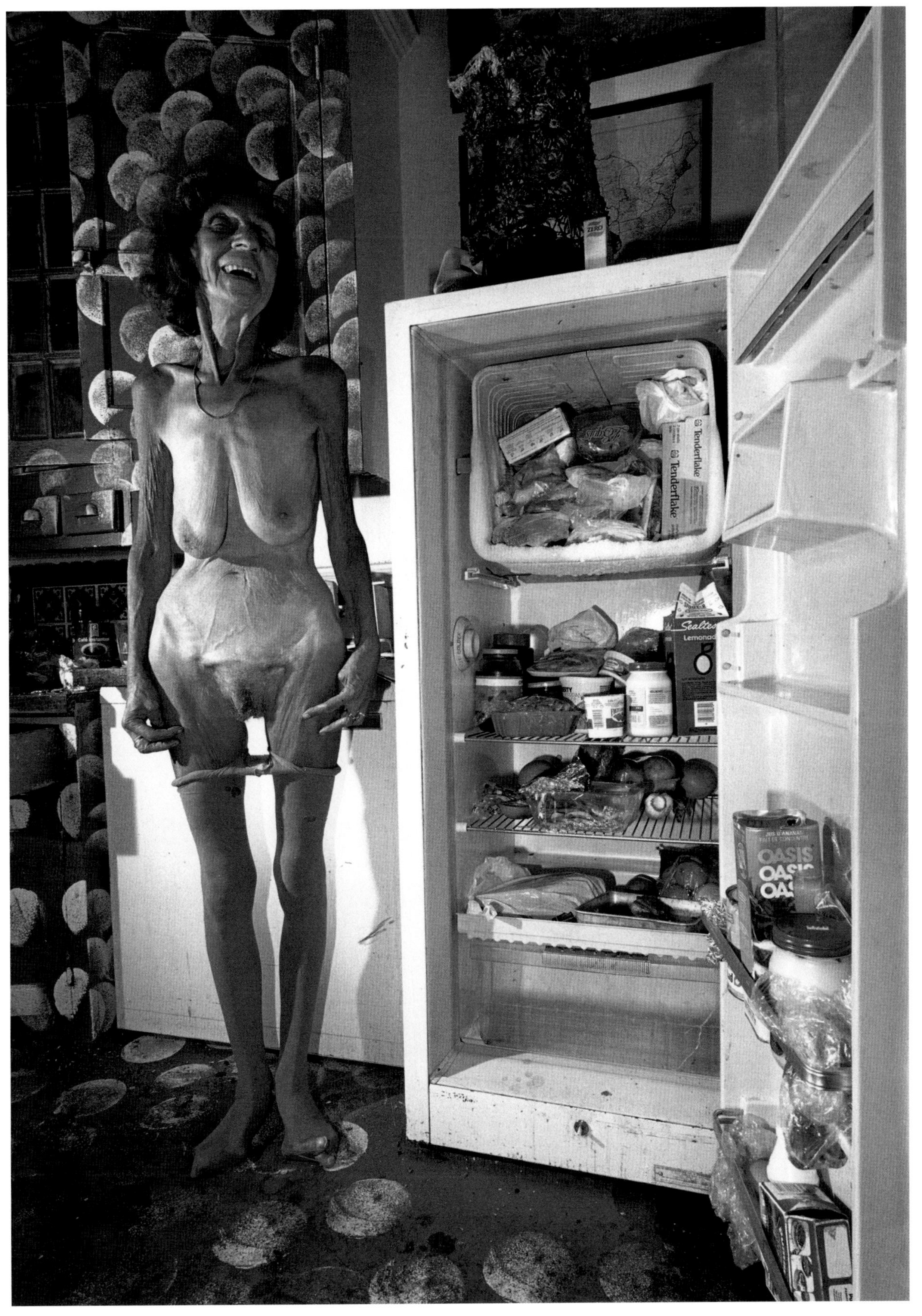




May 3, 1989

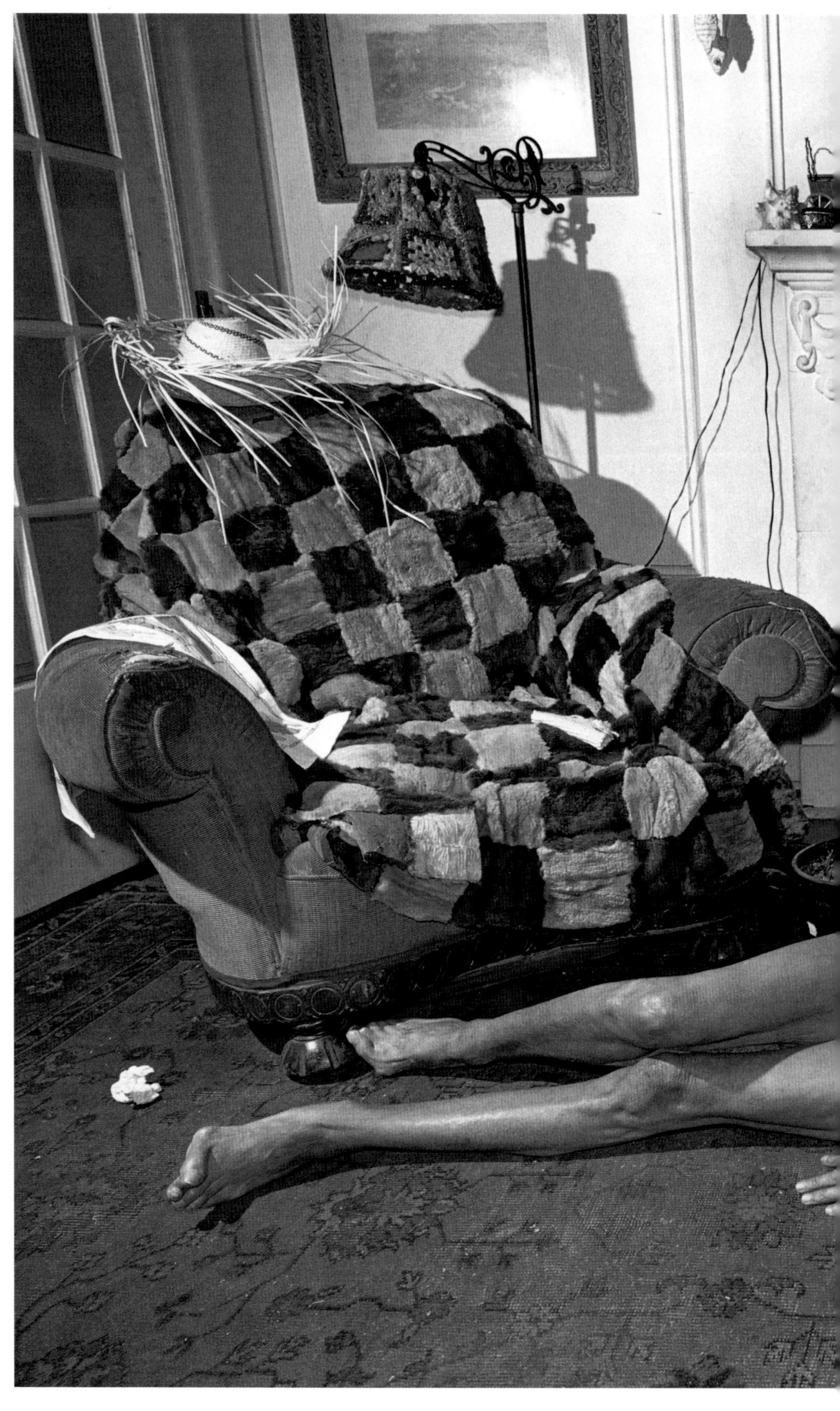

June 4, 1985

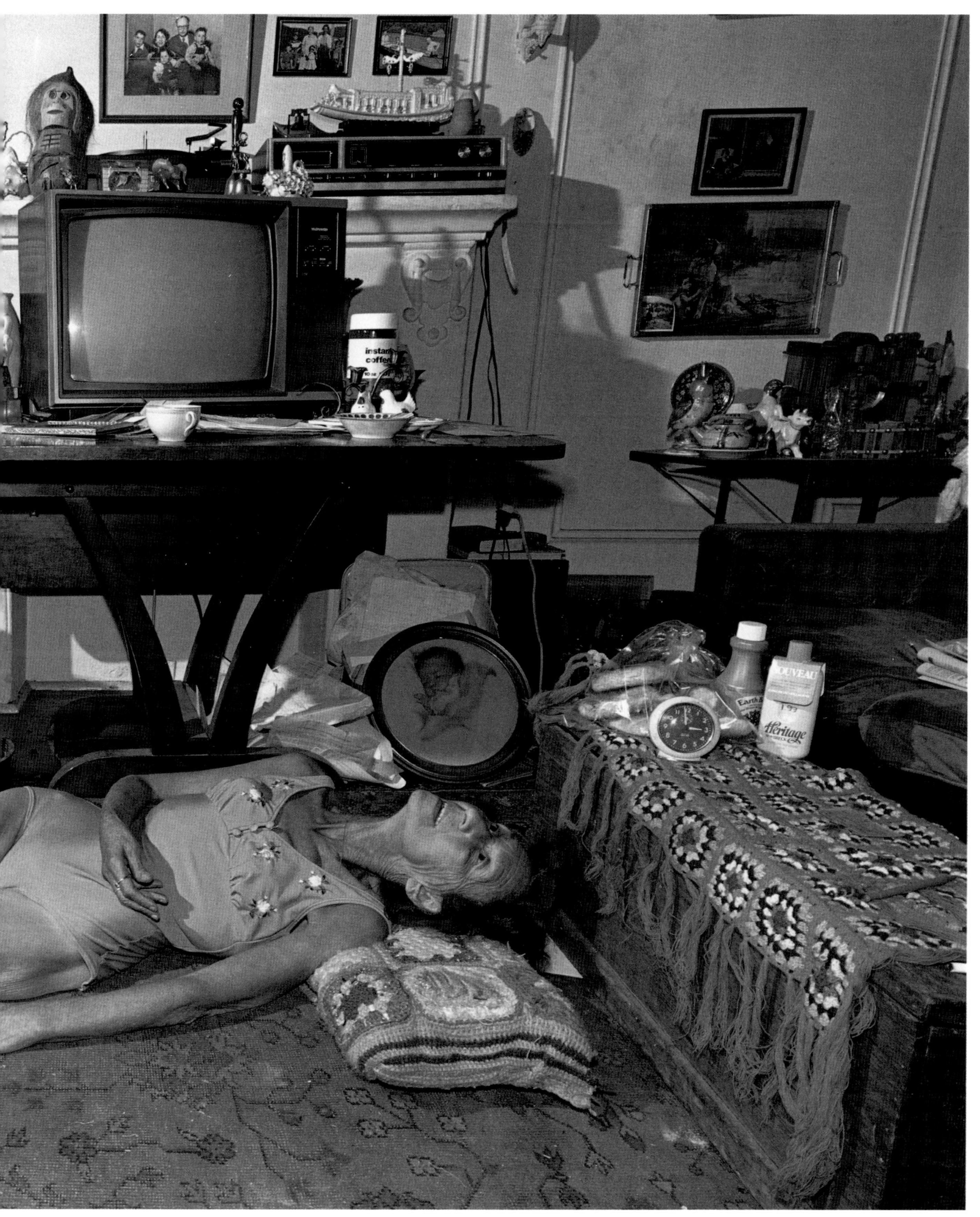
Héritage

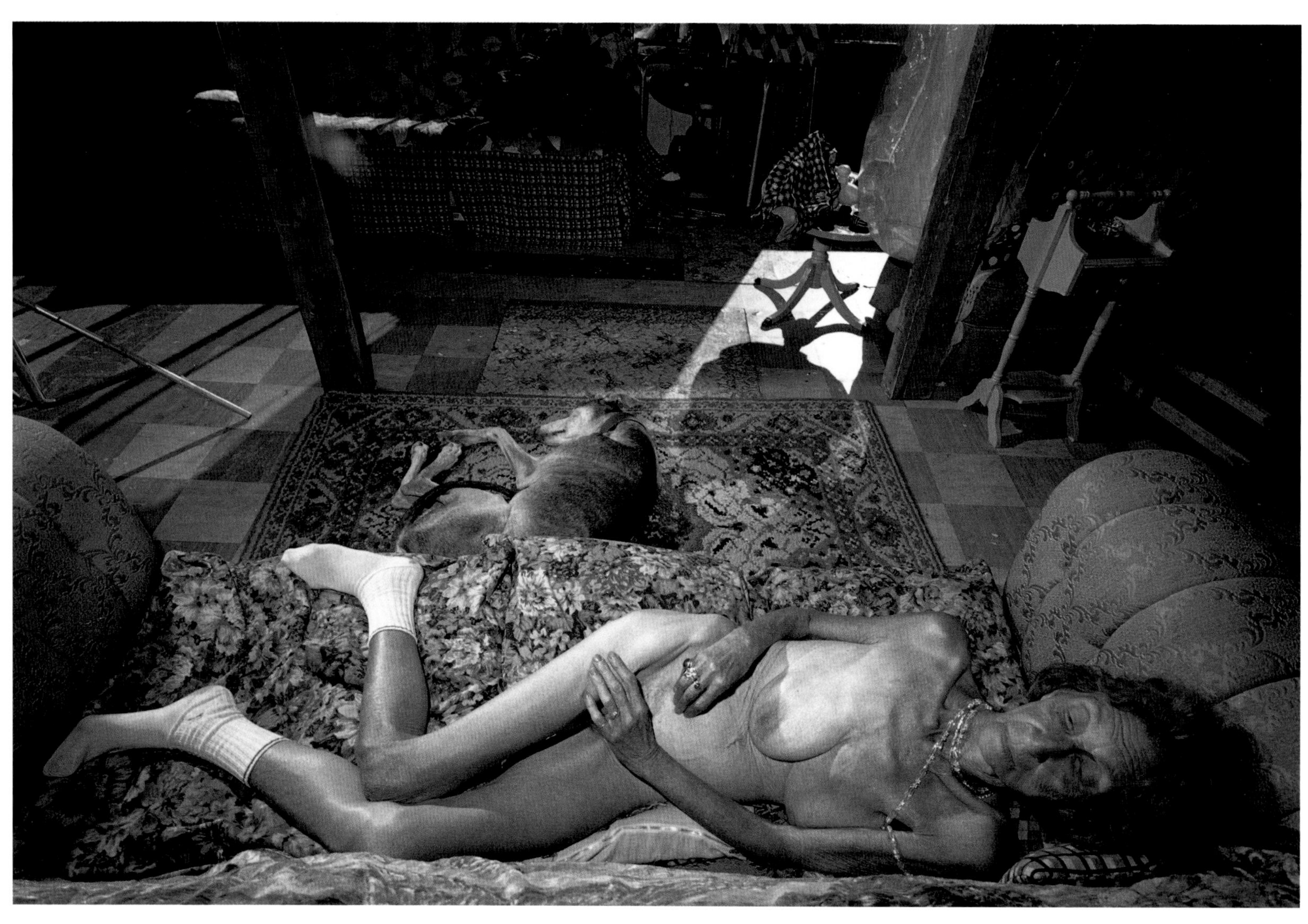

August 29, 1989

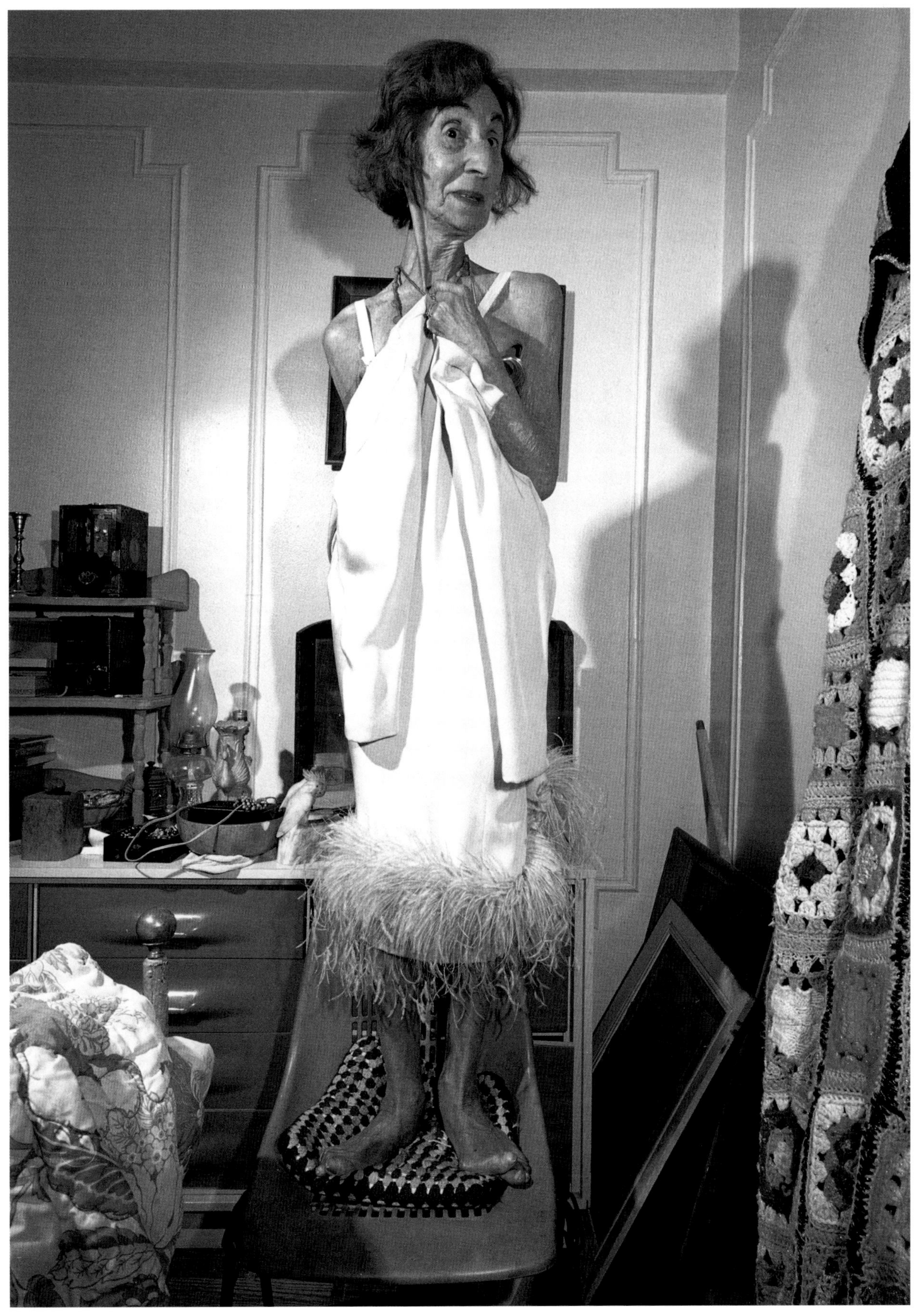



February 9, 1990

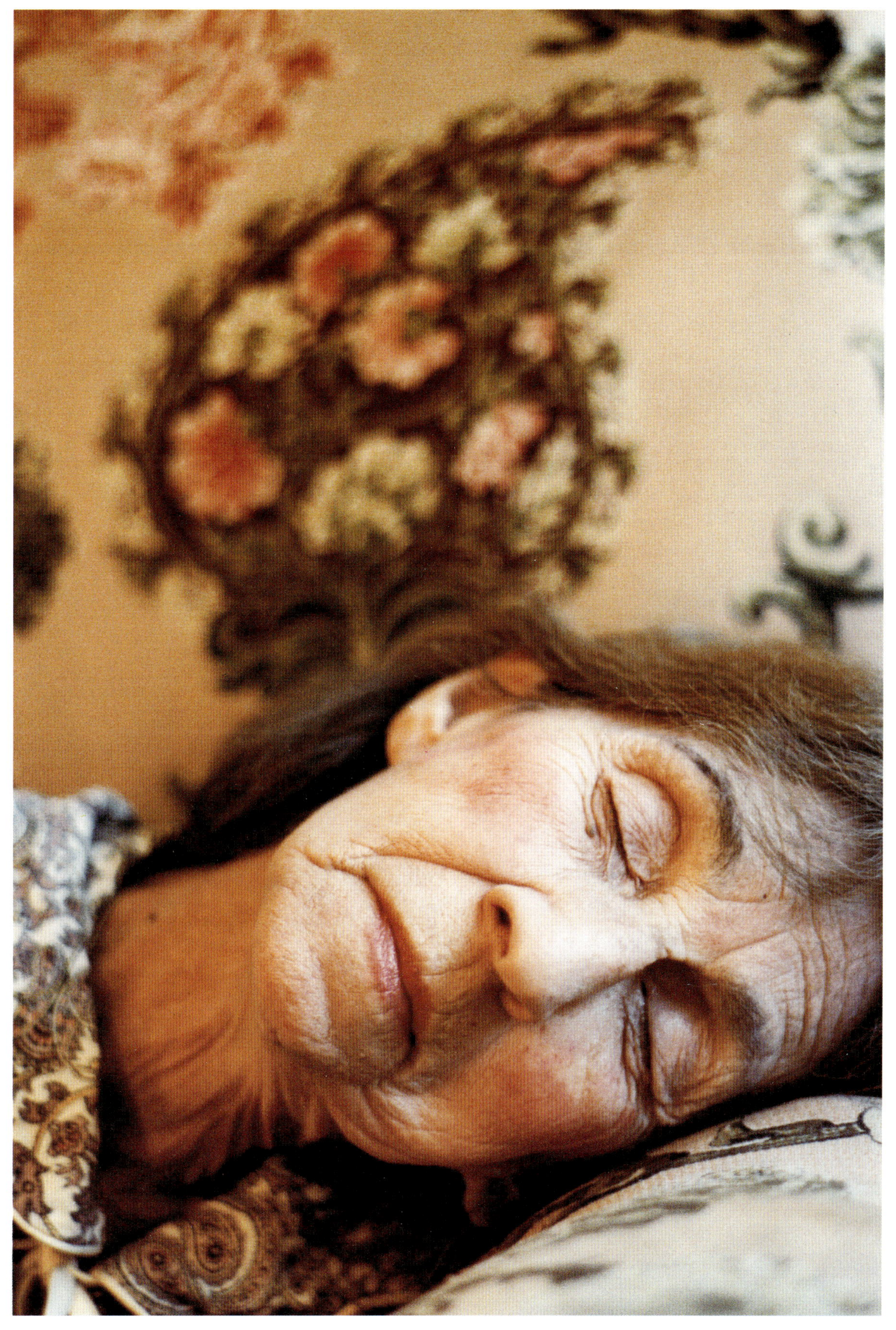



April 18, 1990

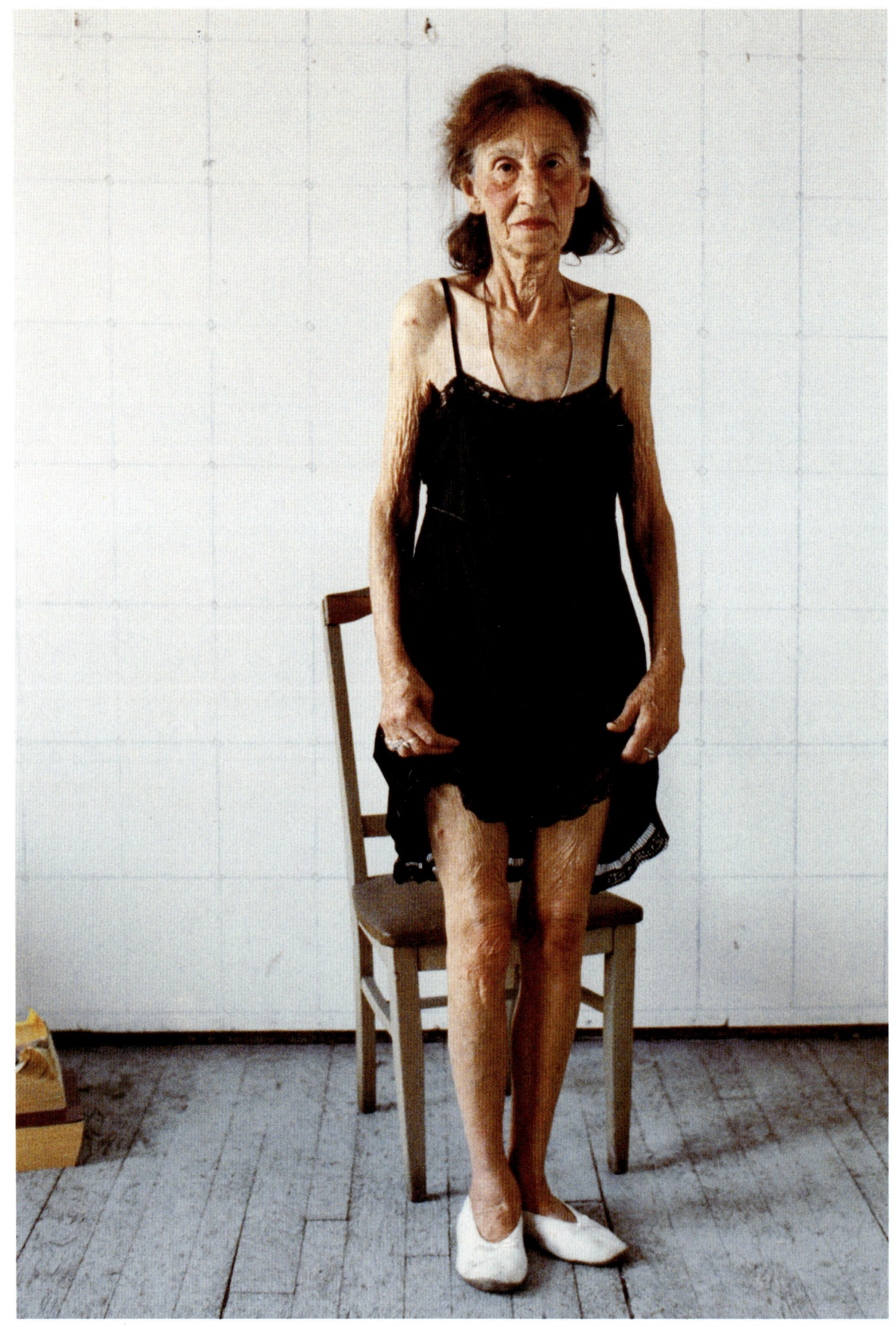



May 21, 1992

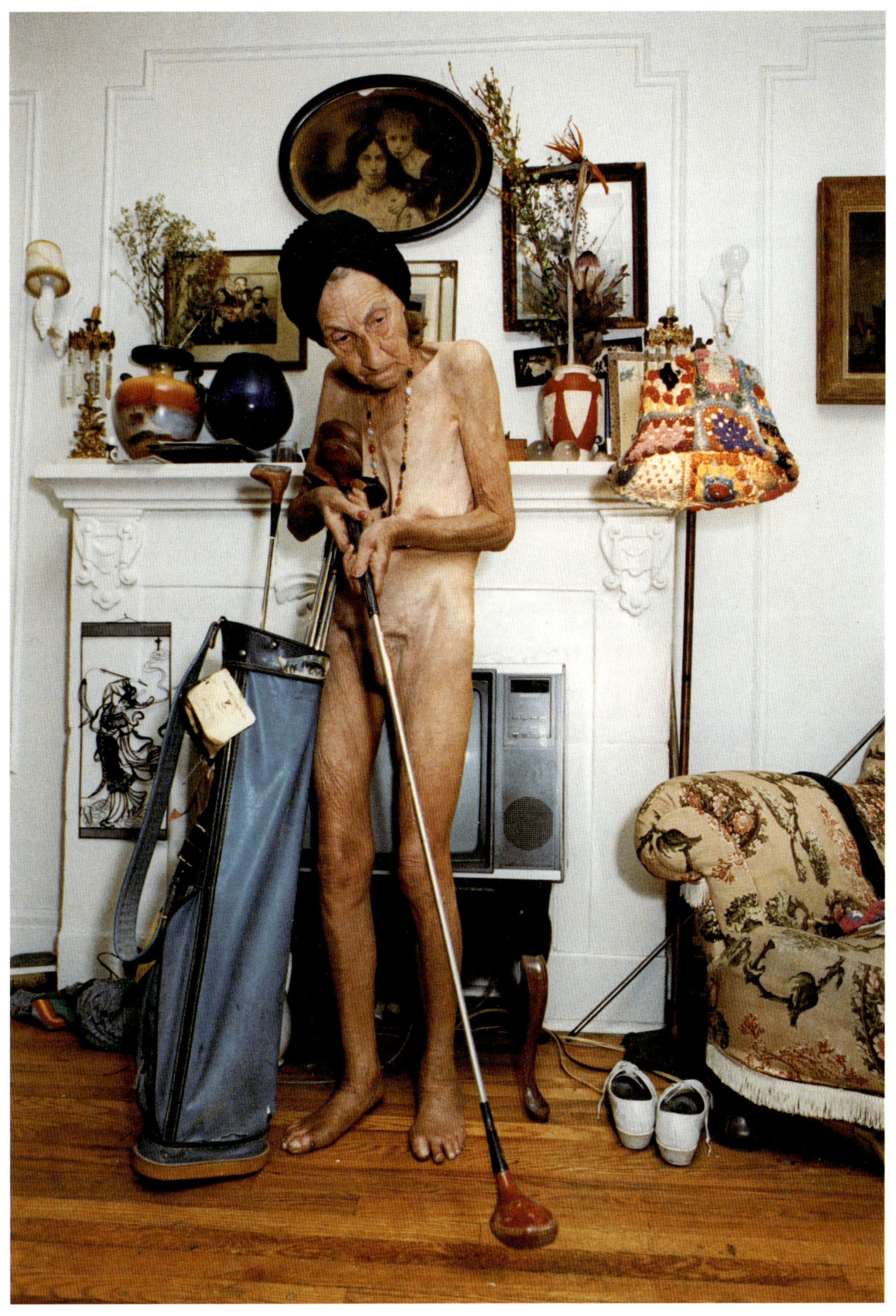



May 30, 1990

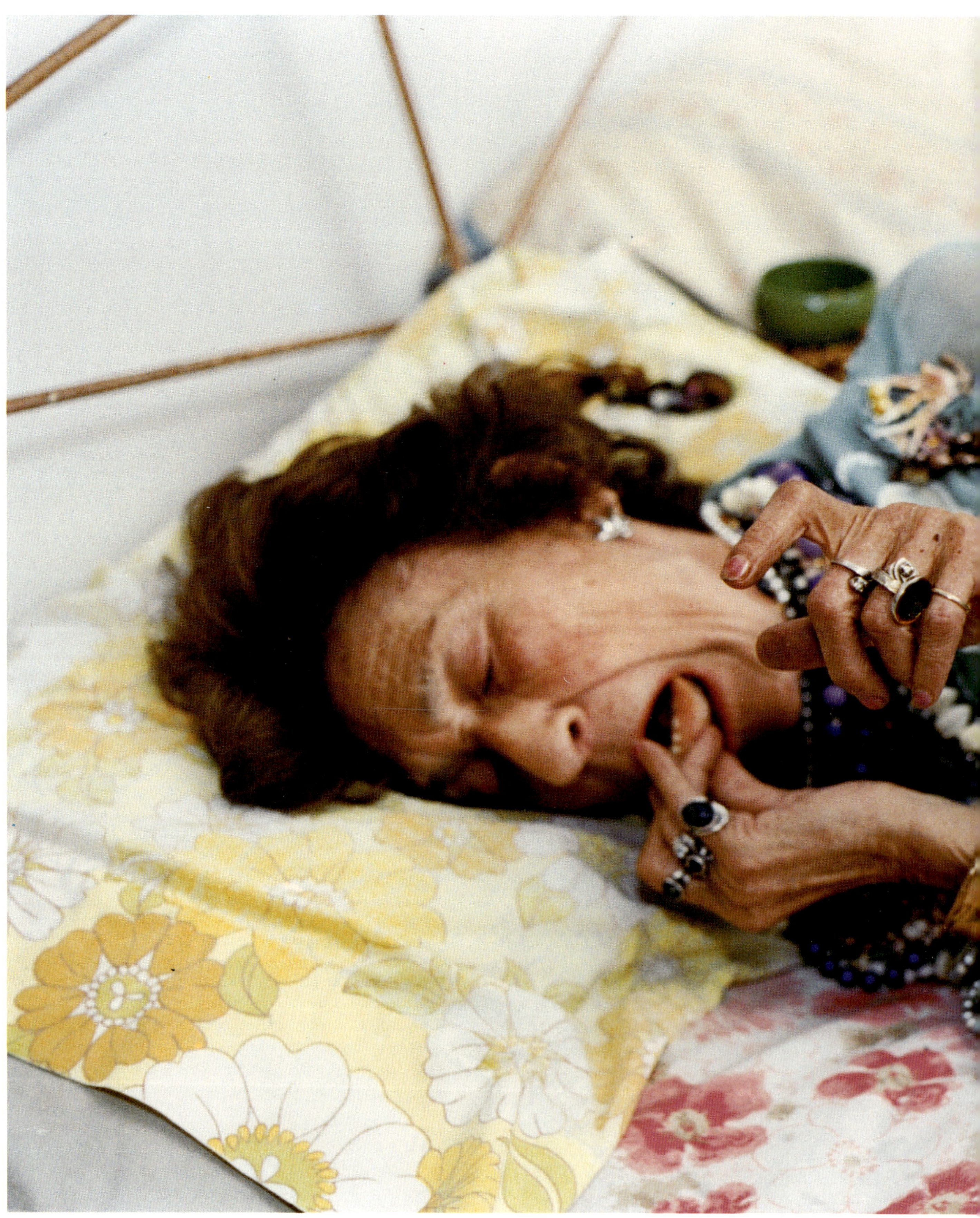

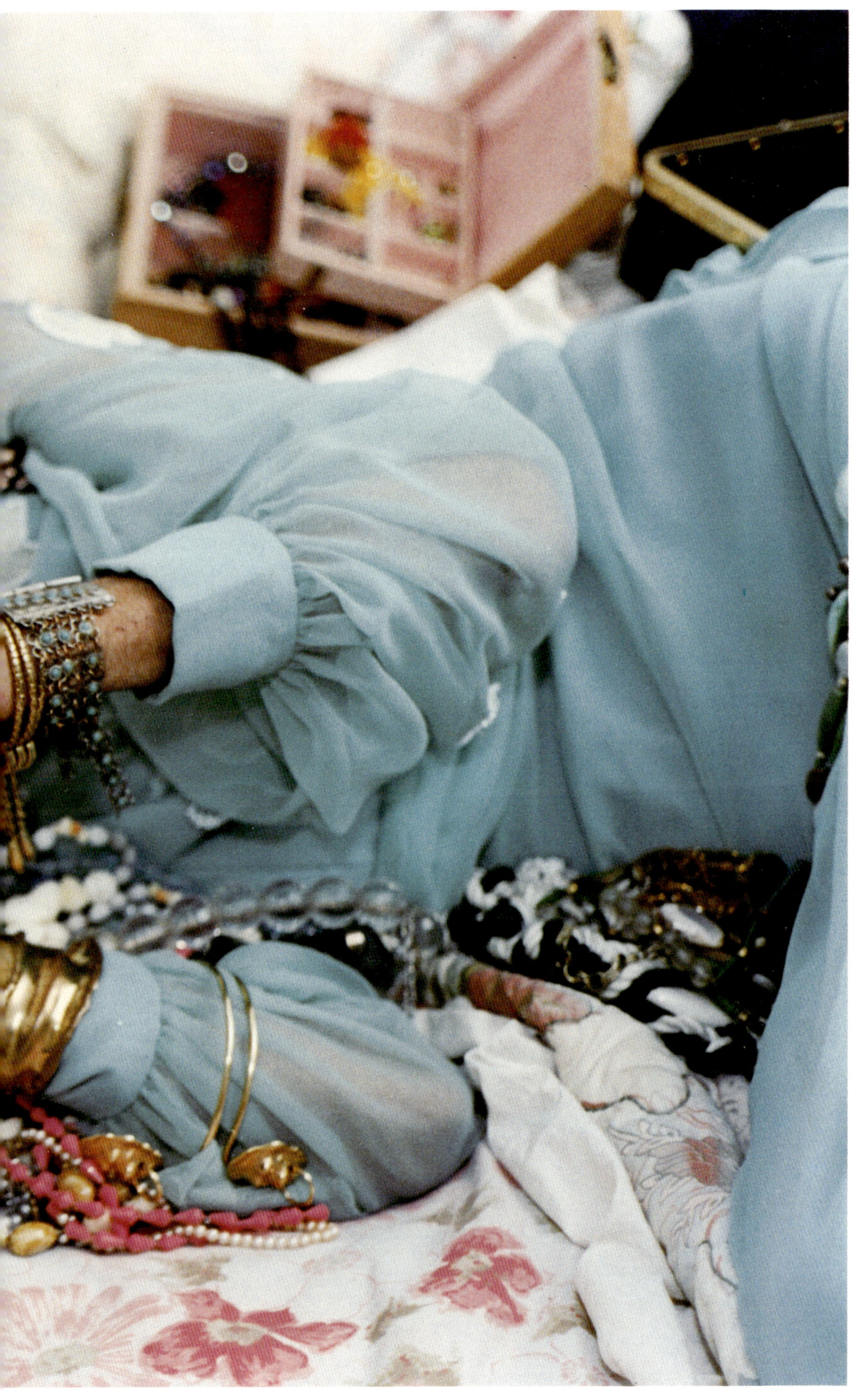

June 8, 1990

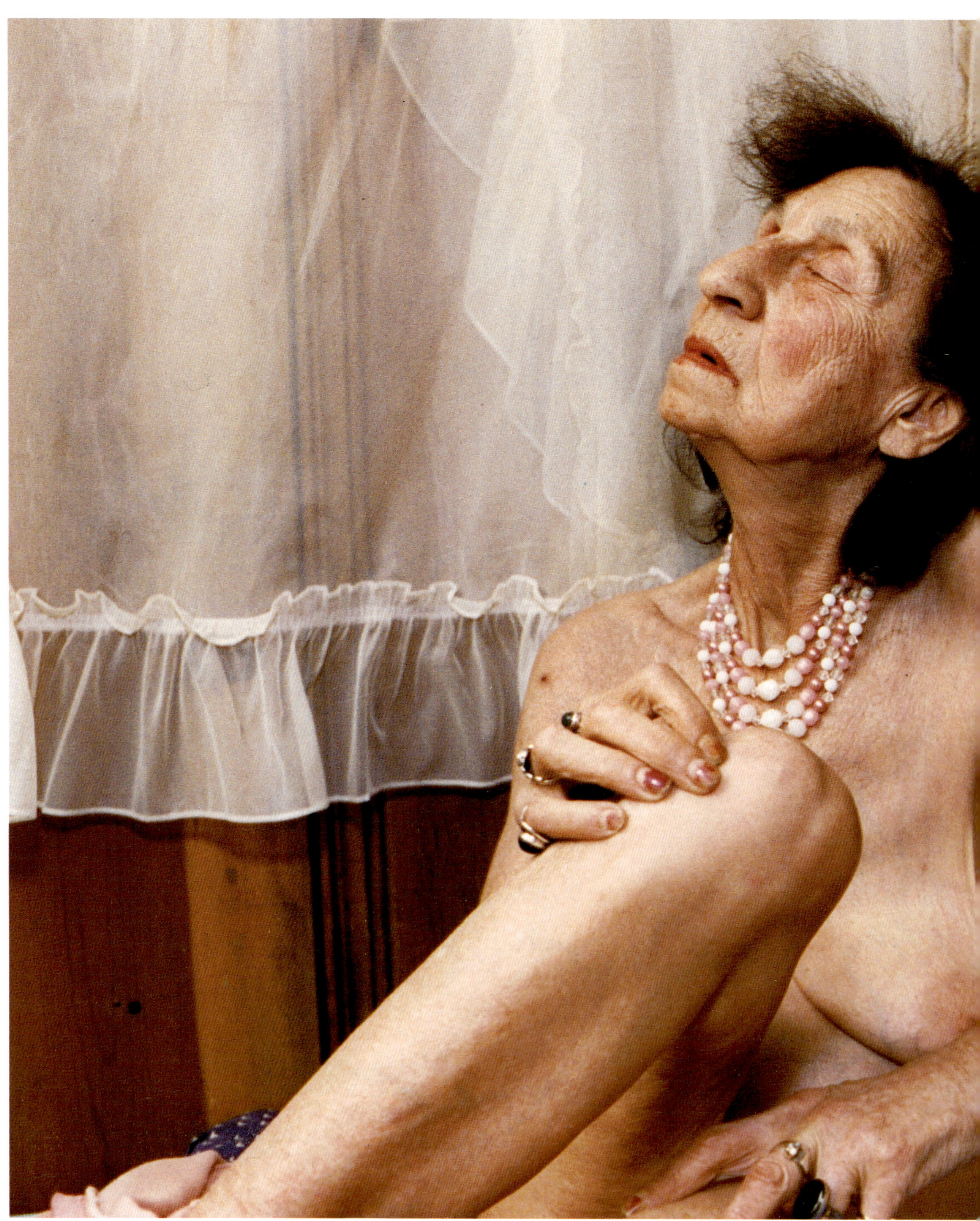

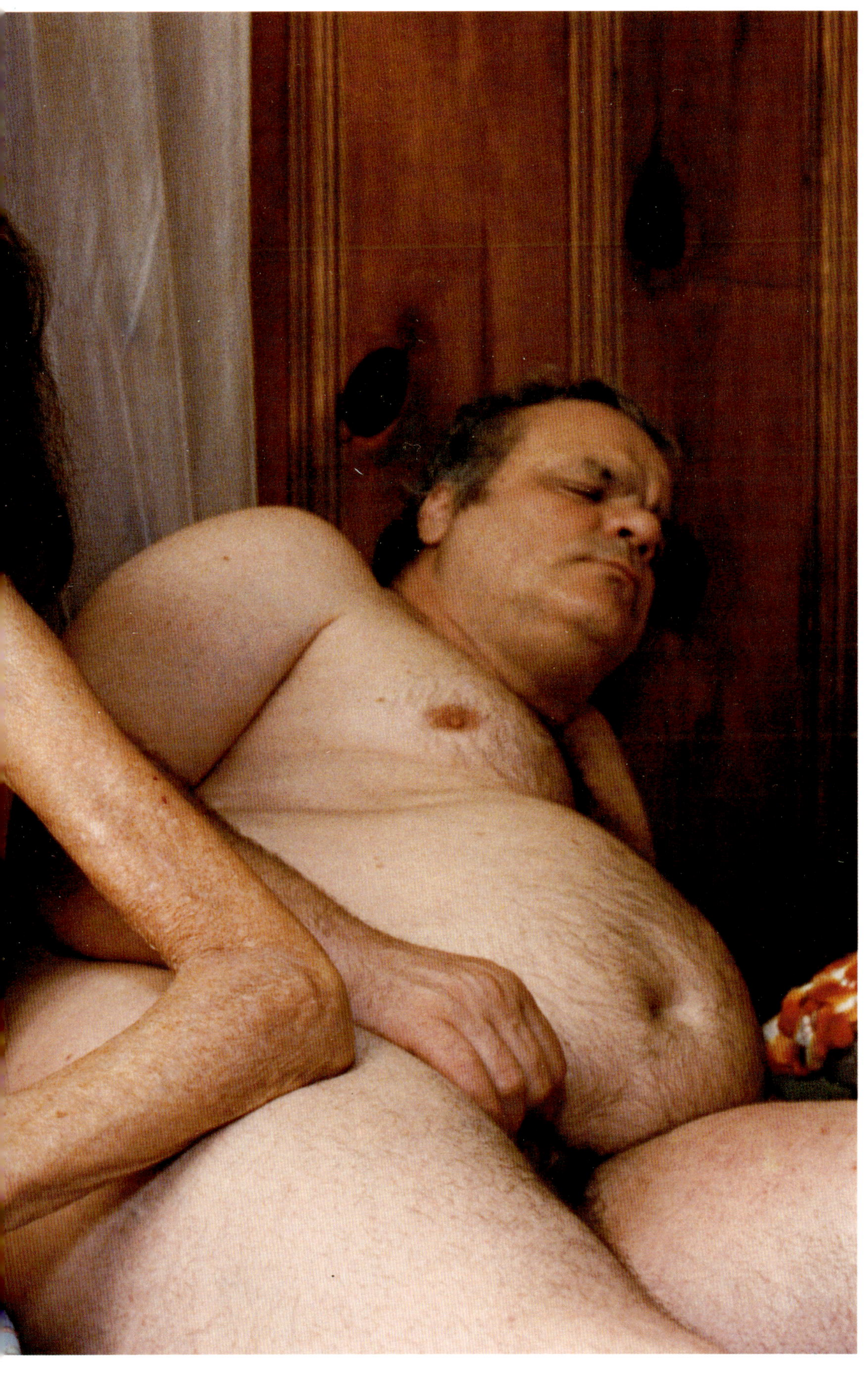

April 24, 1992

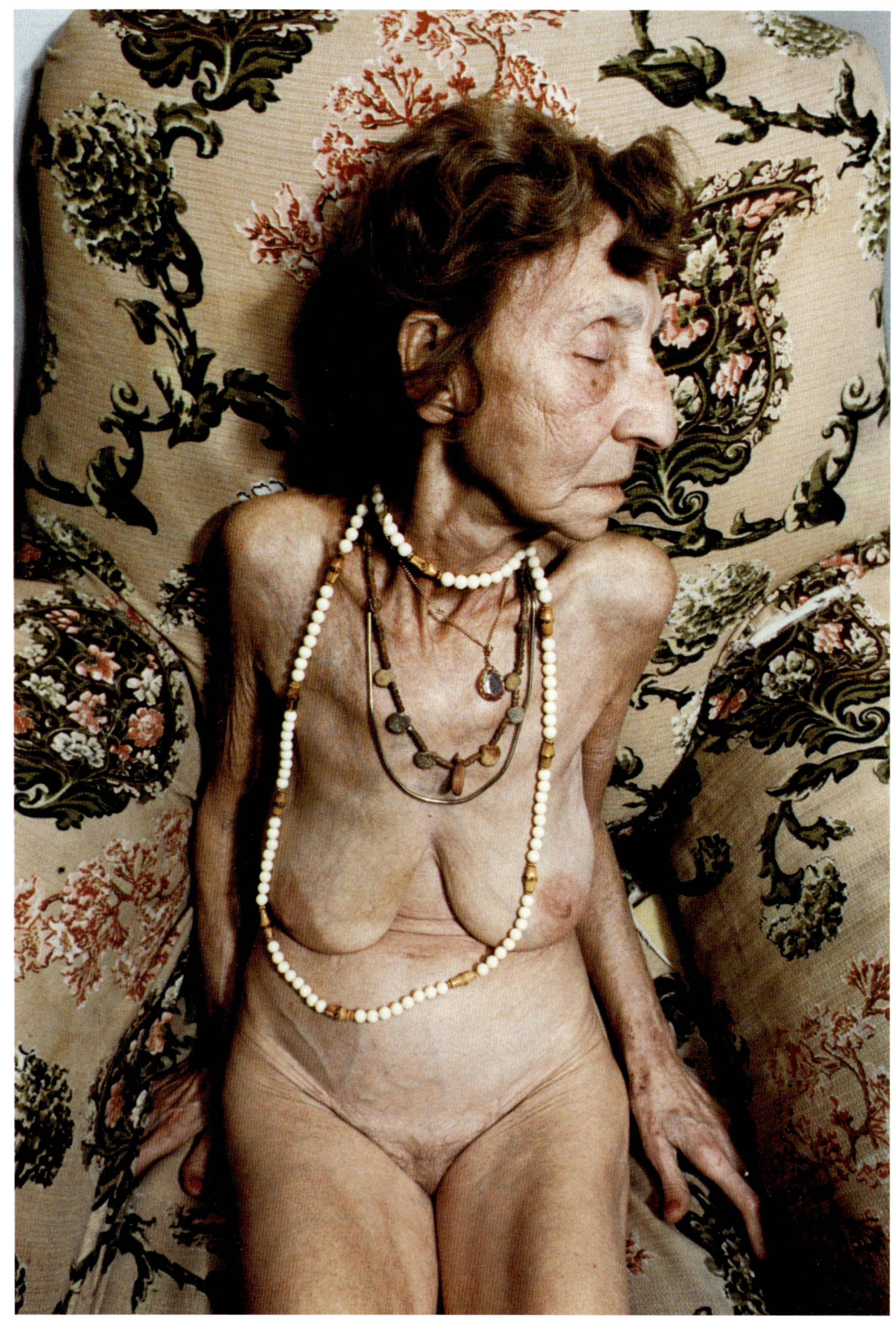



April 11, 1990

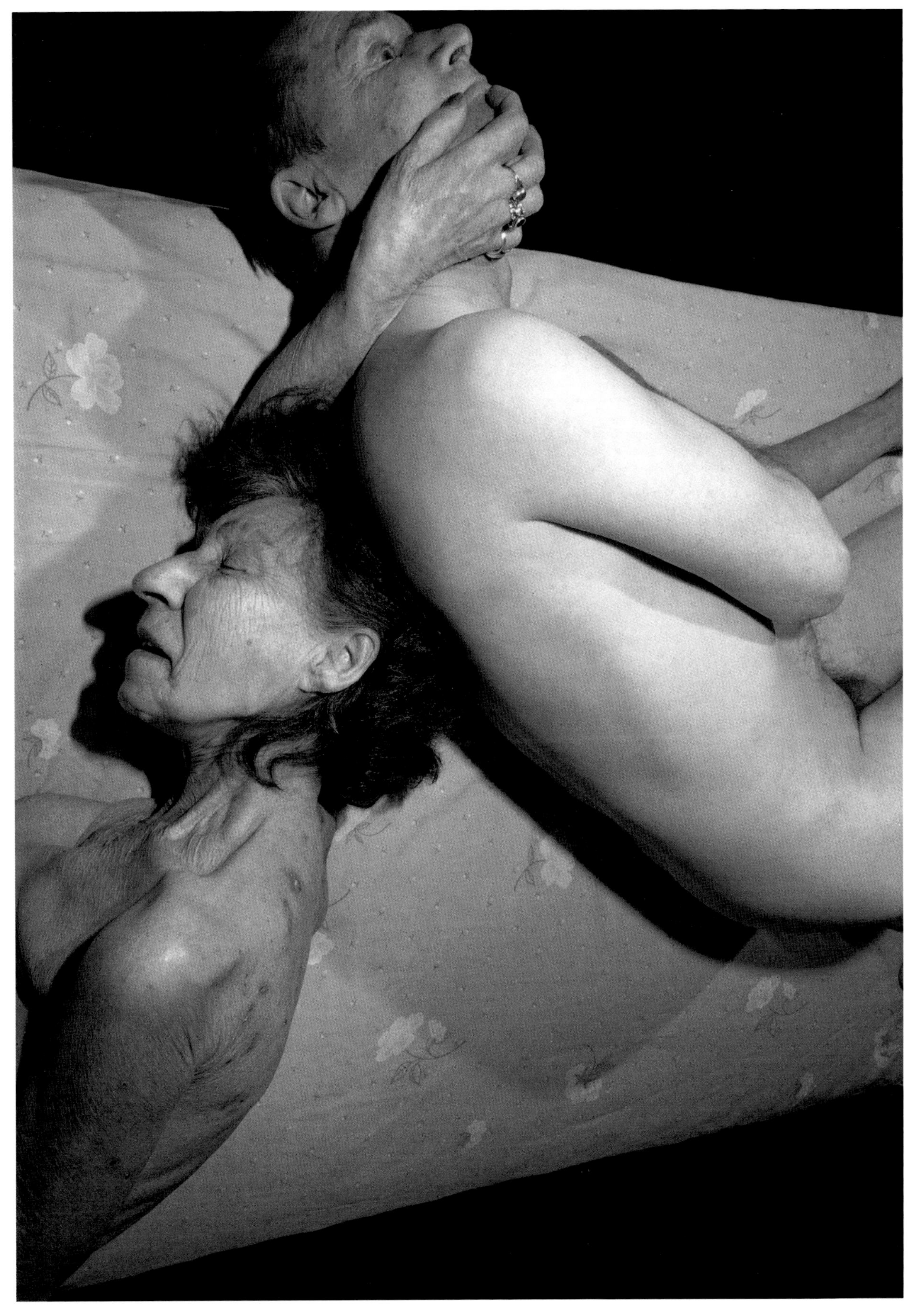



April 13, 1992

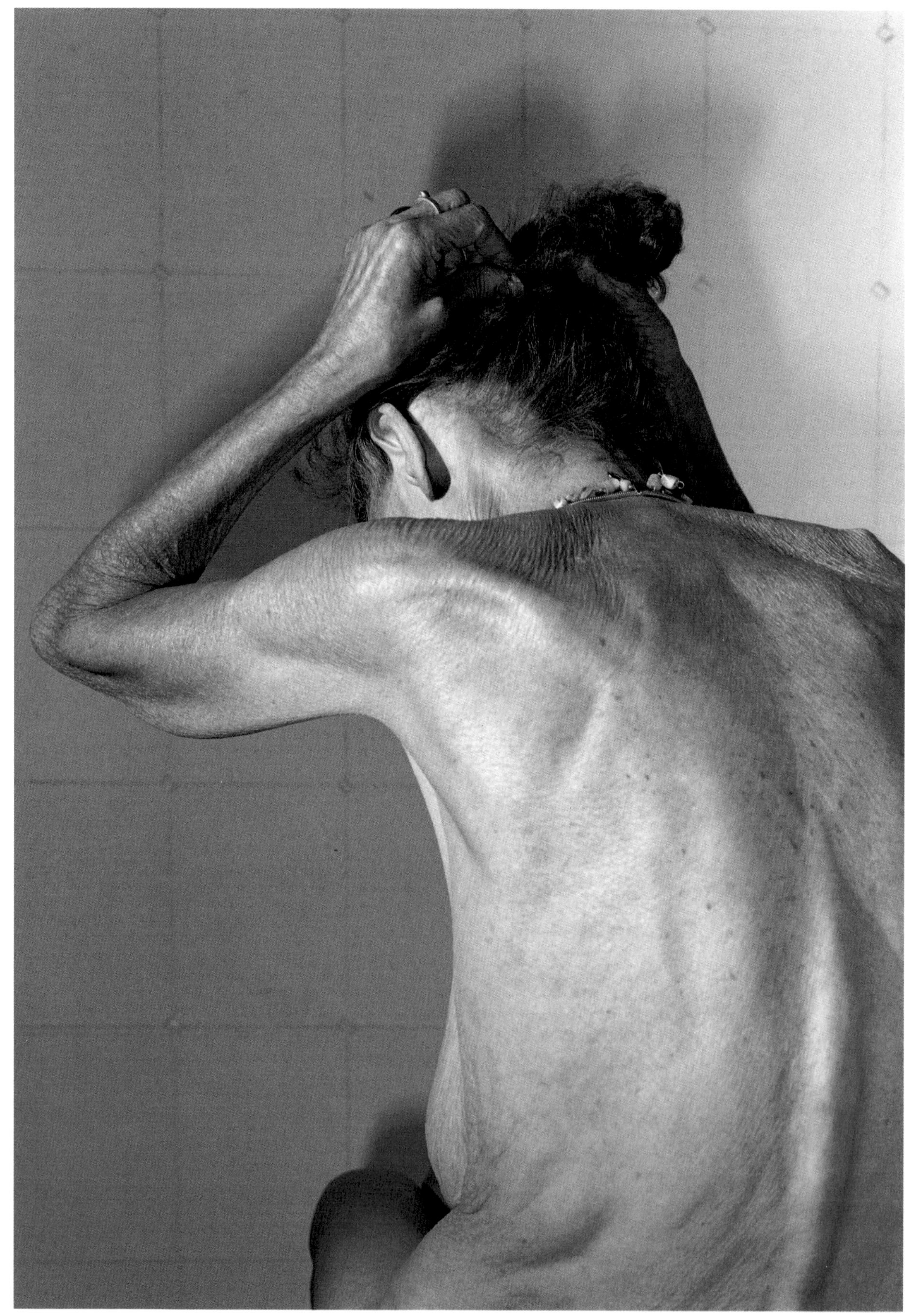



August 29, 1991

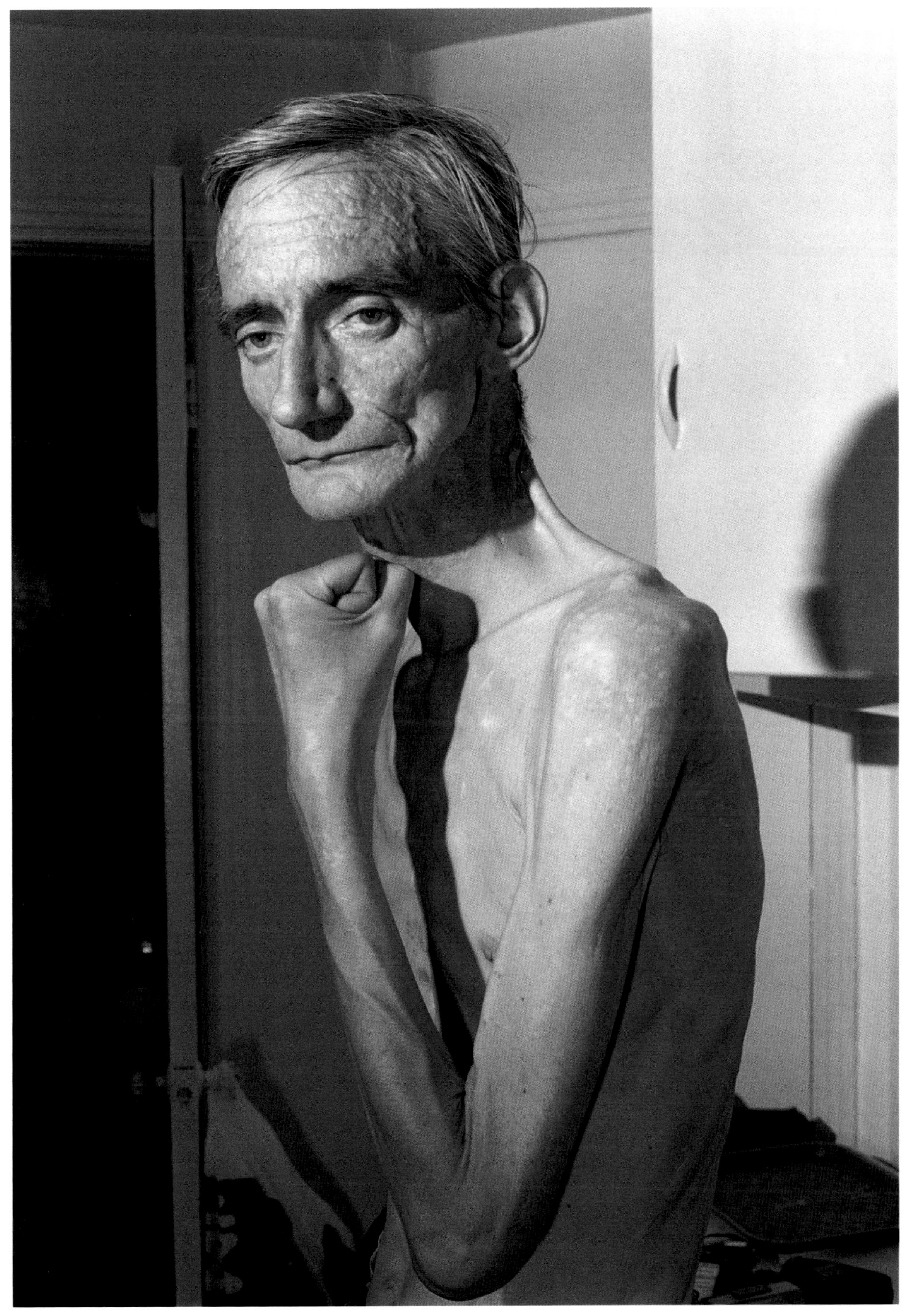



July 7, 1991

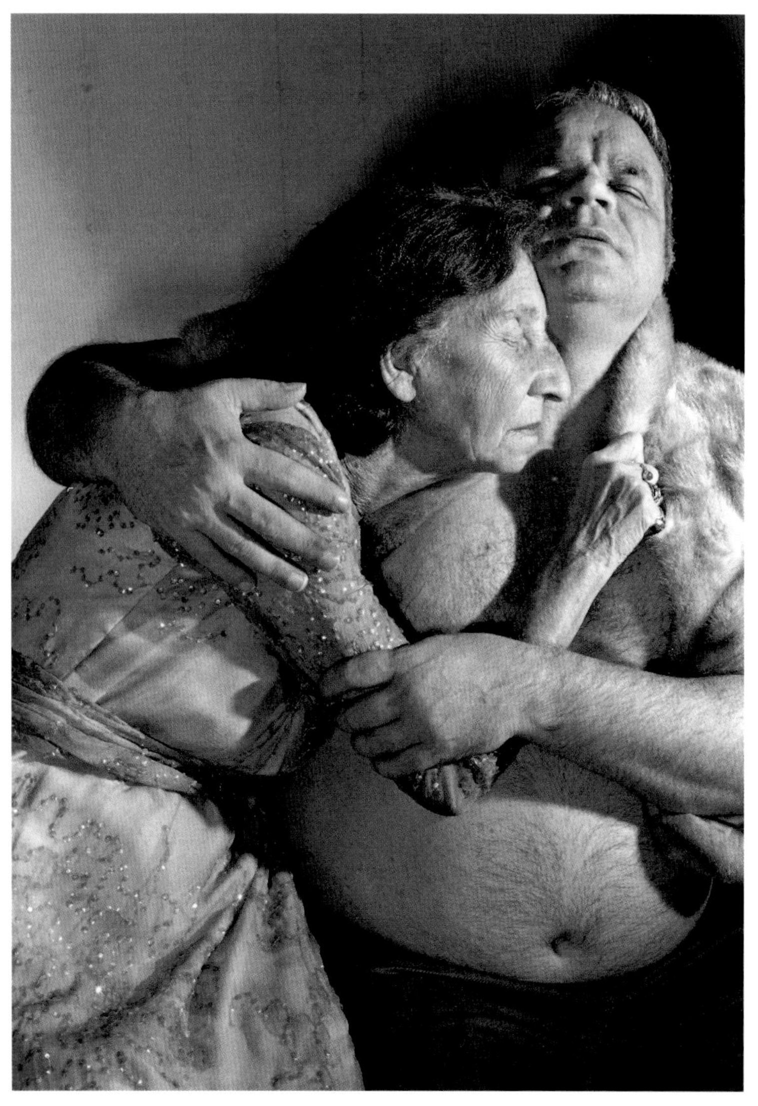

November 14, 1991

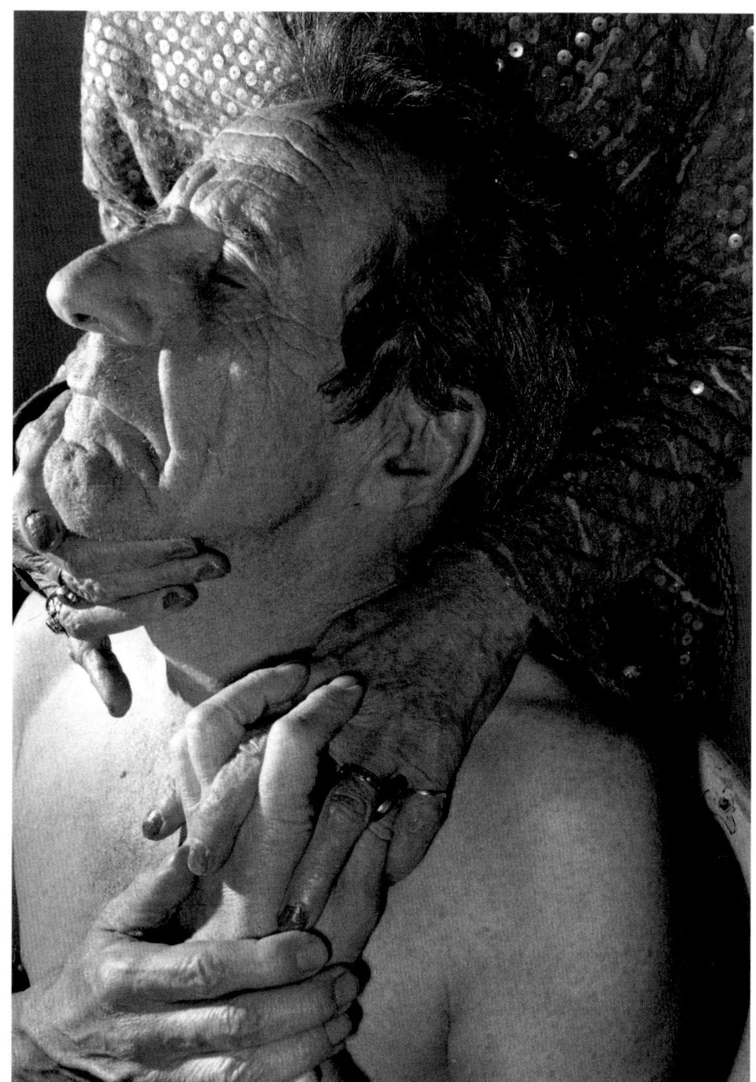

November 21, 1991

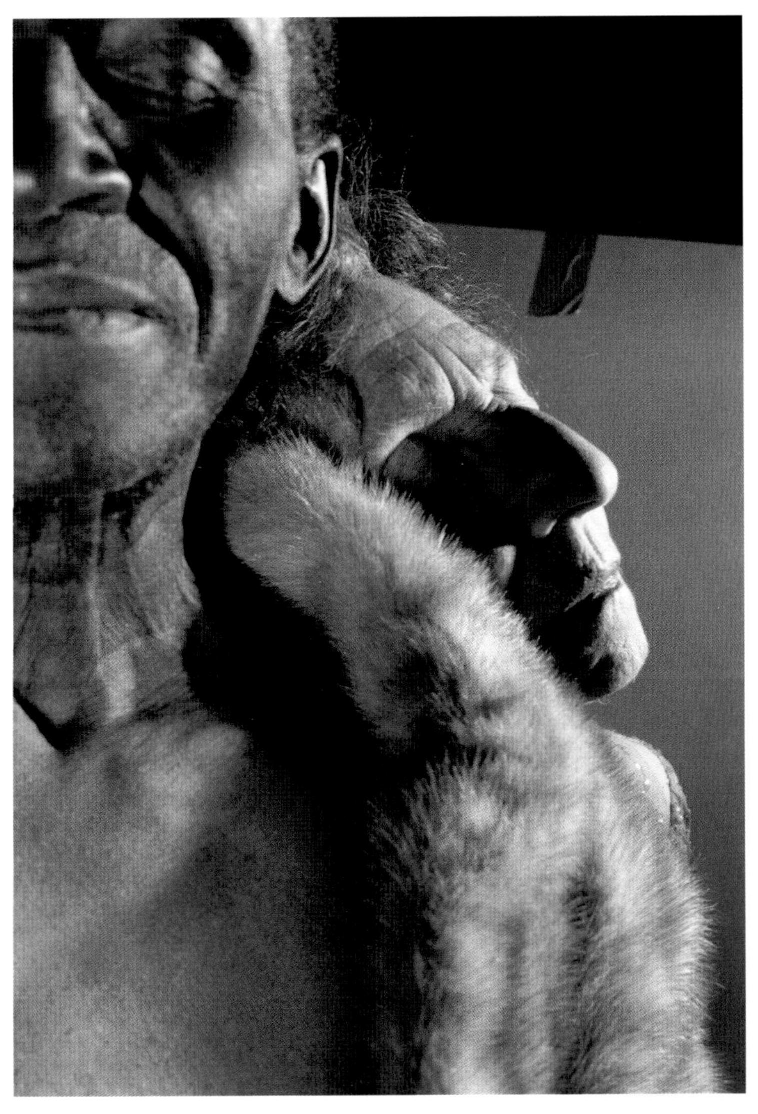

October 23, 1991

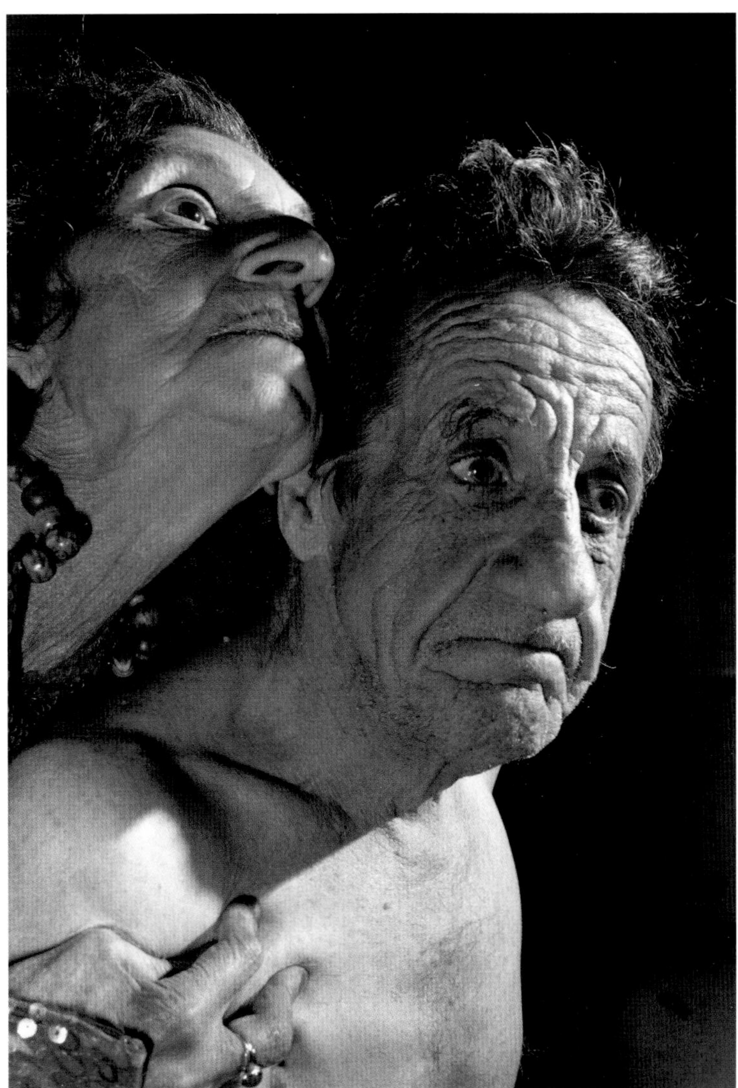

November 21, 1991

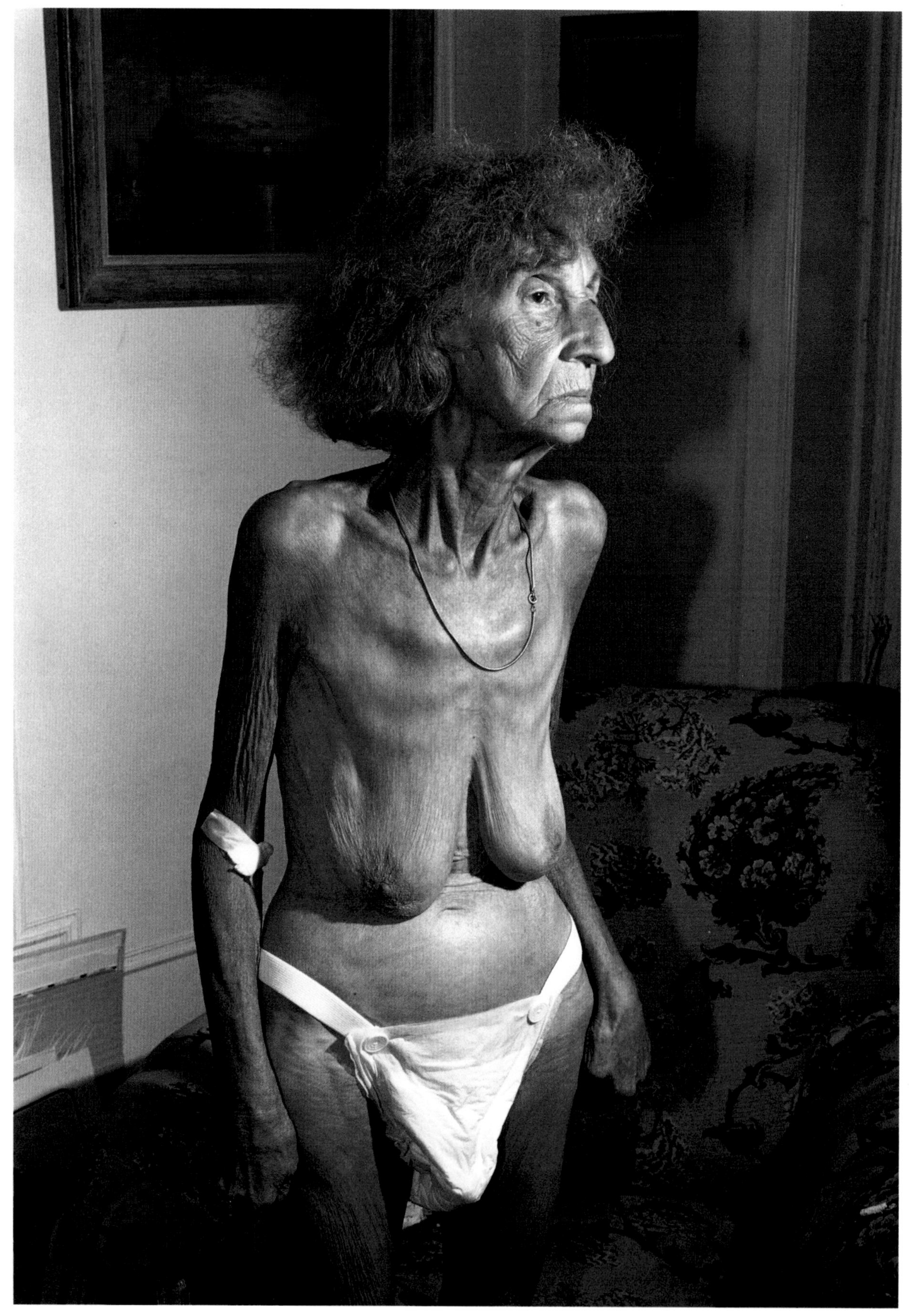



June 6, 1989

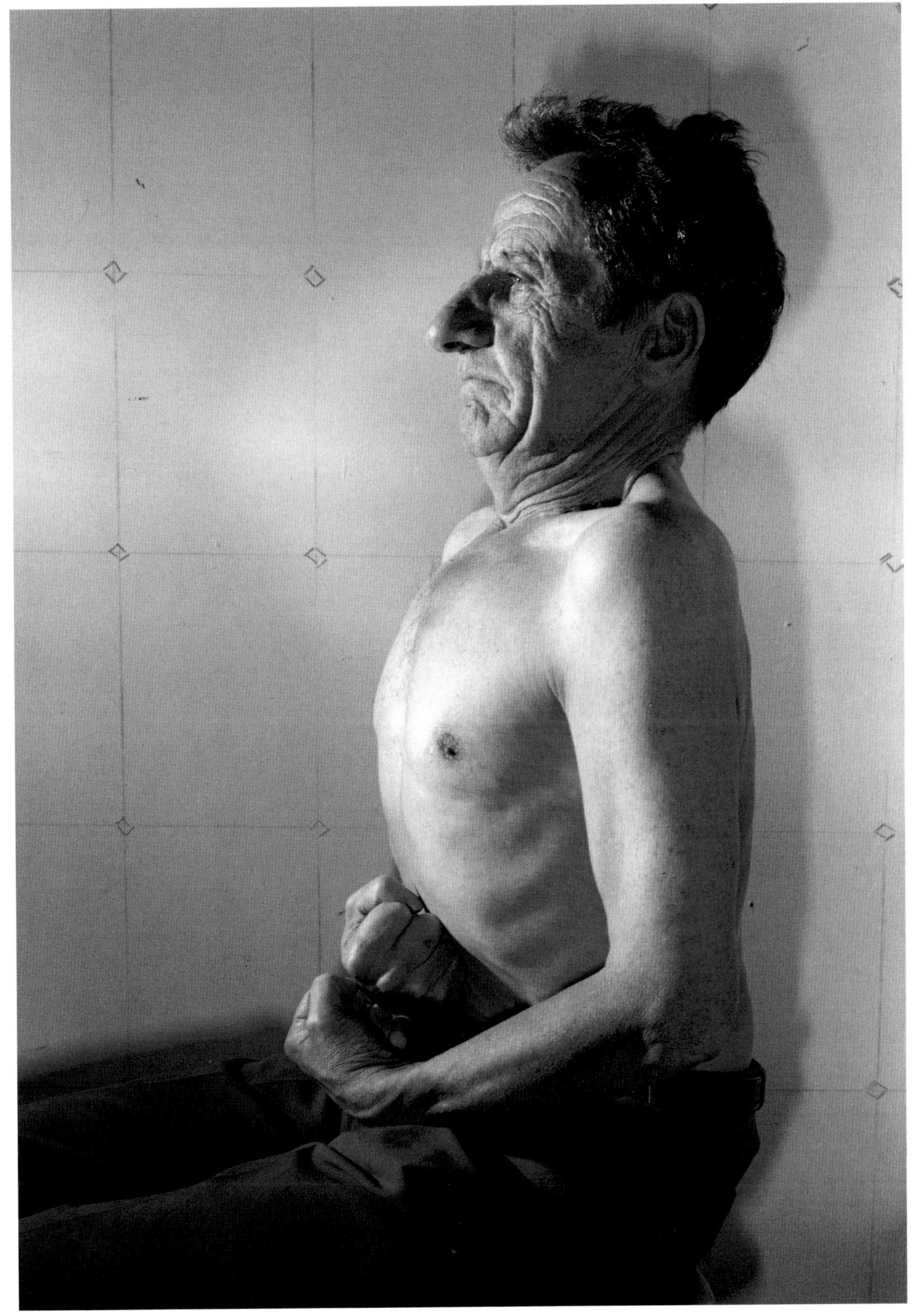



October 11, 1991

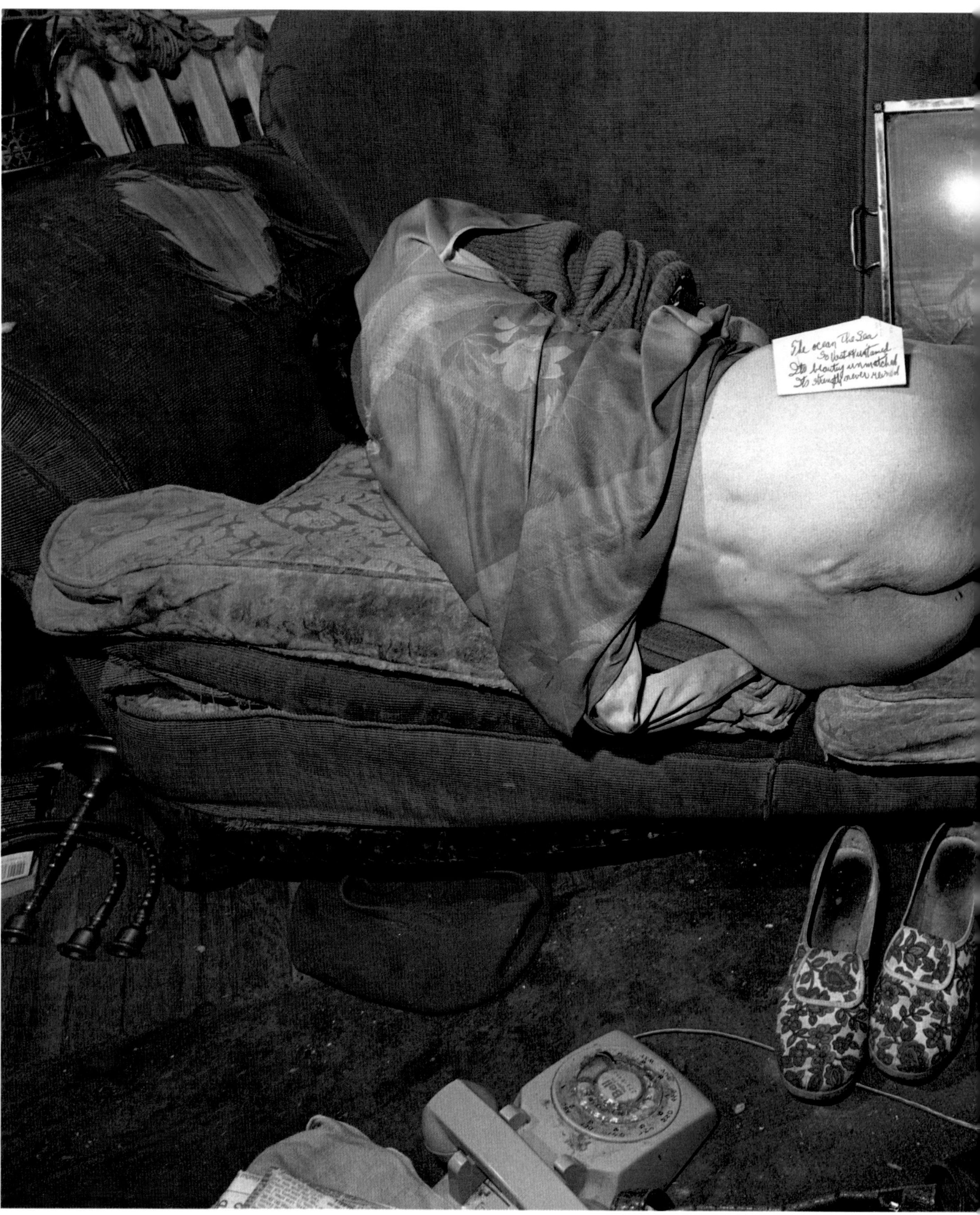

The ocean The Sea
So vast & untamed
Its beauty unmatched
Its strength never marred

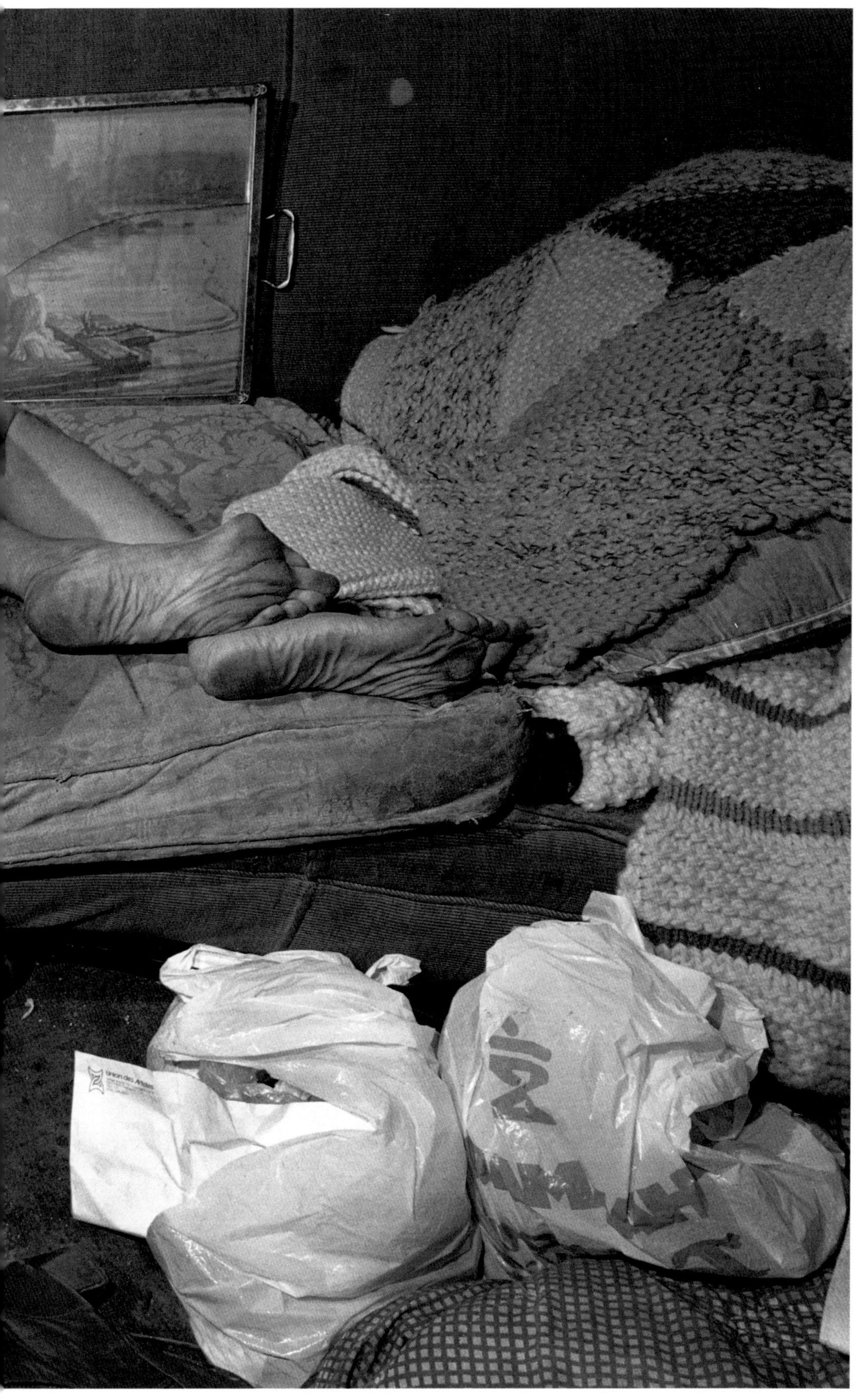

March 15, 1988

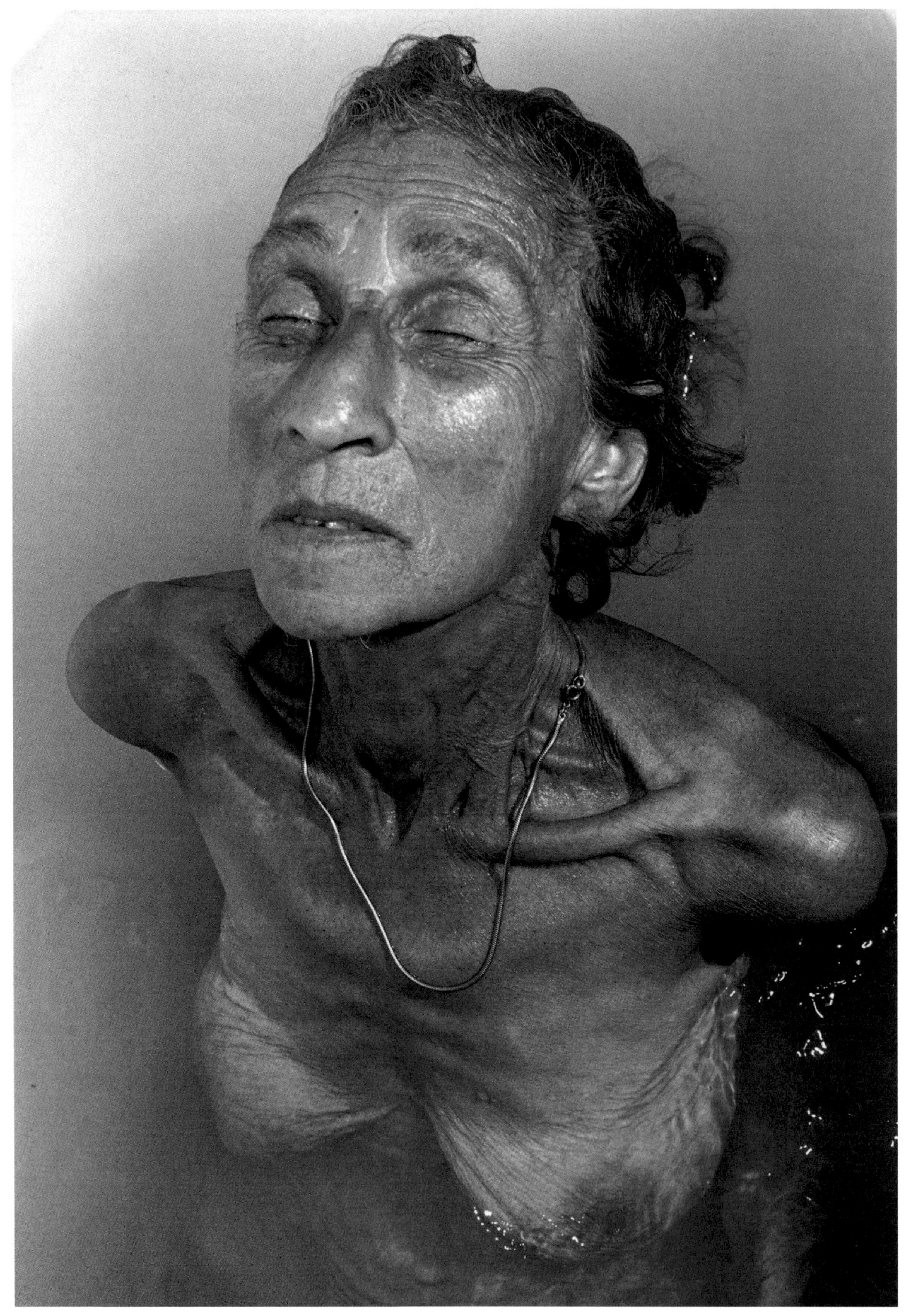



May 31, 1989

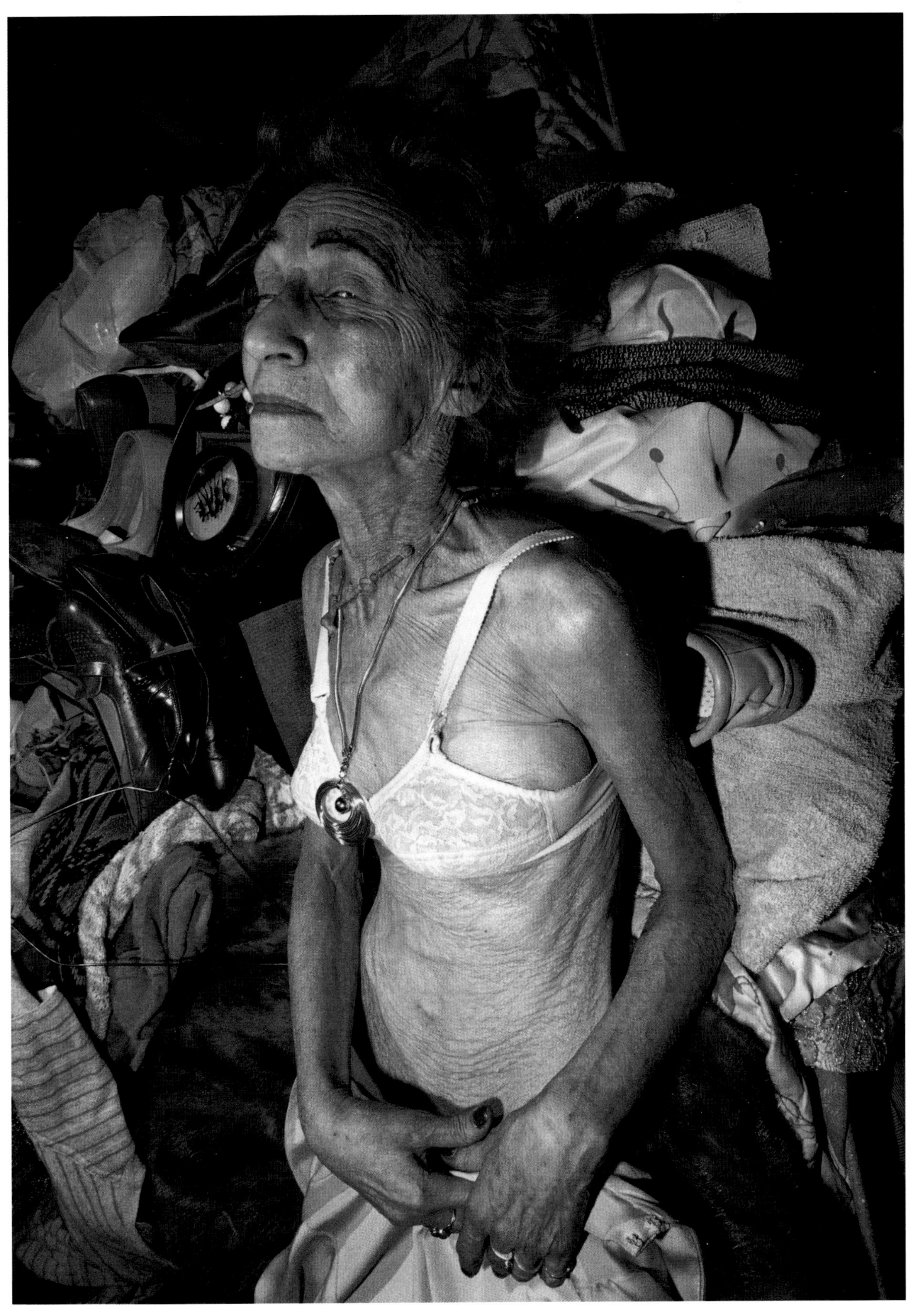



February 9, 1990

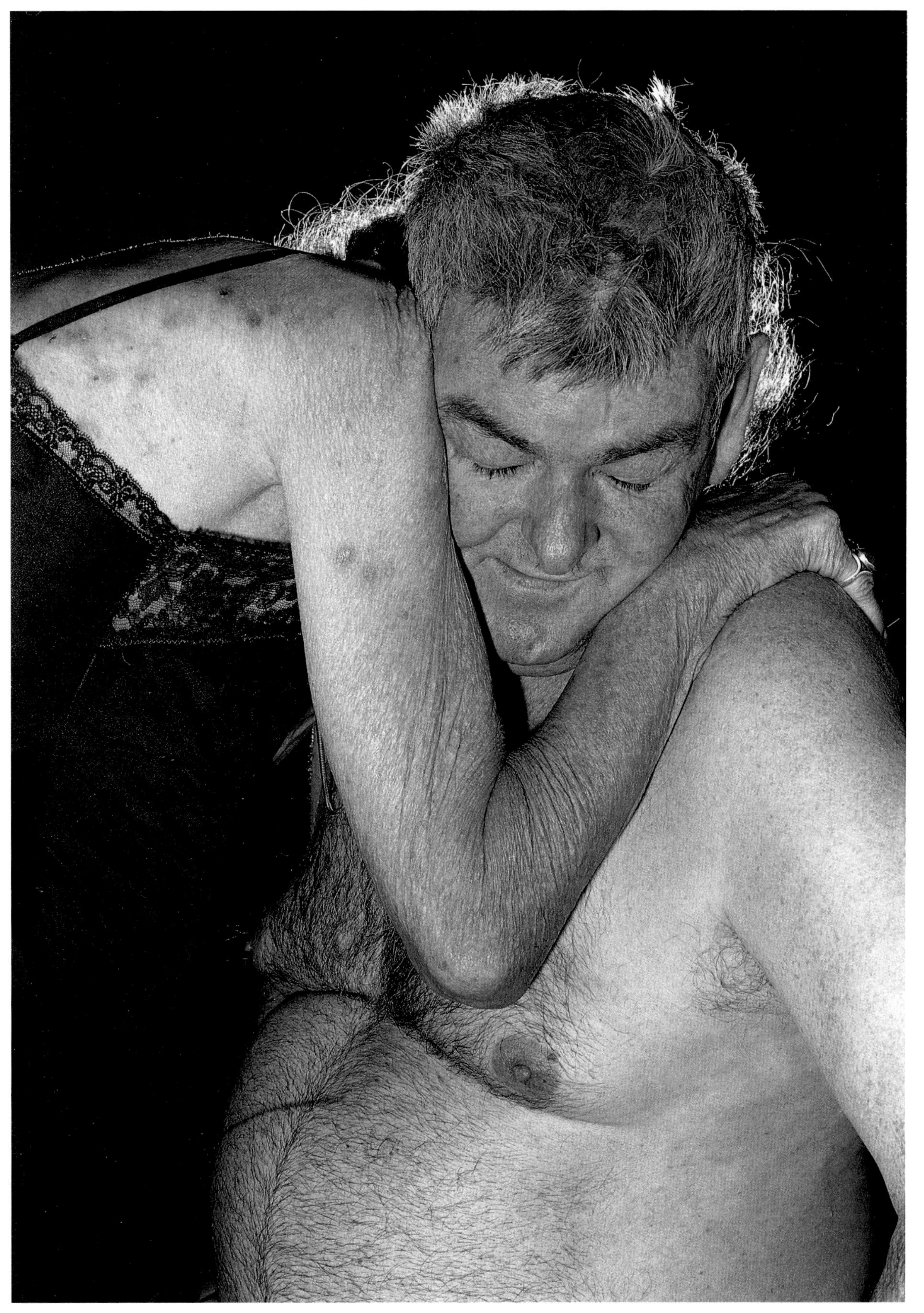



May 20, 1992

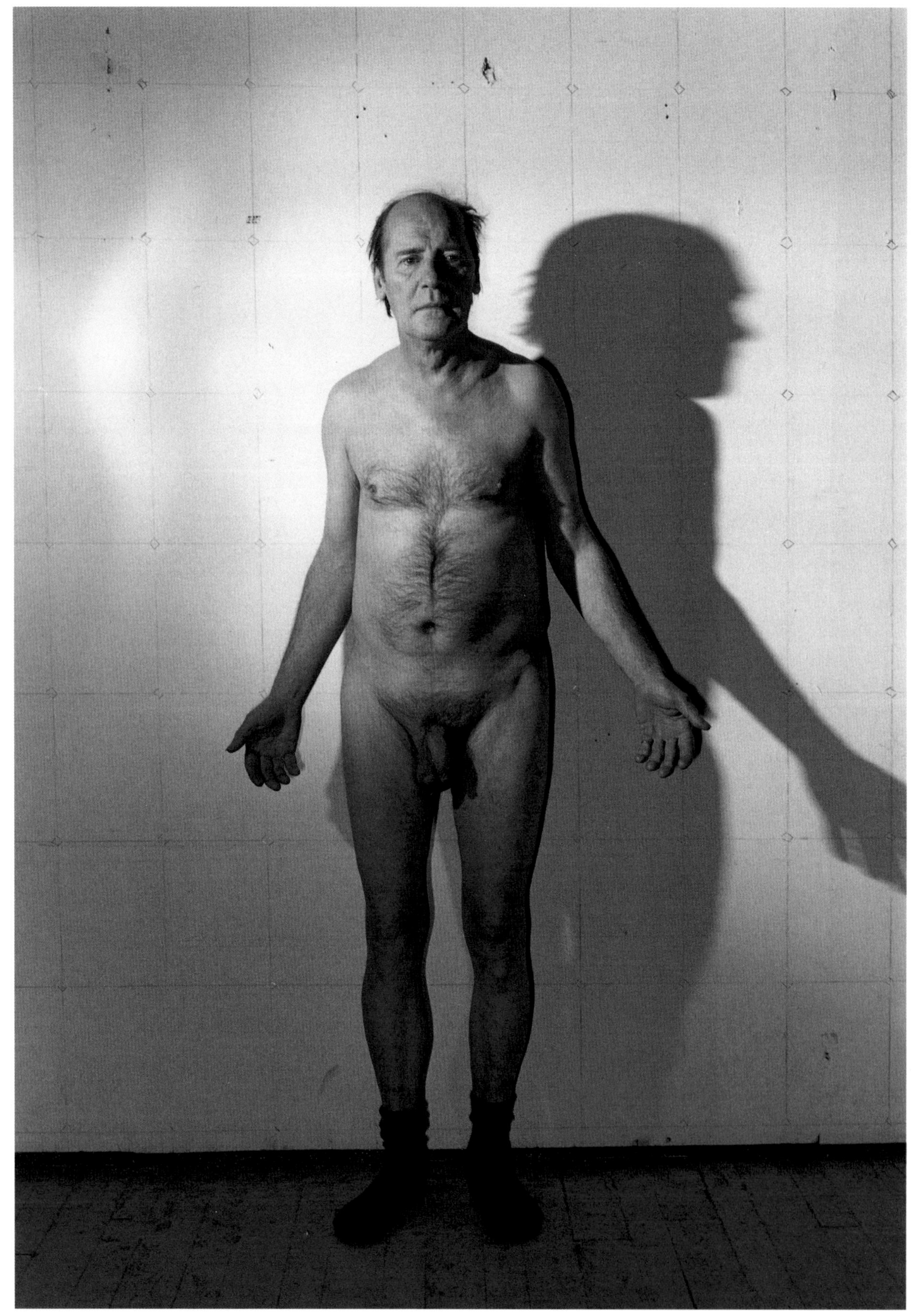

December 17, 1991

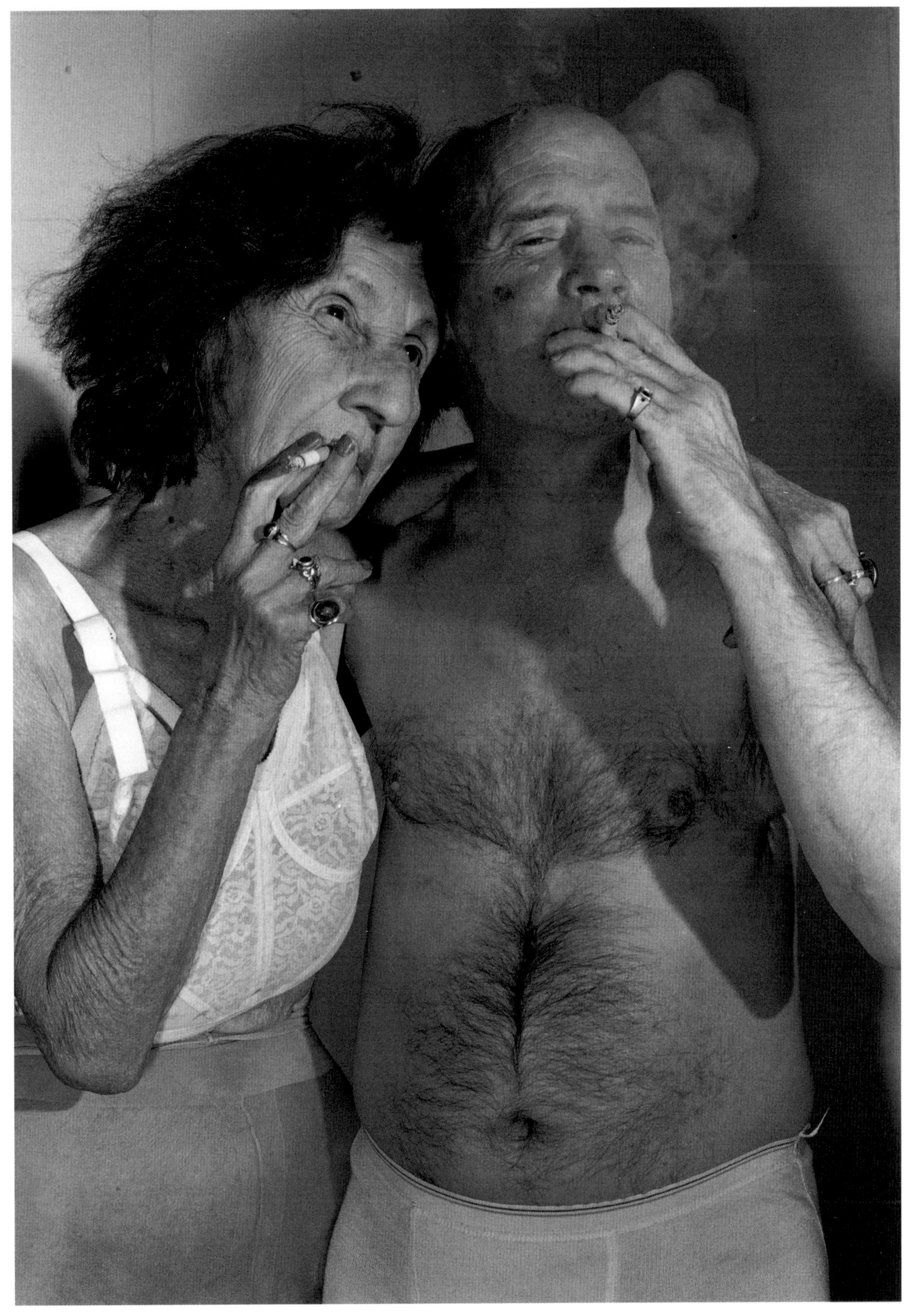



December 4, 1991

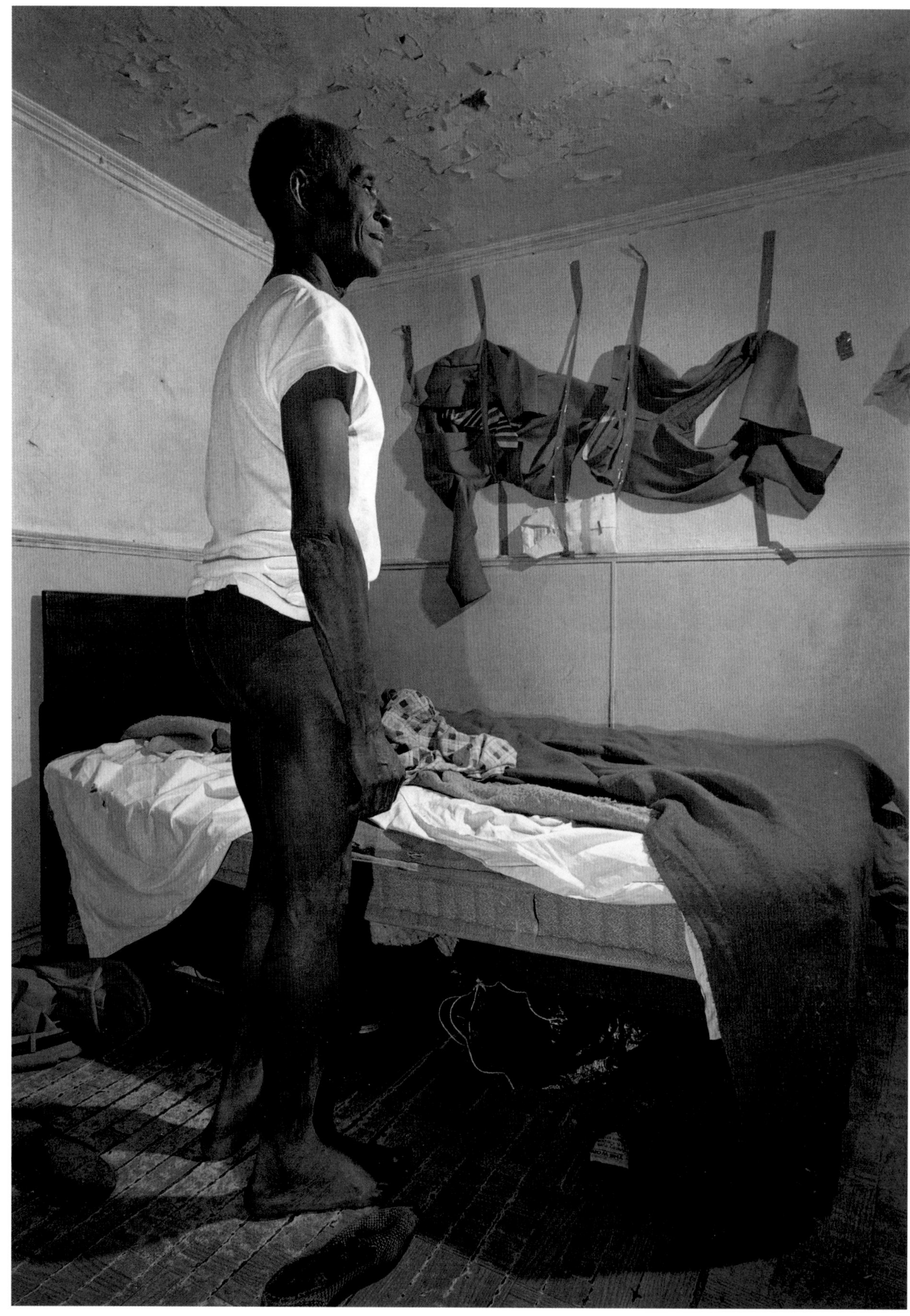



January 27, 1987

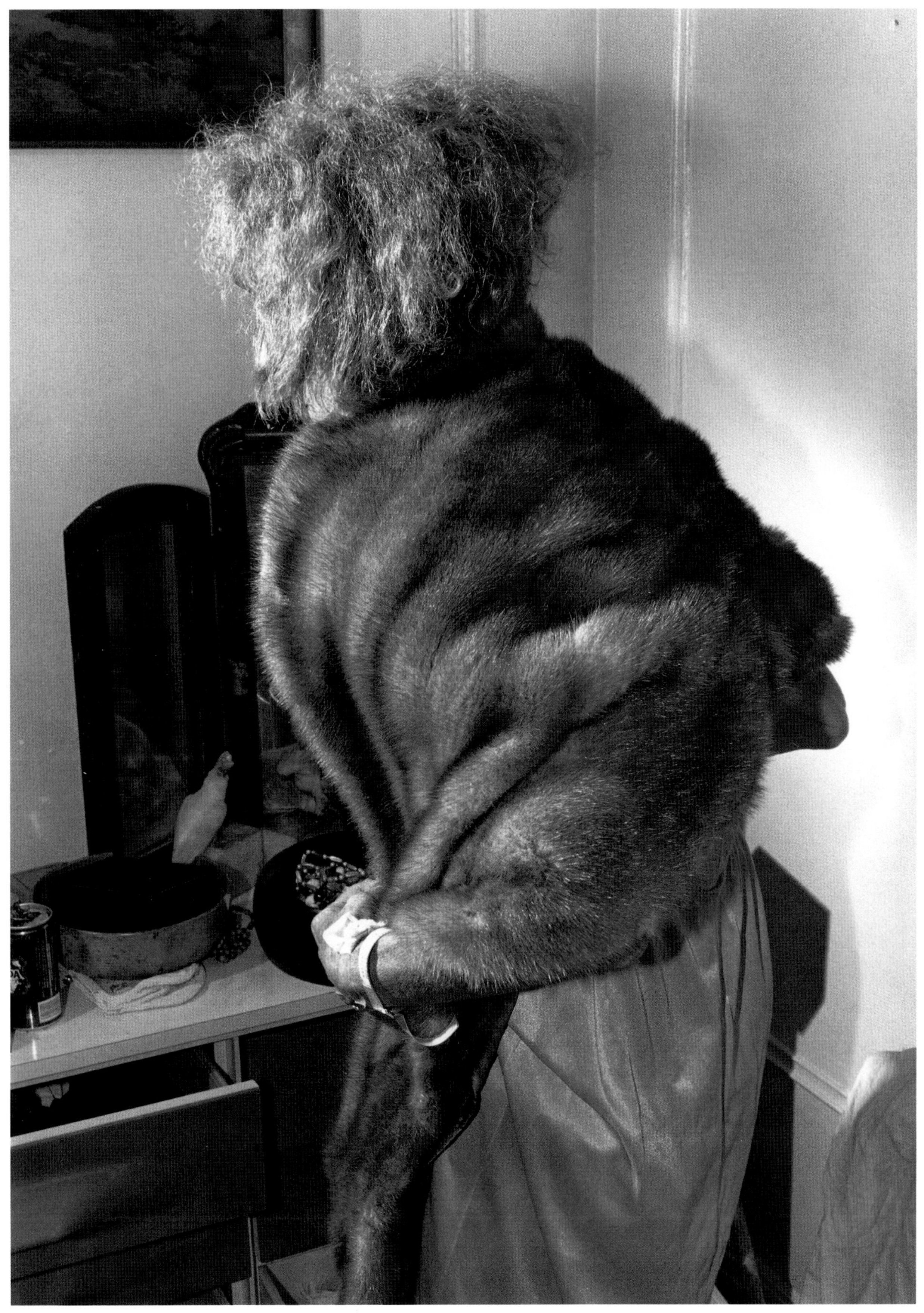



June 13, 1989

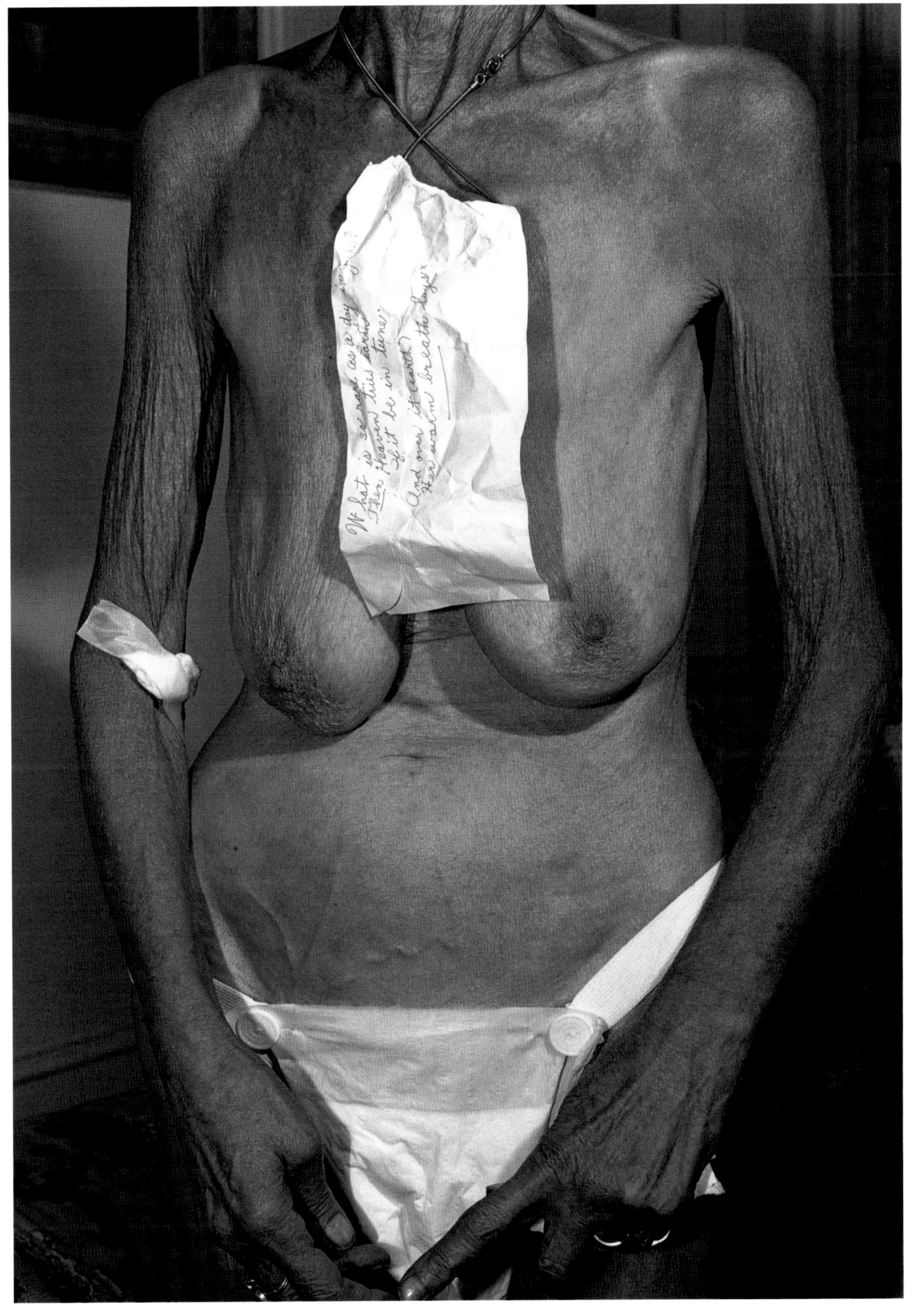
What is so rare as a day in June?
Then Heaven tries earth
If it be in tune;
And over it (earth)
Her warm breath lays



June 7, 1989

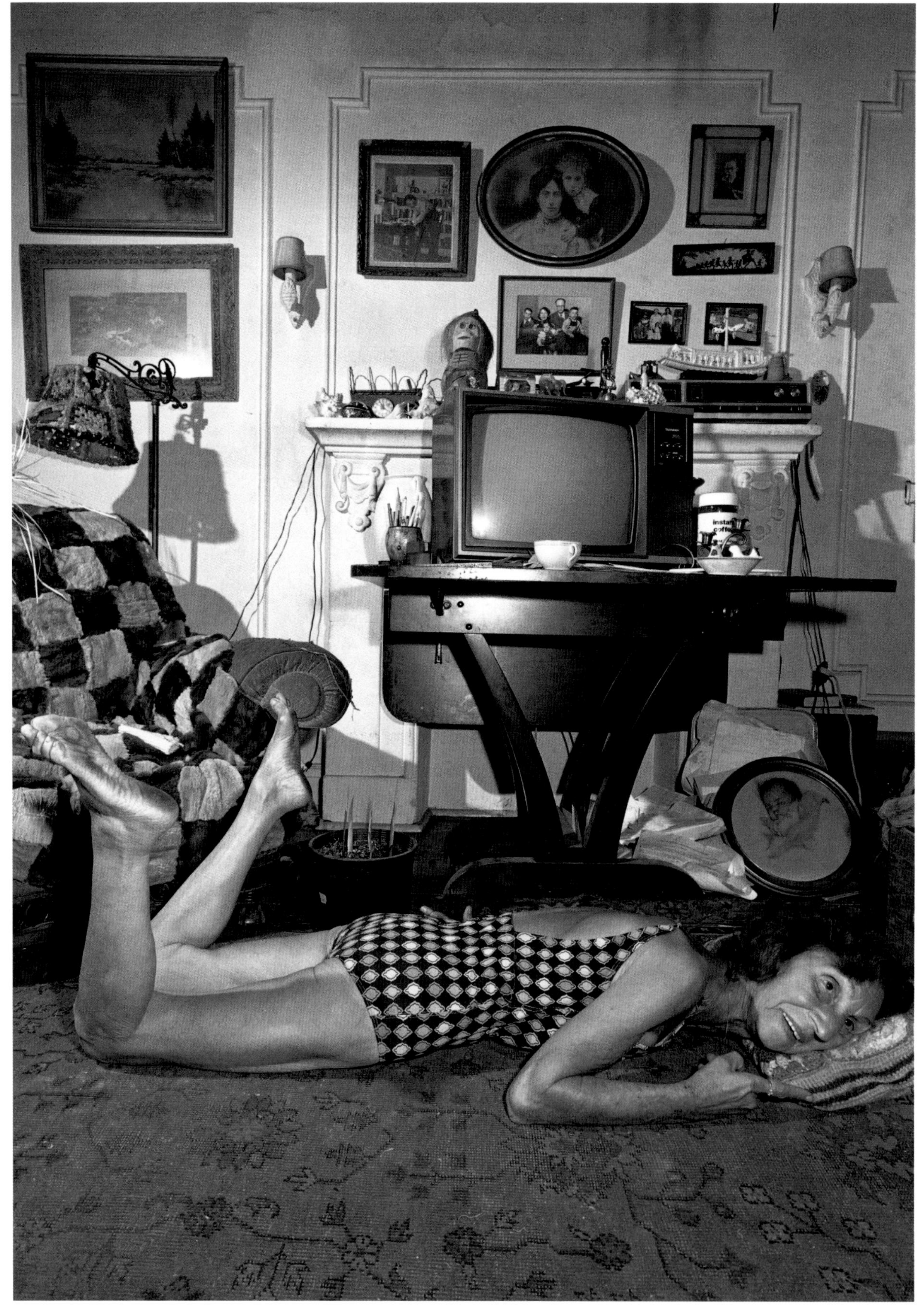



June 14, 1985

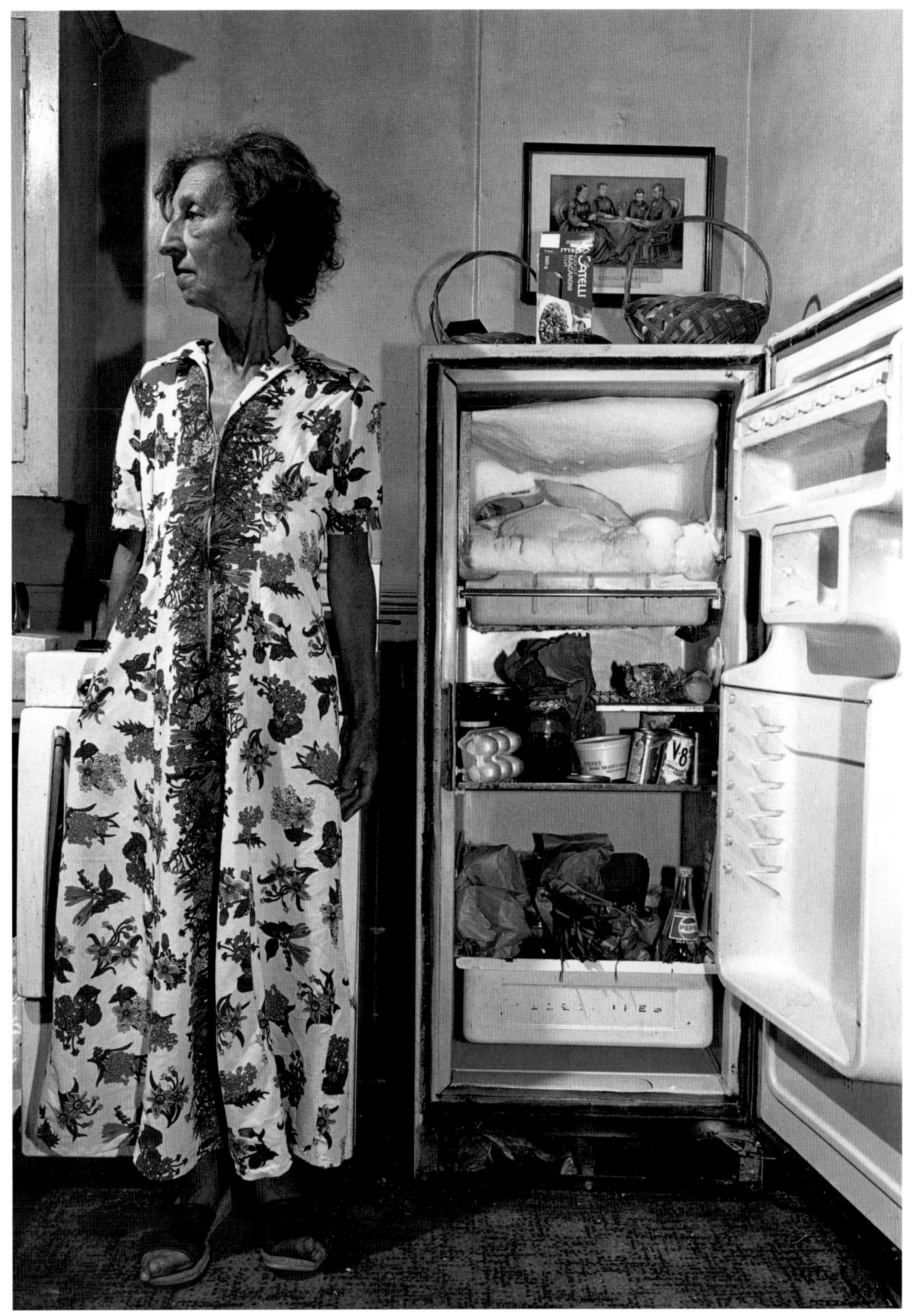




July 24, 1982

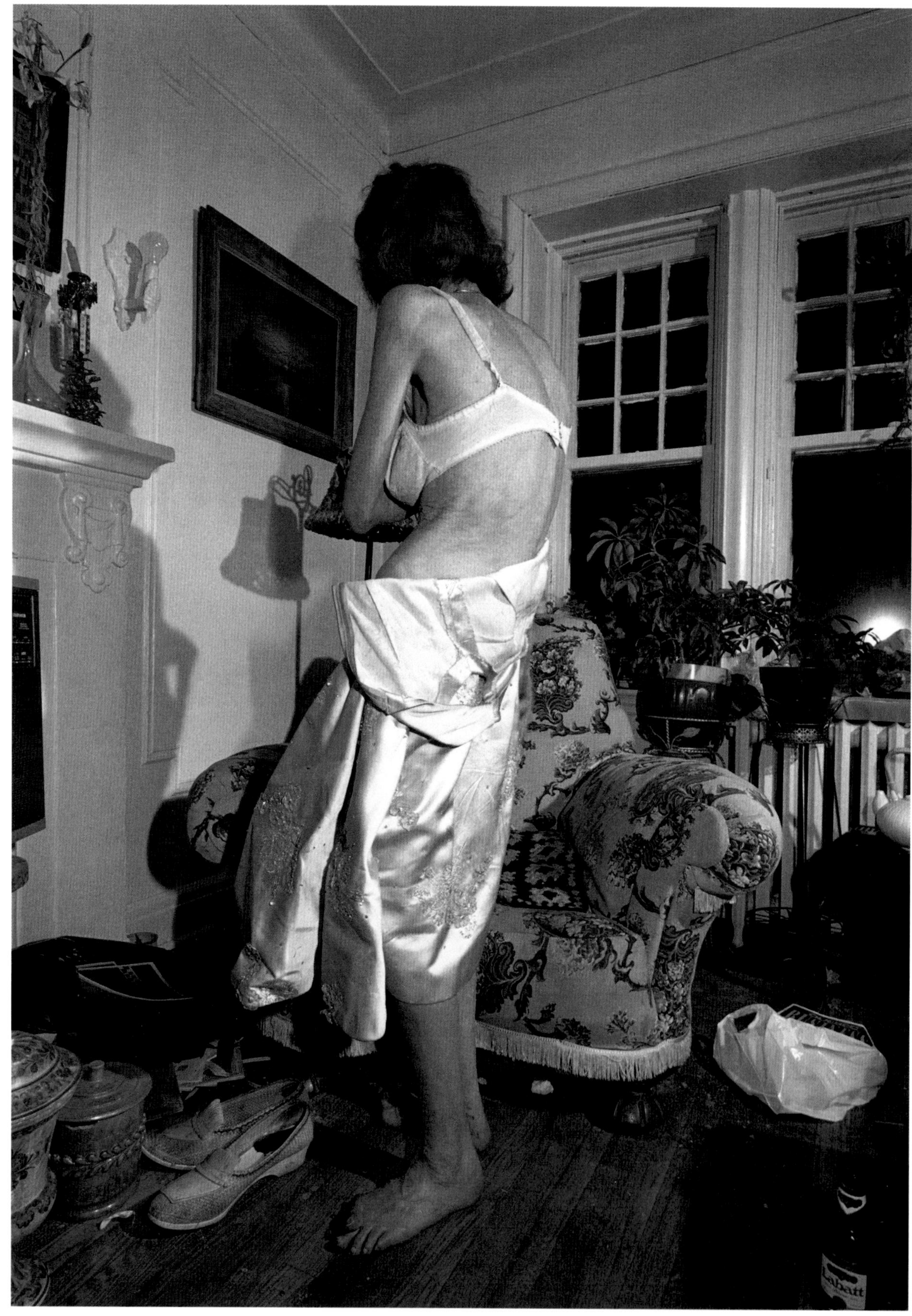




February 7, 1989

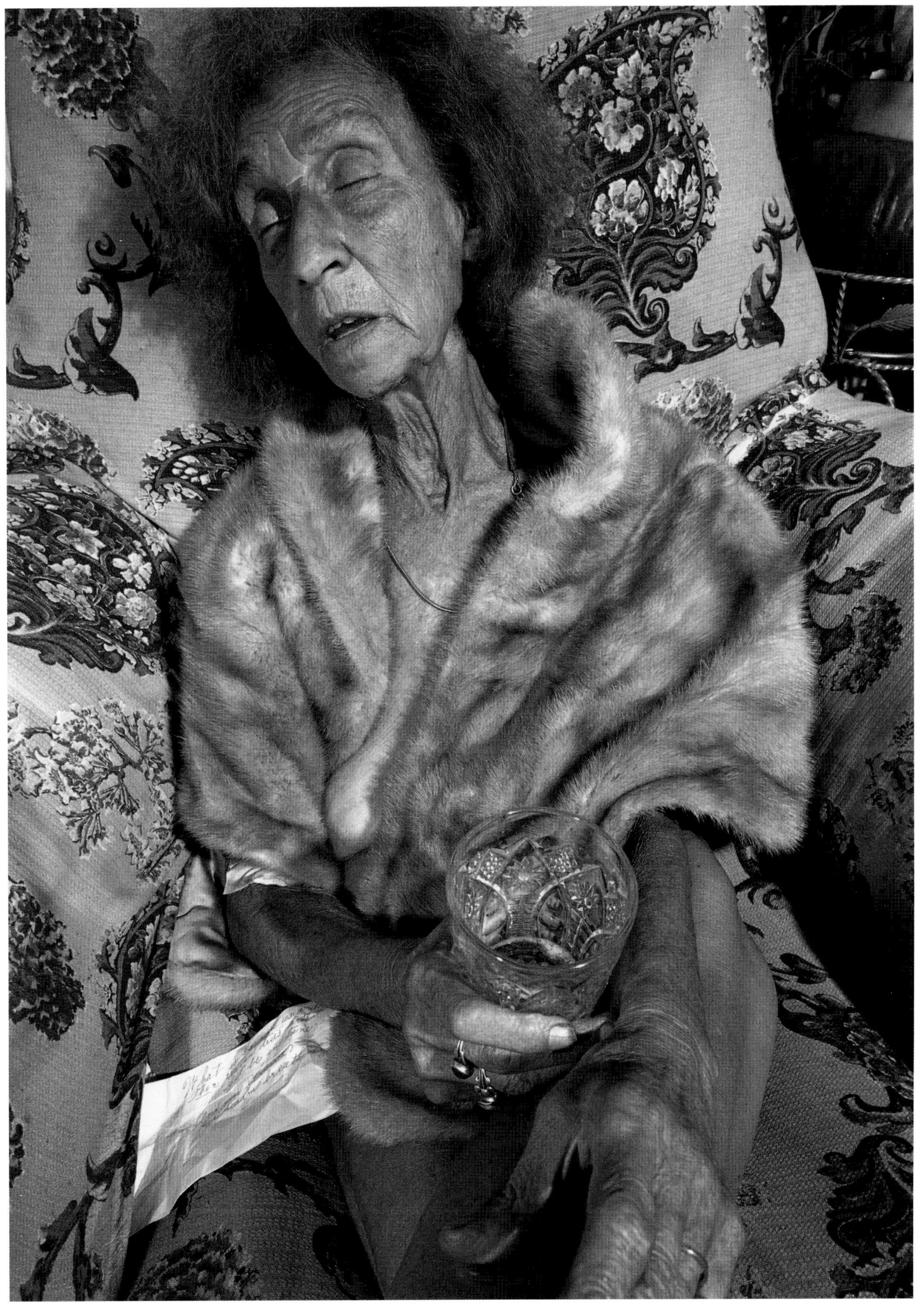

July 7, 1989

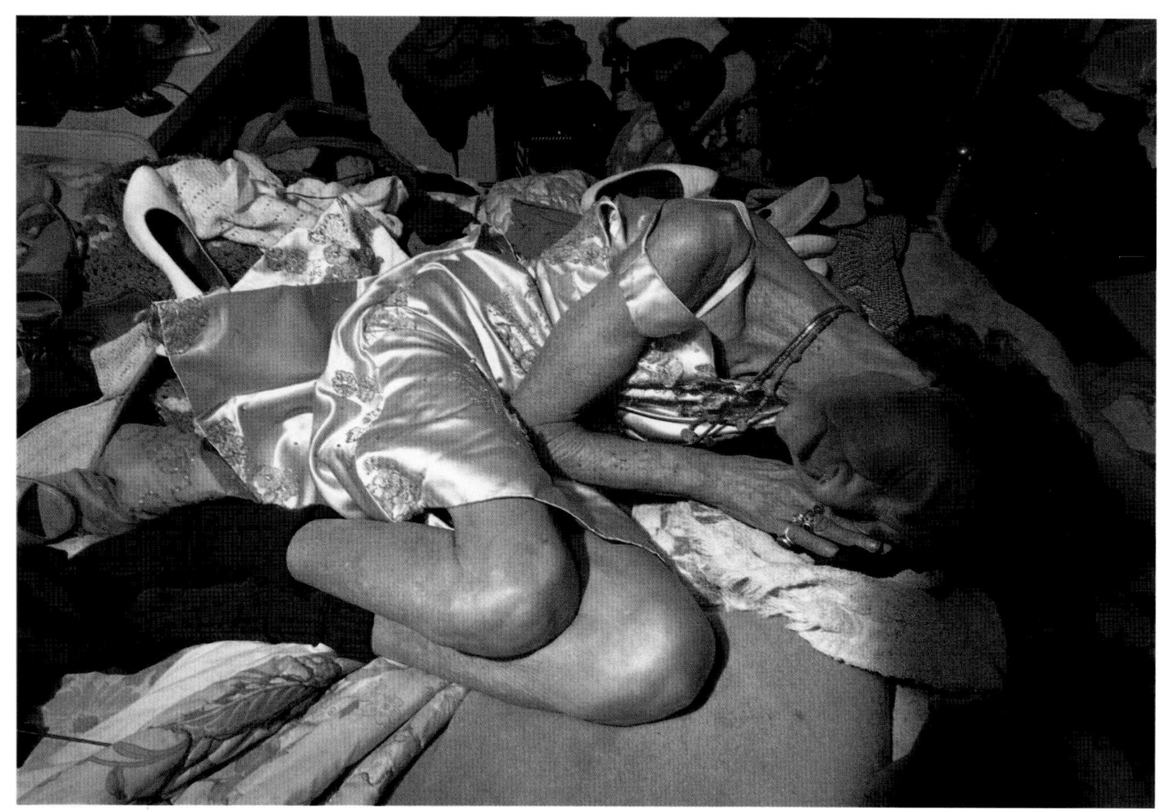

January 28, 1990

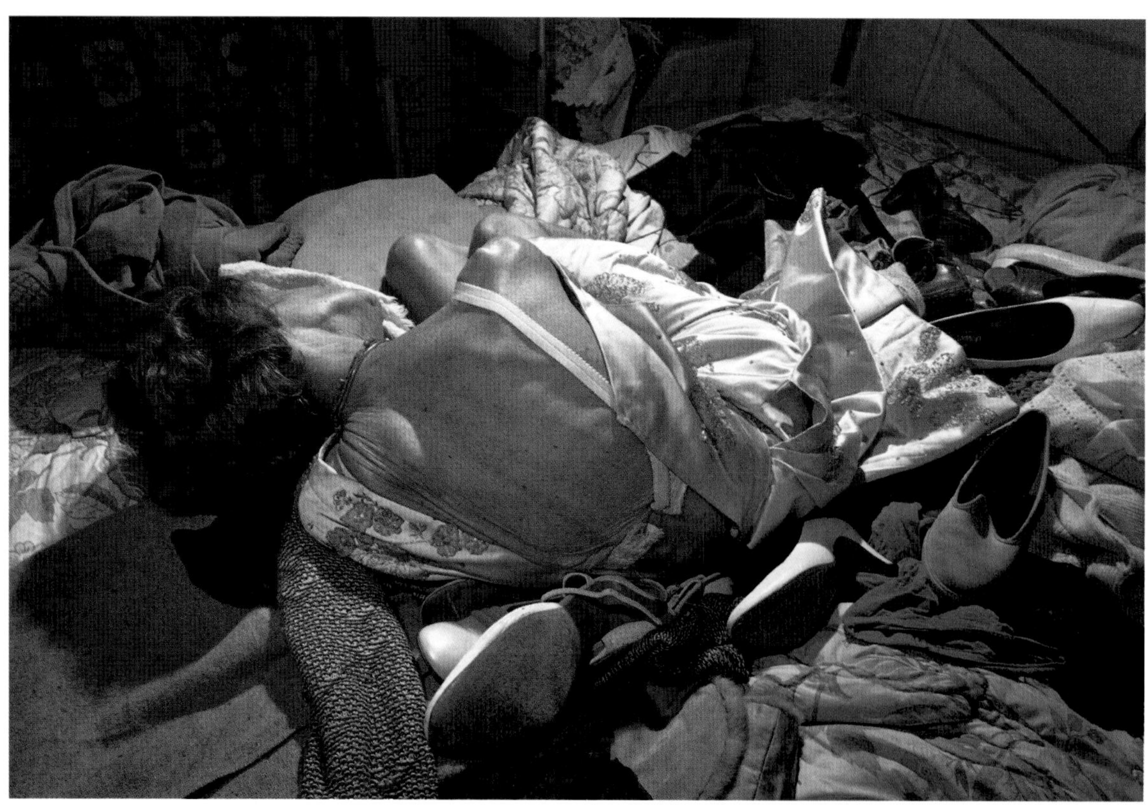



January 28, 1990

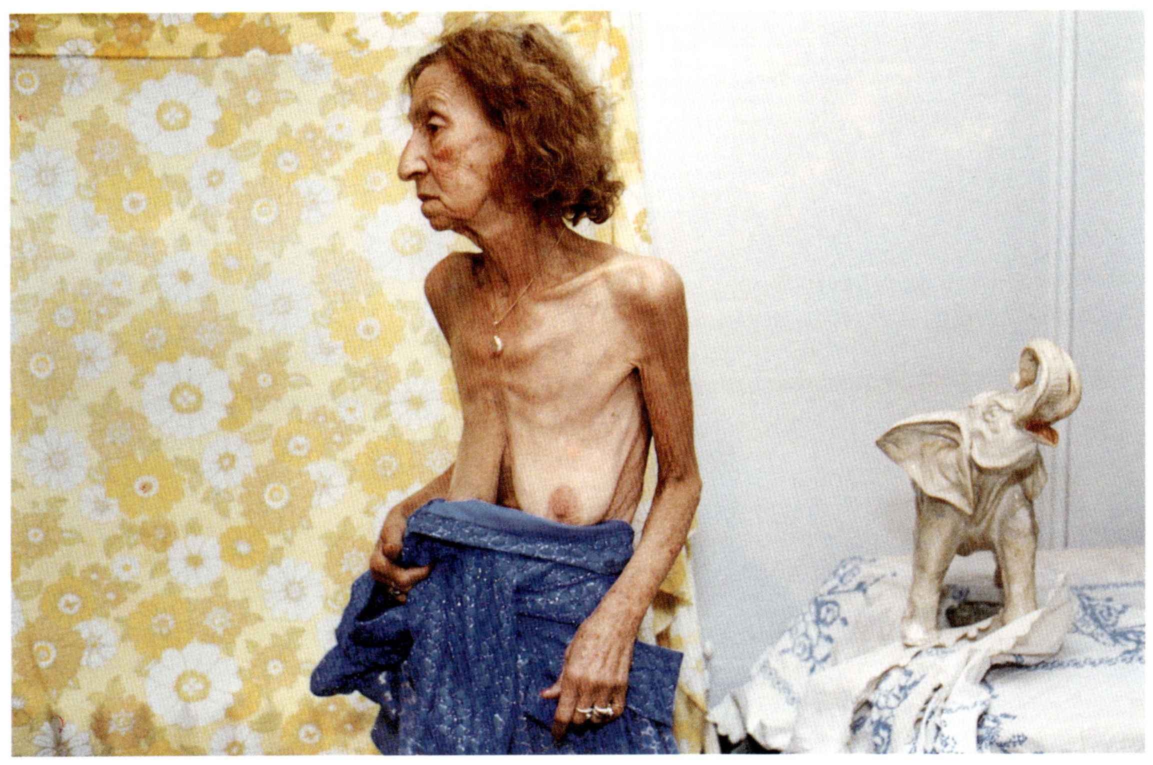

May 18, 1990

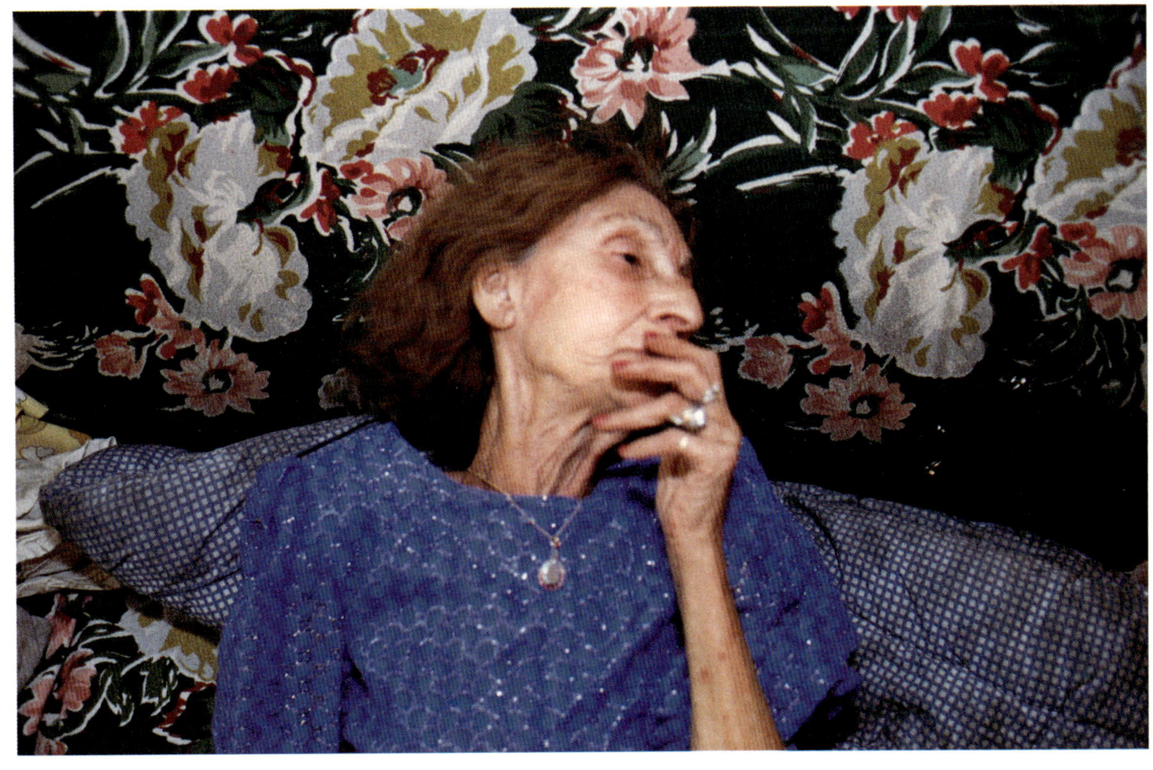

May 18, 1990

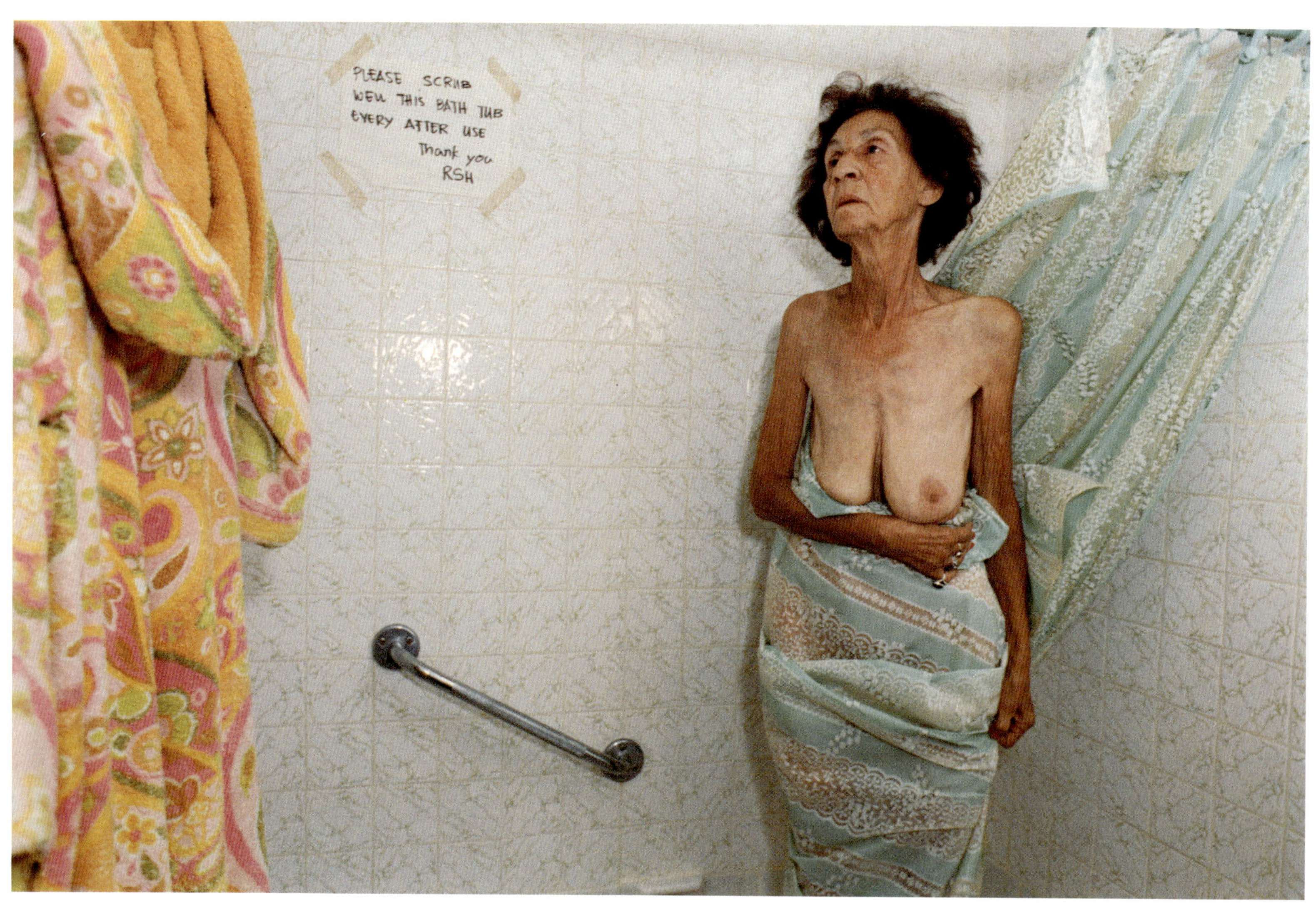


October 10, 1991

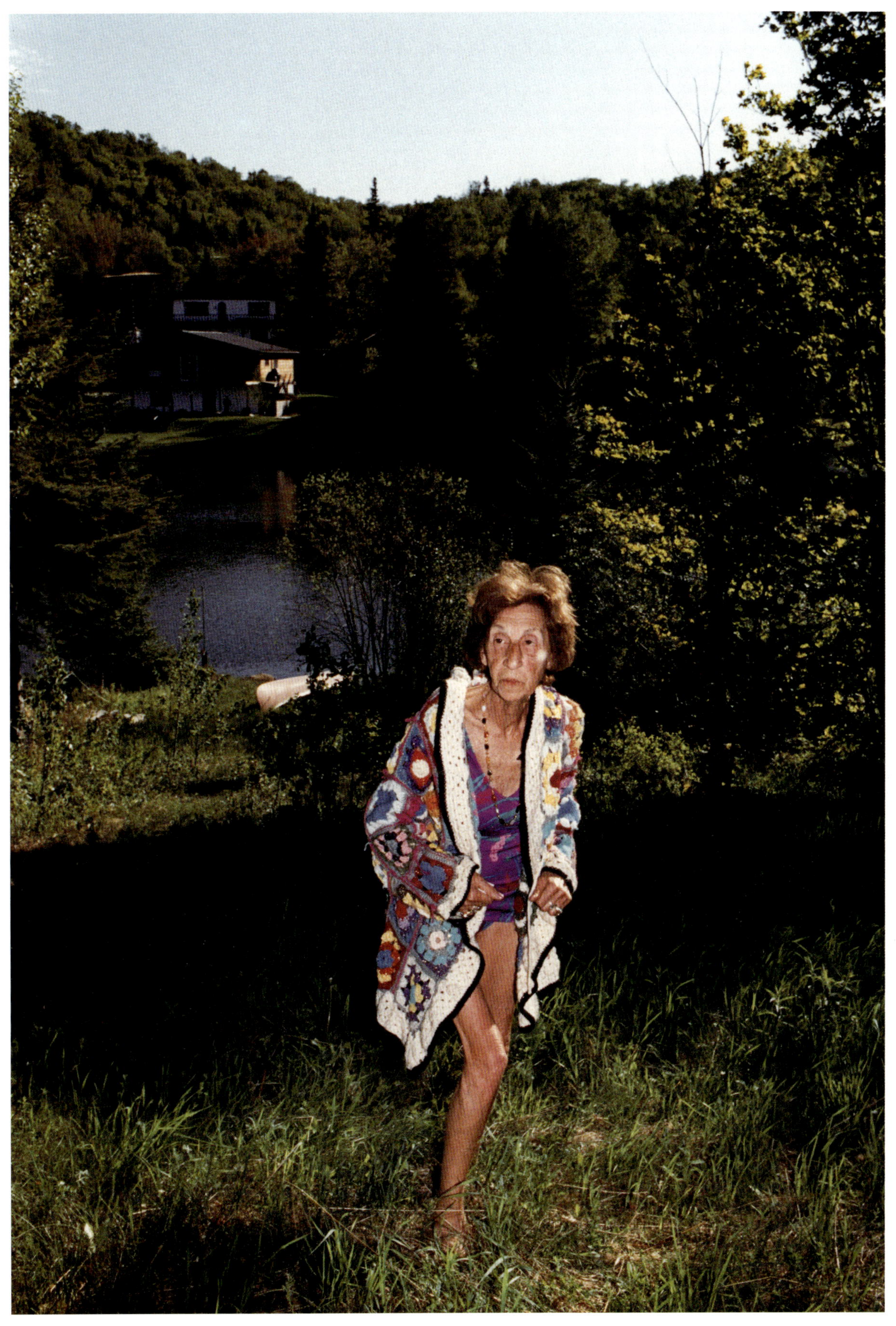



June 1, 1990

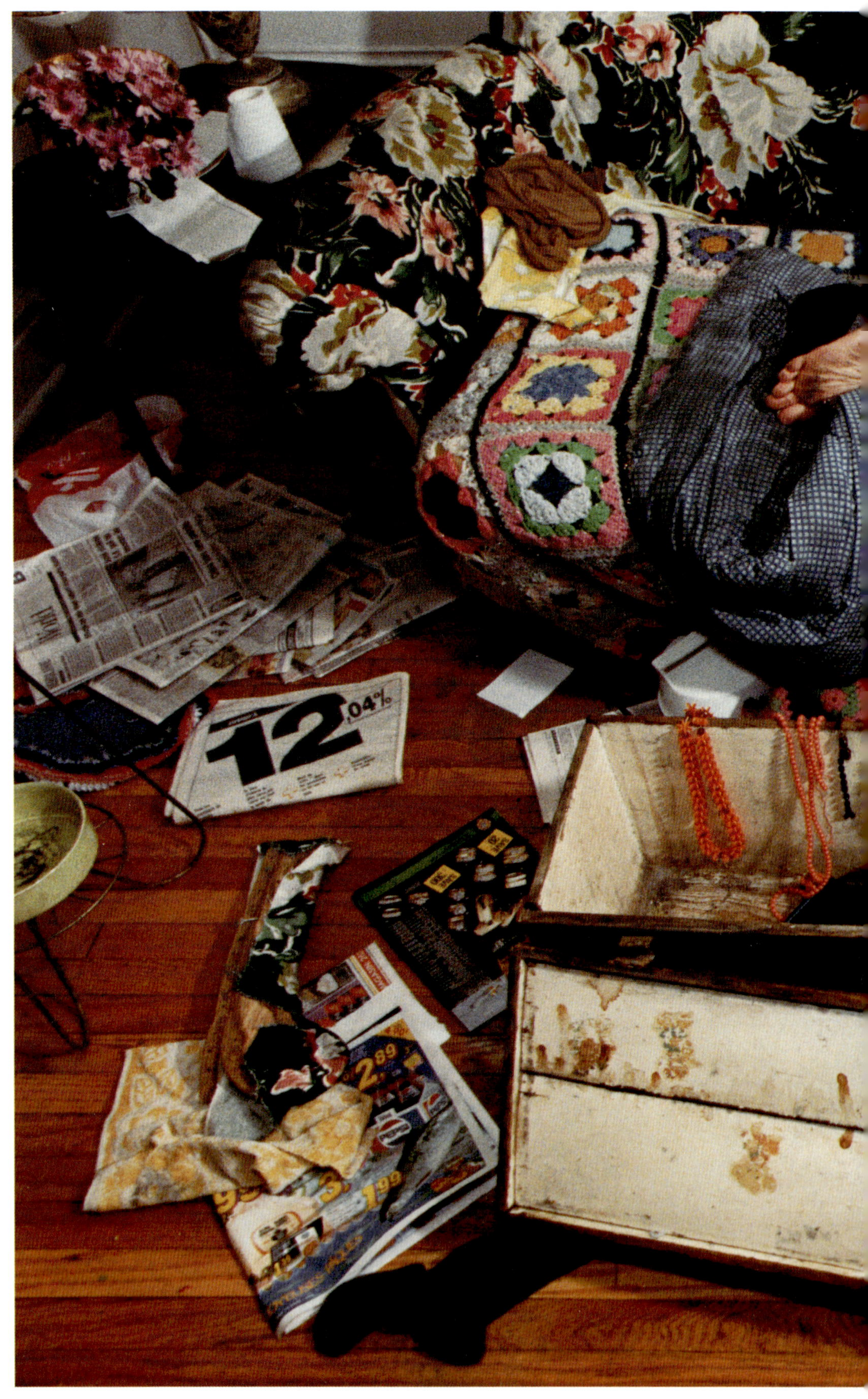




April 11, 1990

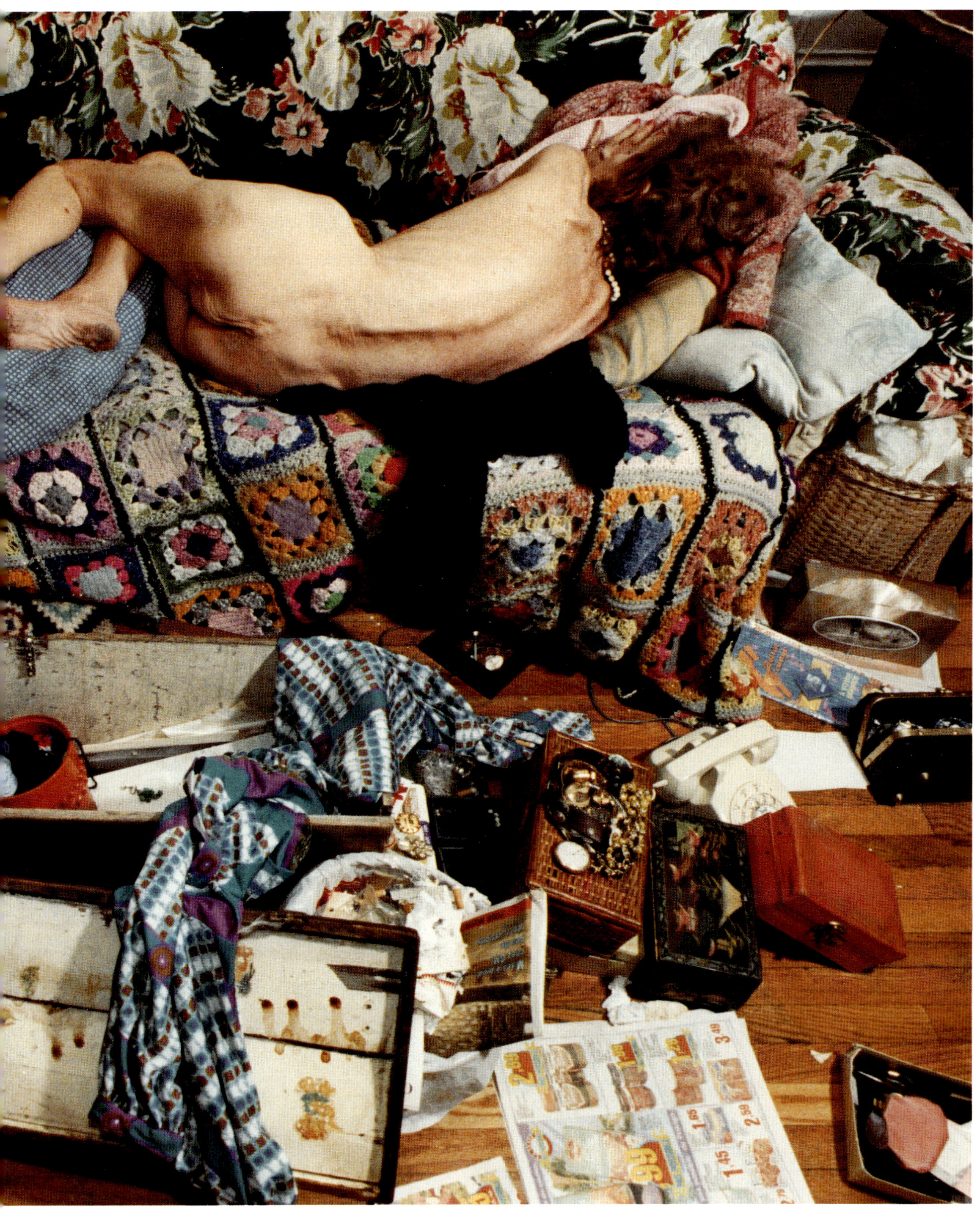

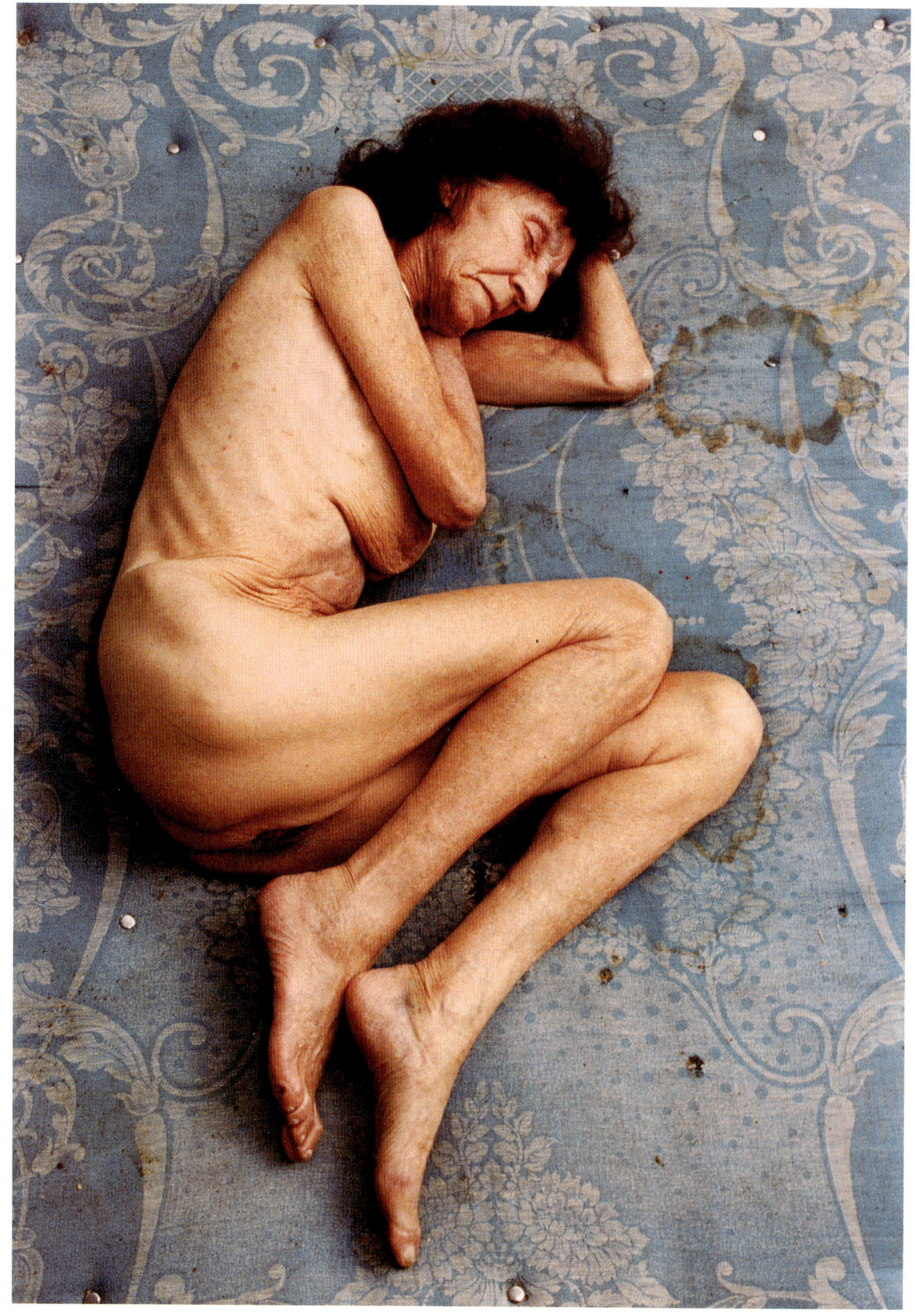

April 27, 1991

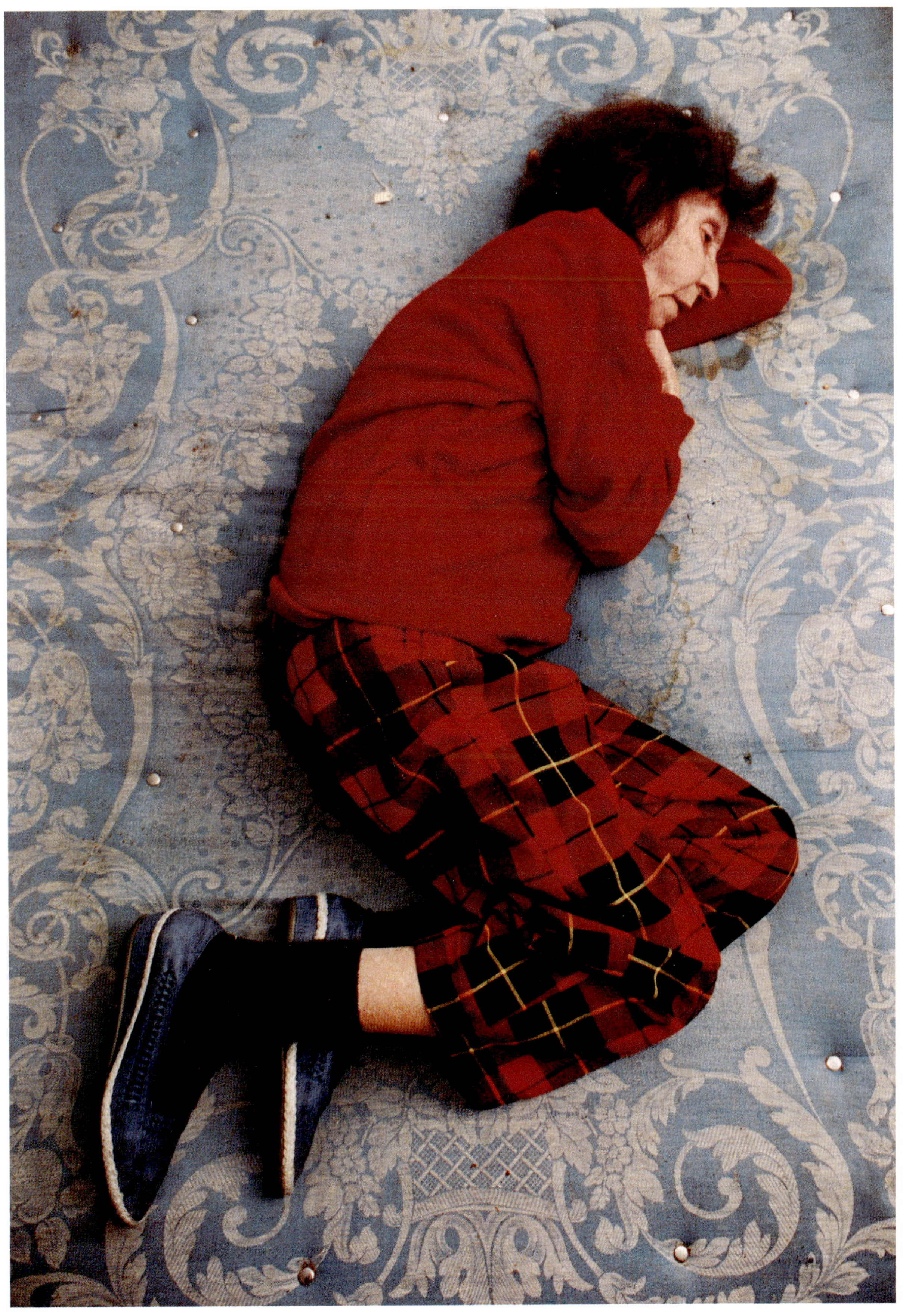



April 27, 1991

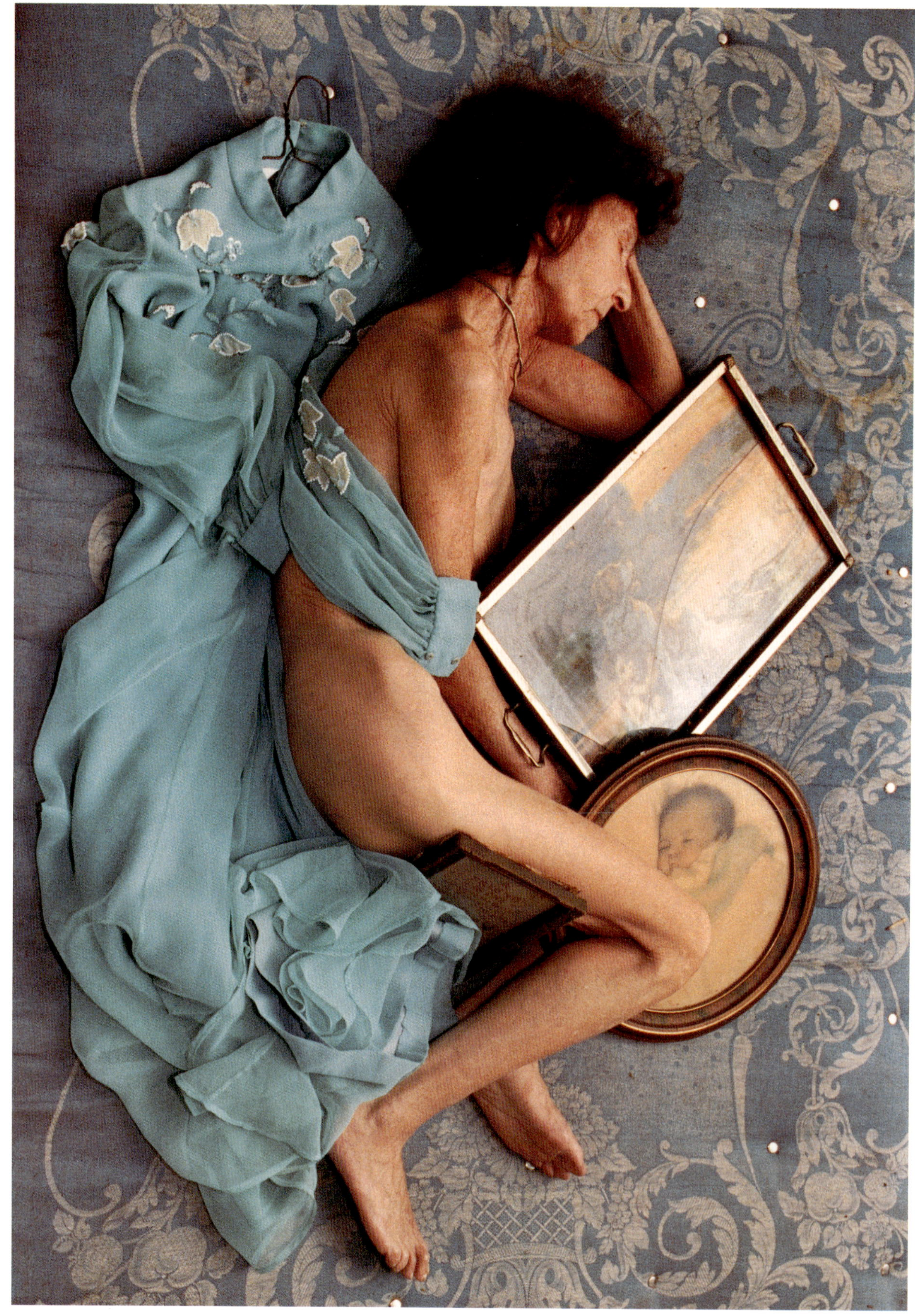



April 27, 1991

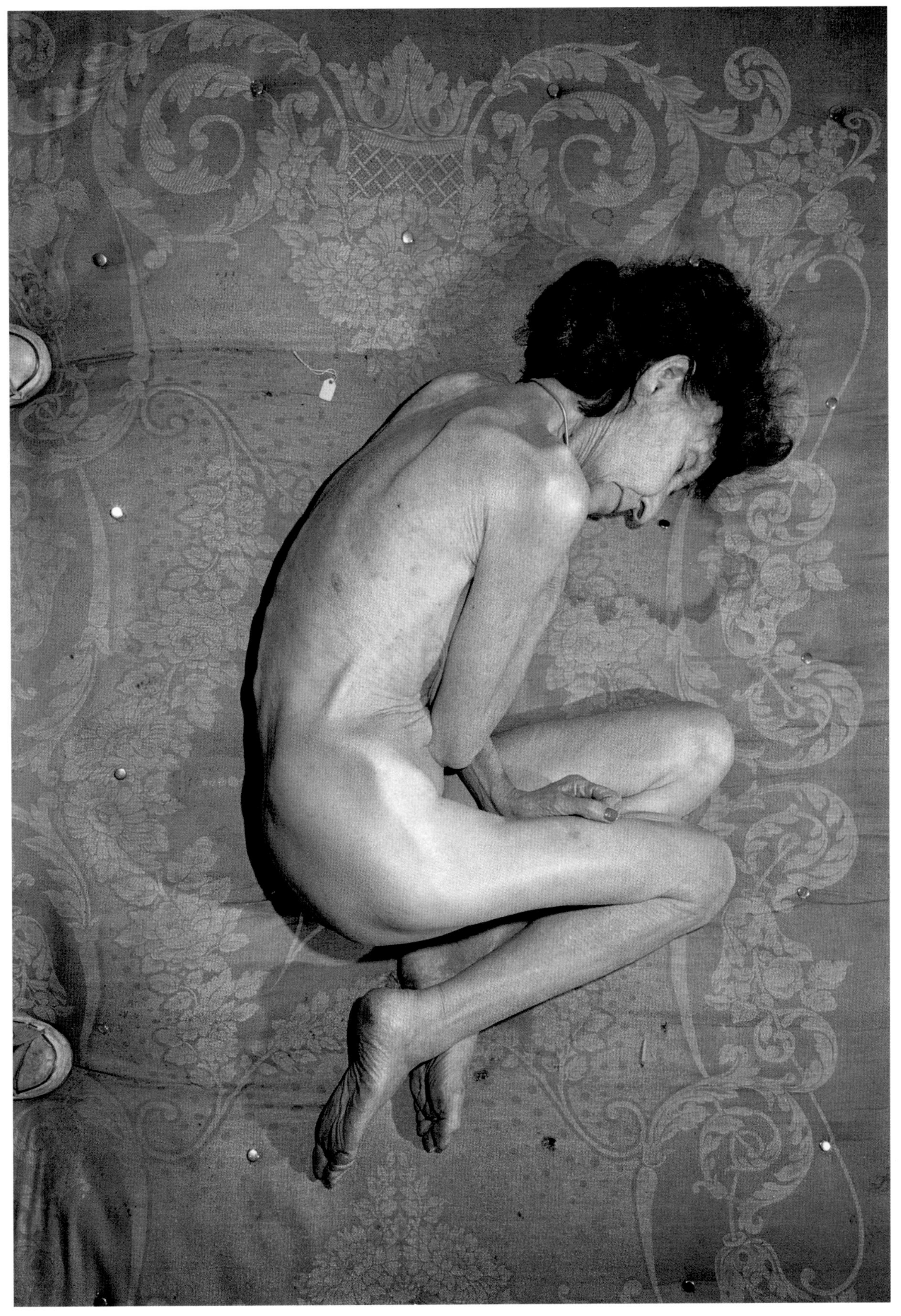



April 27, 1991

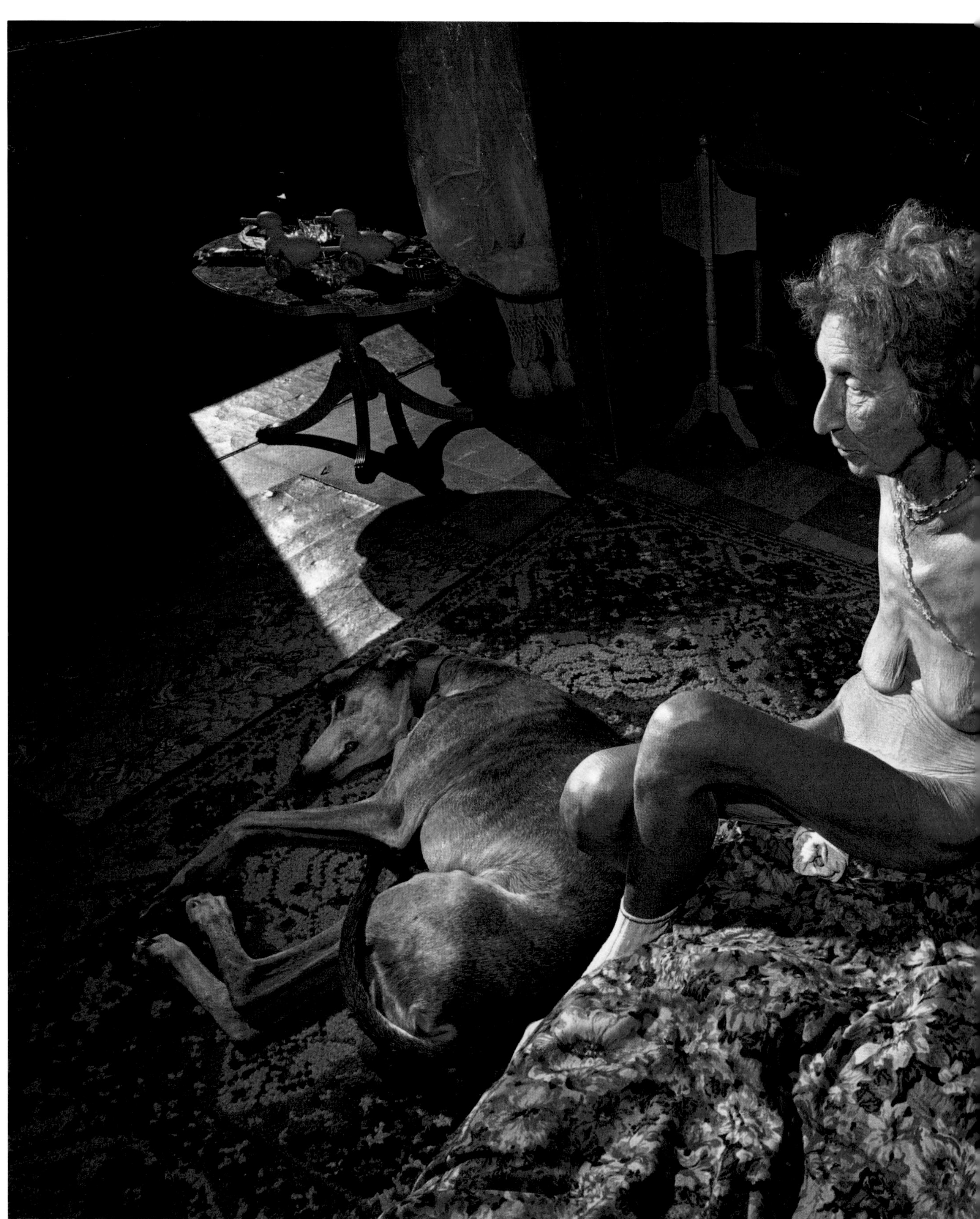

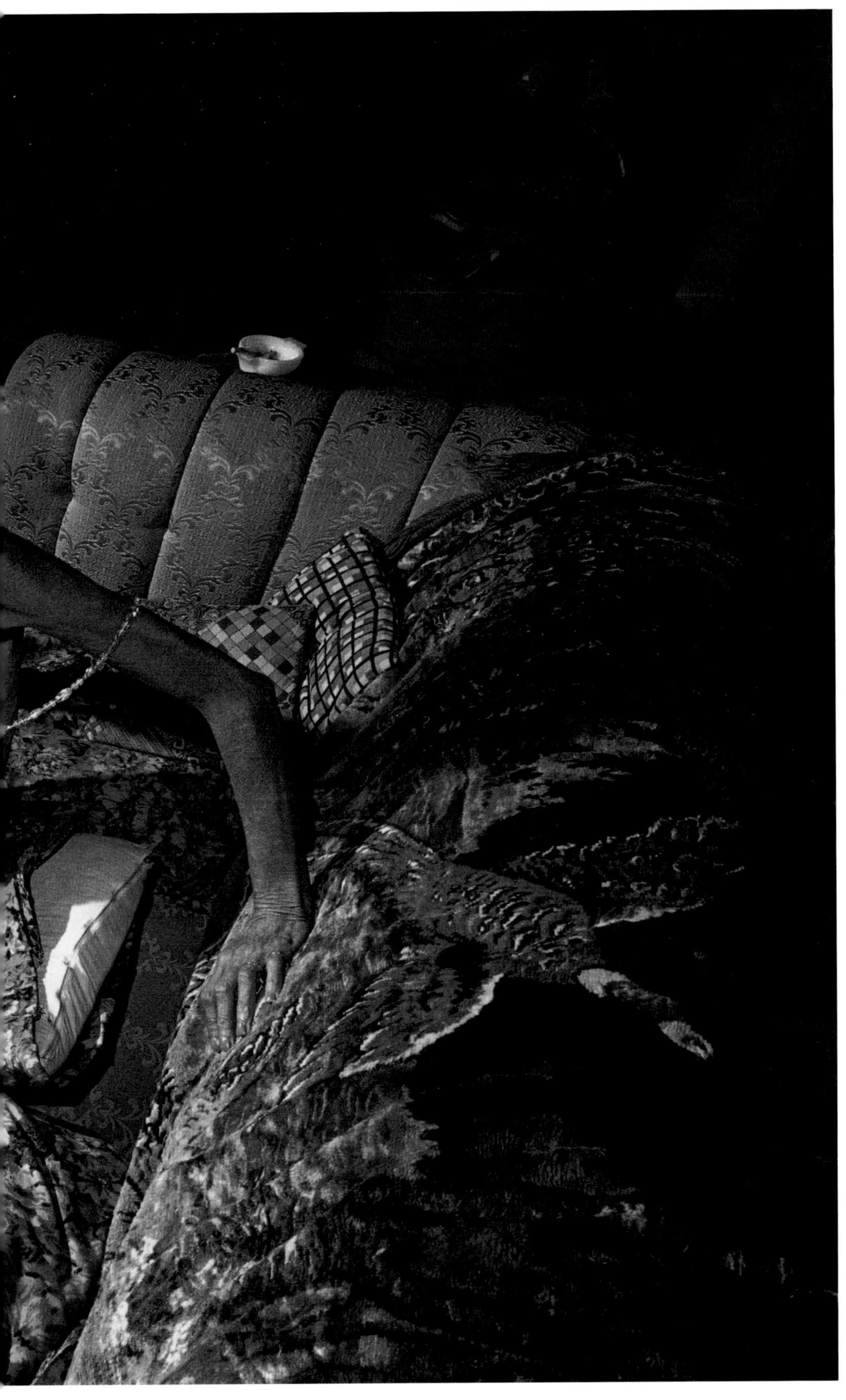

August 24, 1989

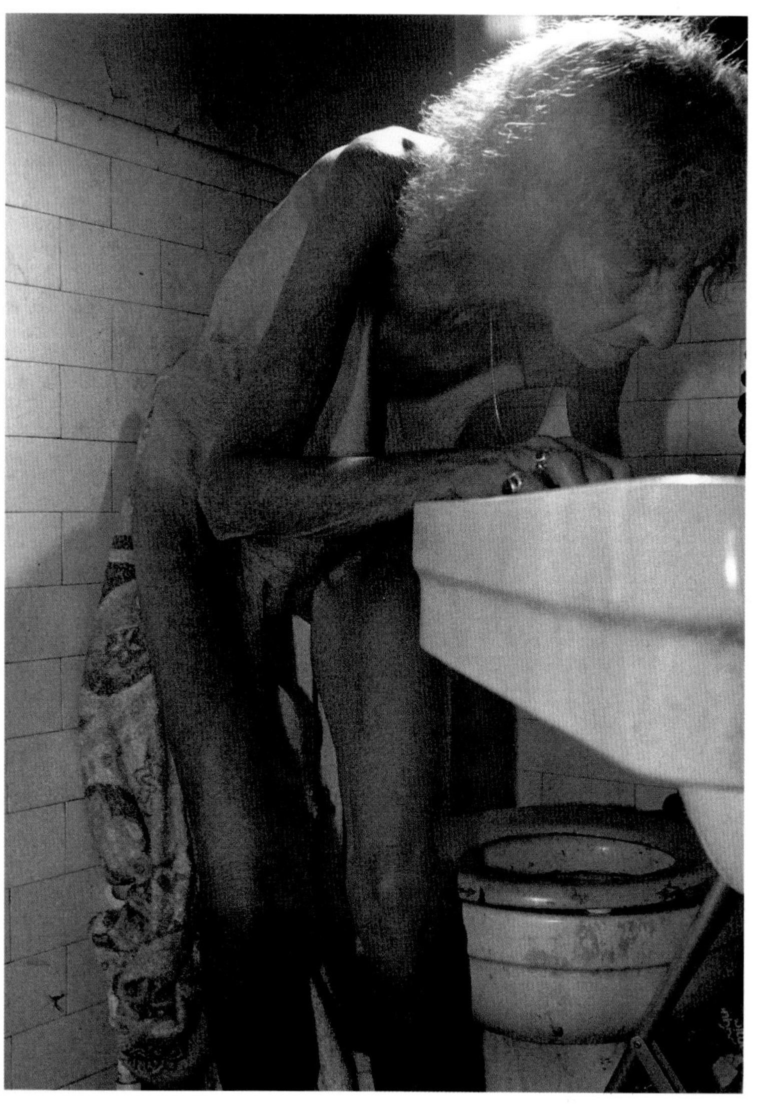

May 31, 1989

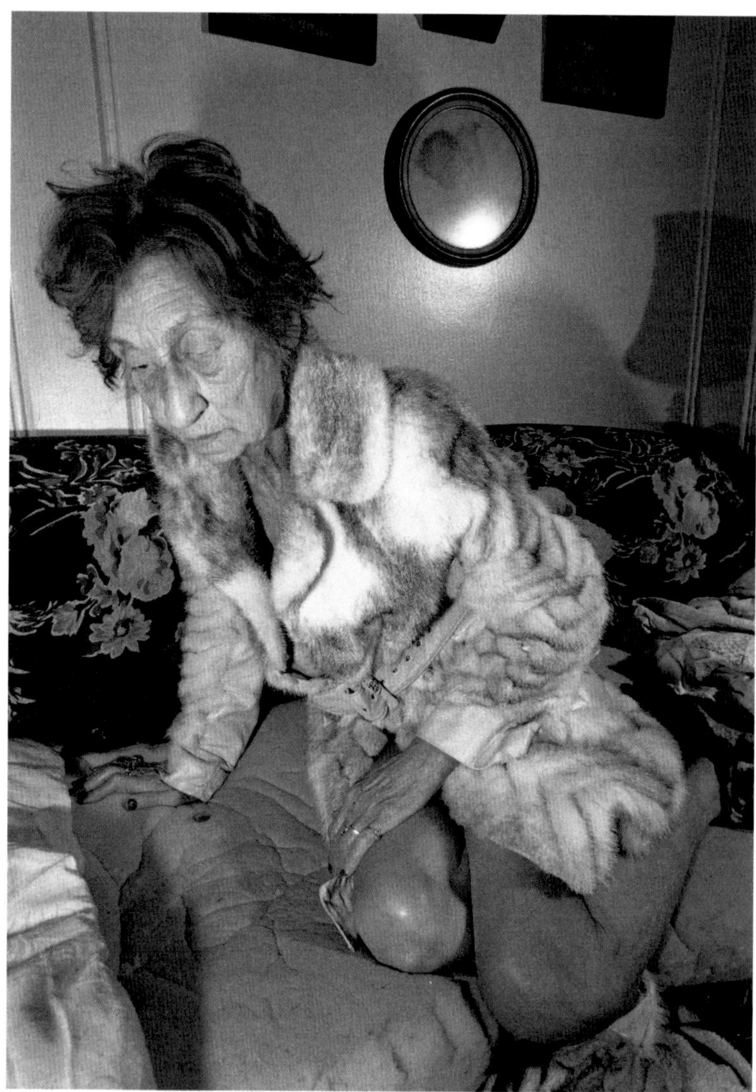

June 6, 1990

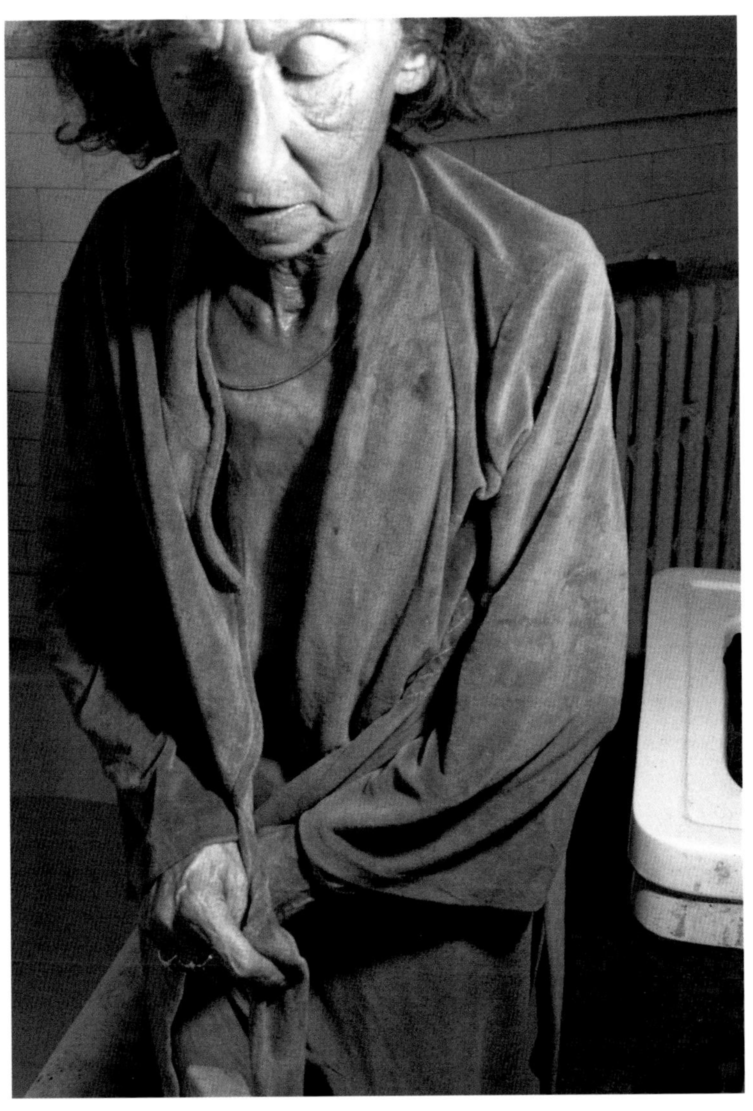

May 24, 1989

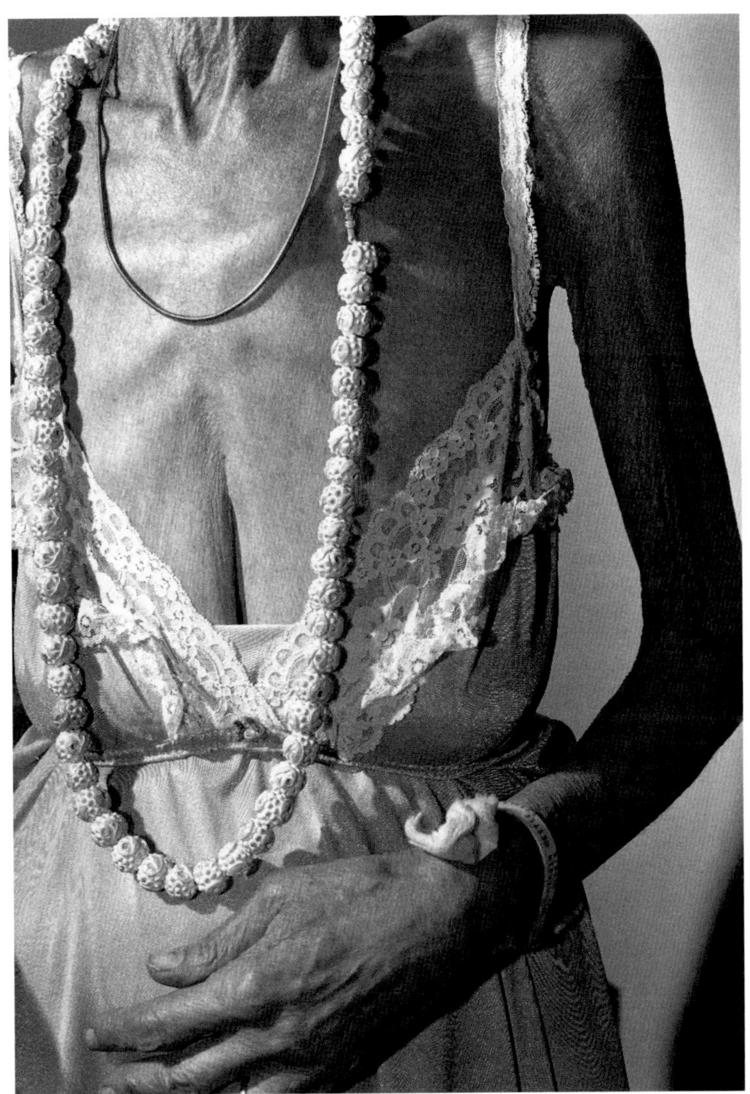

June 13, 1989

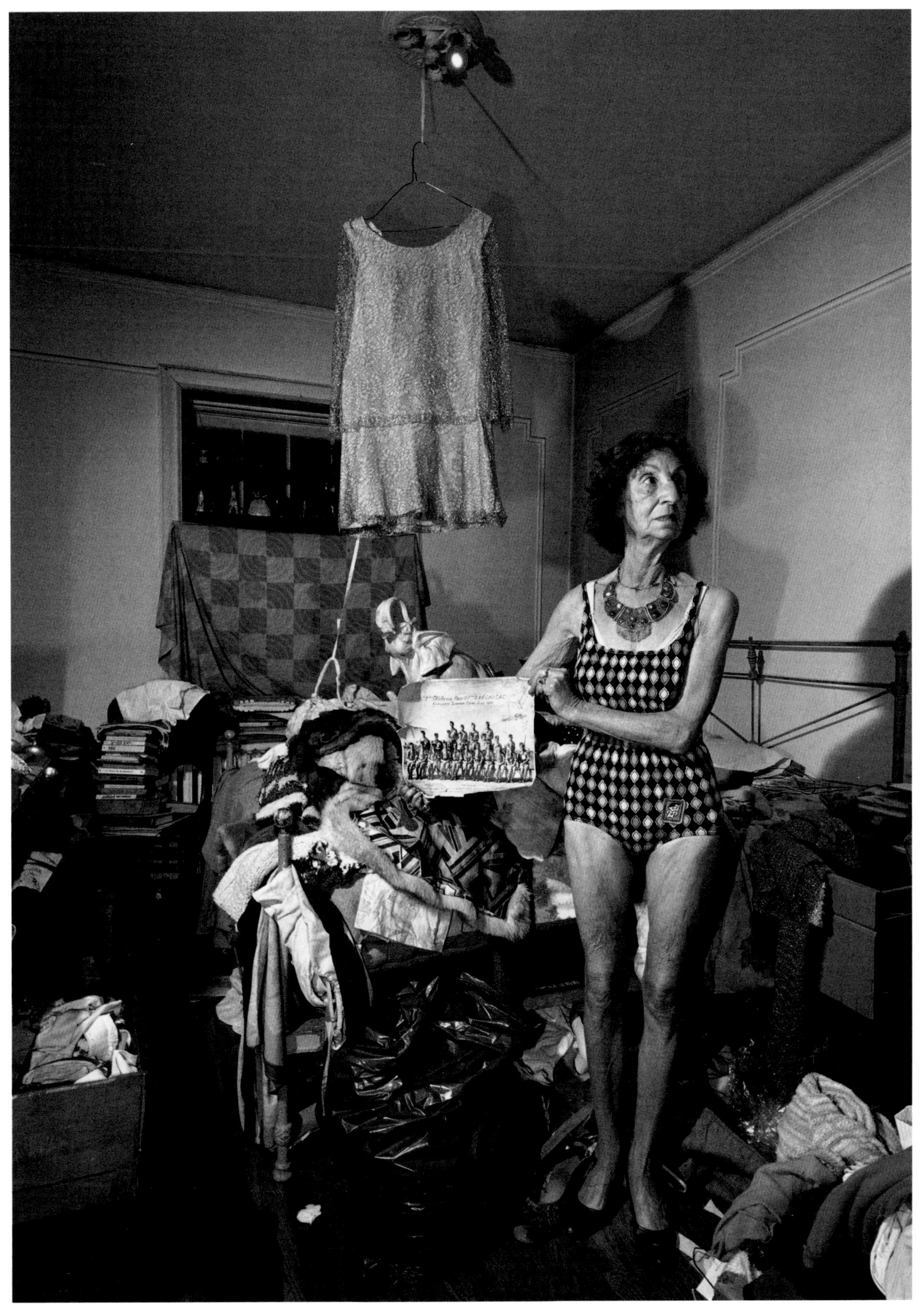



November 21, 1986

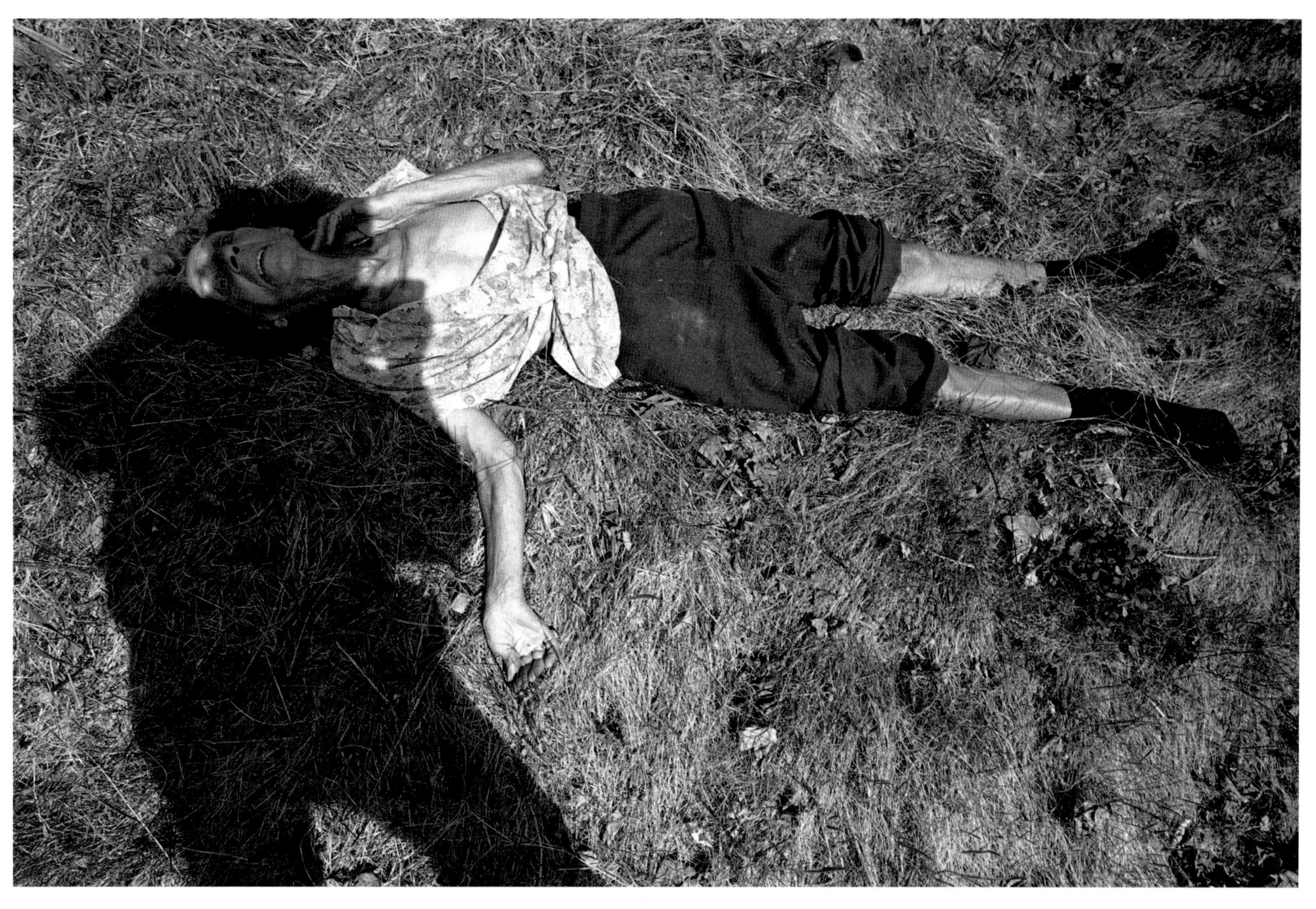

May 17, 1989

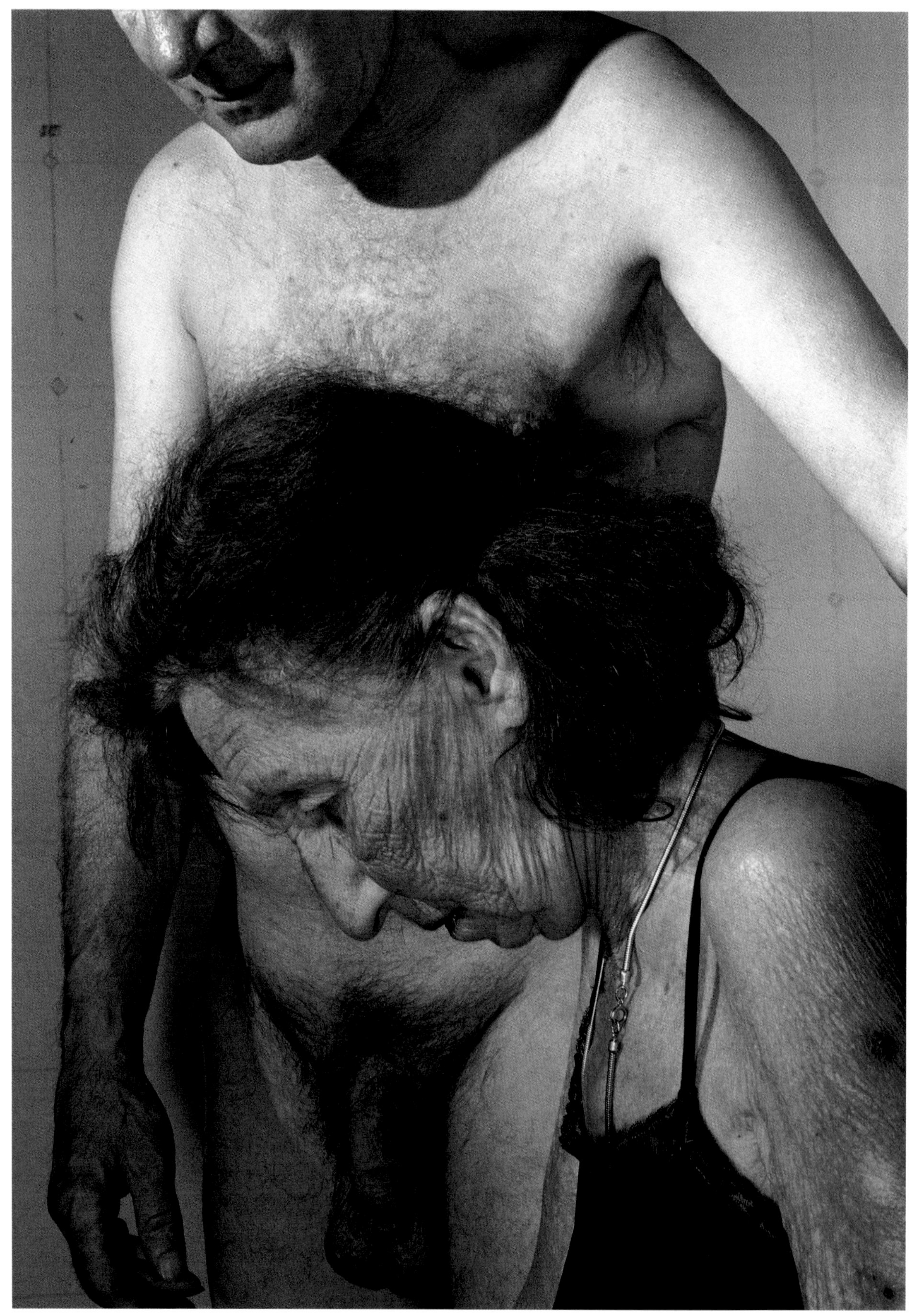



May 21, 1992

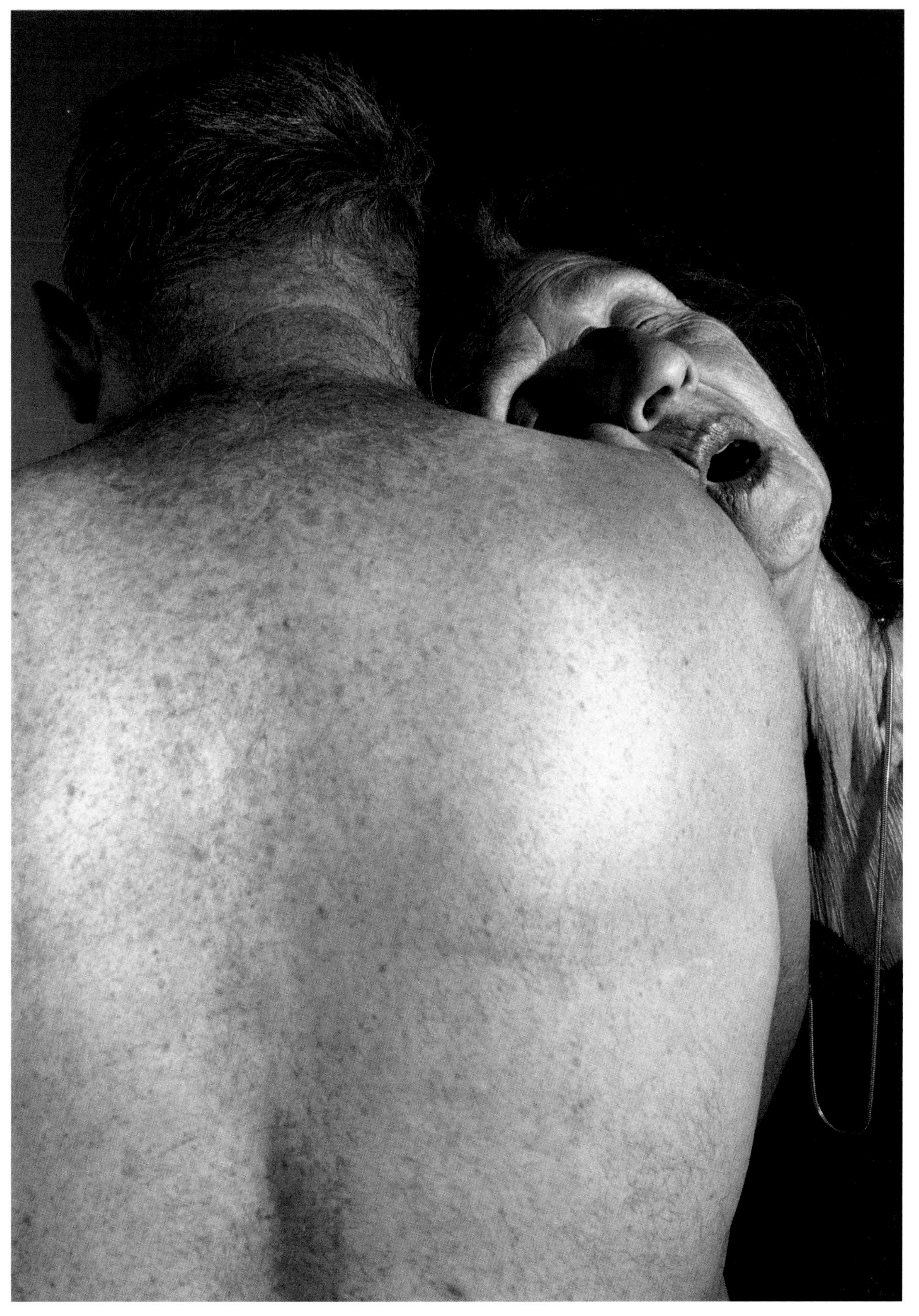



May 20, 1992

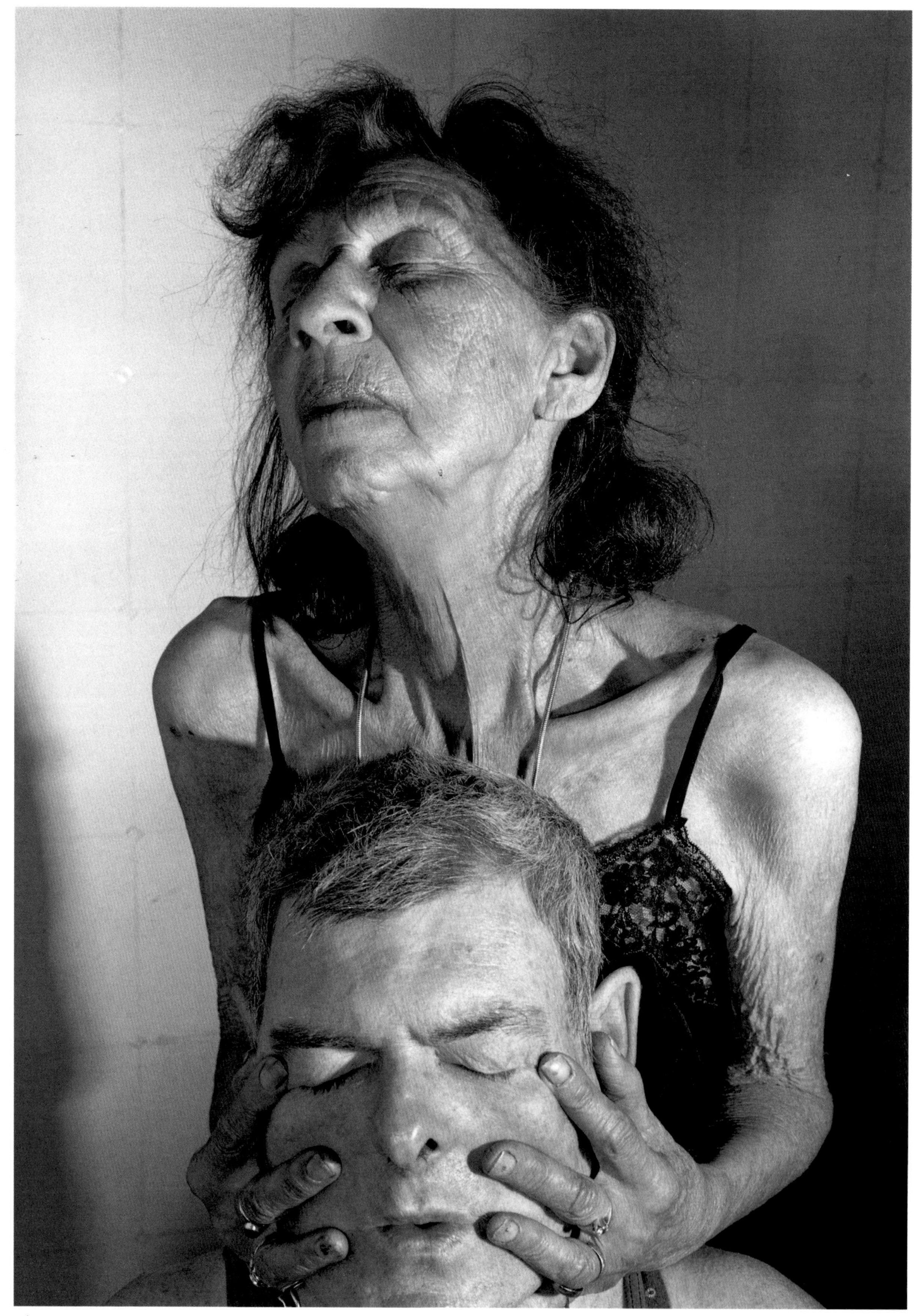



May 20, 1992

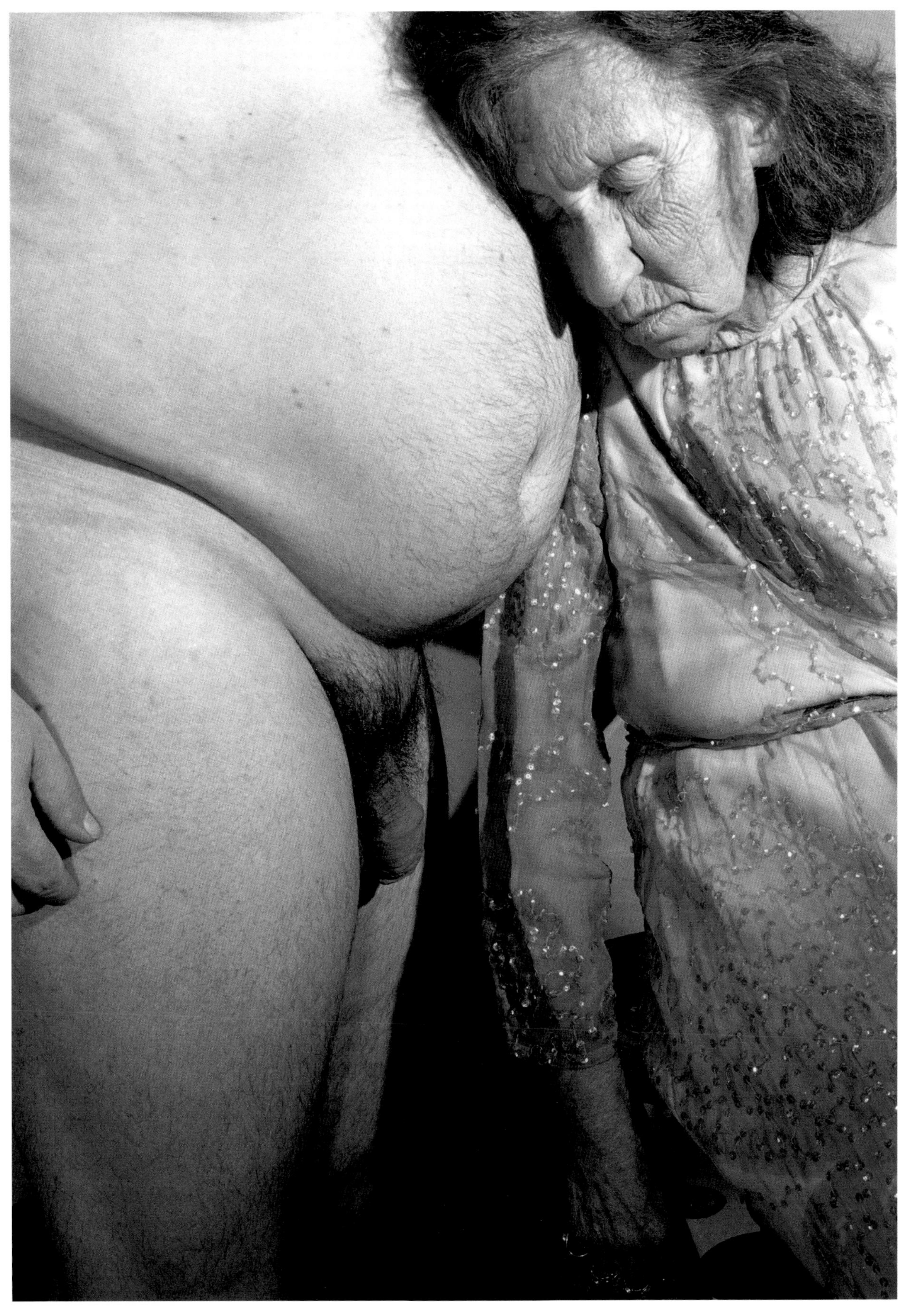



May 27, 1992

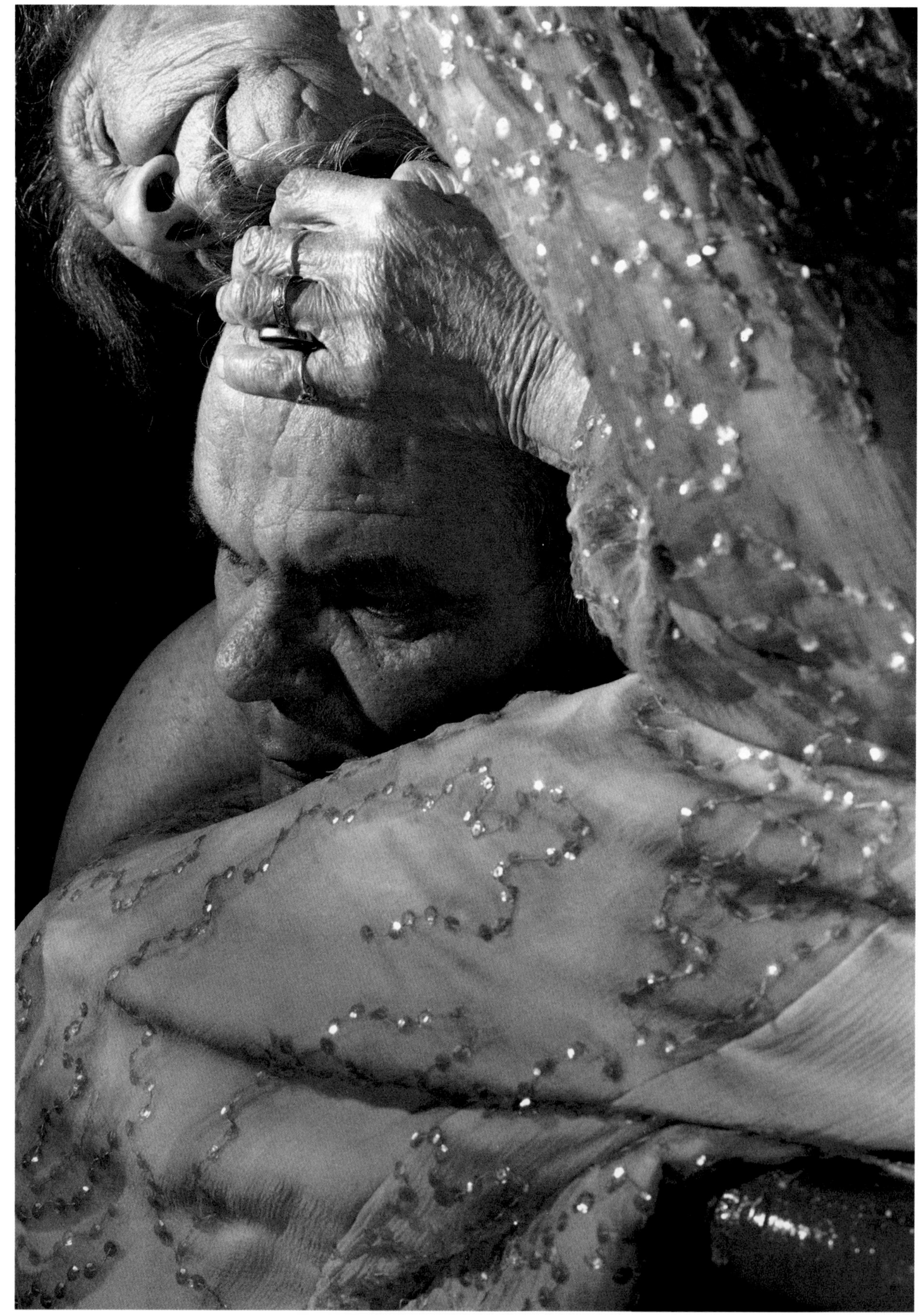

May 27, 1992

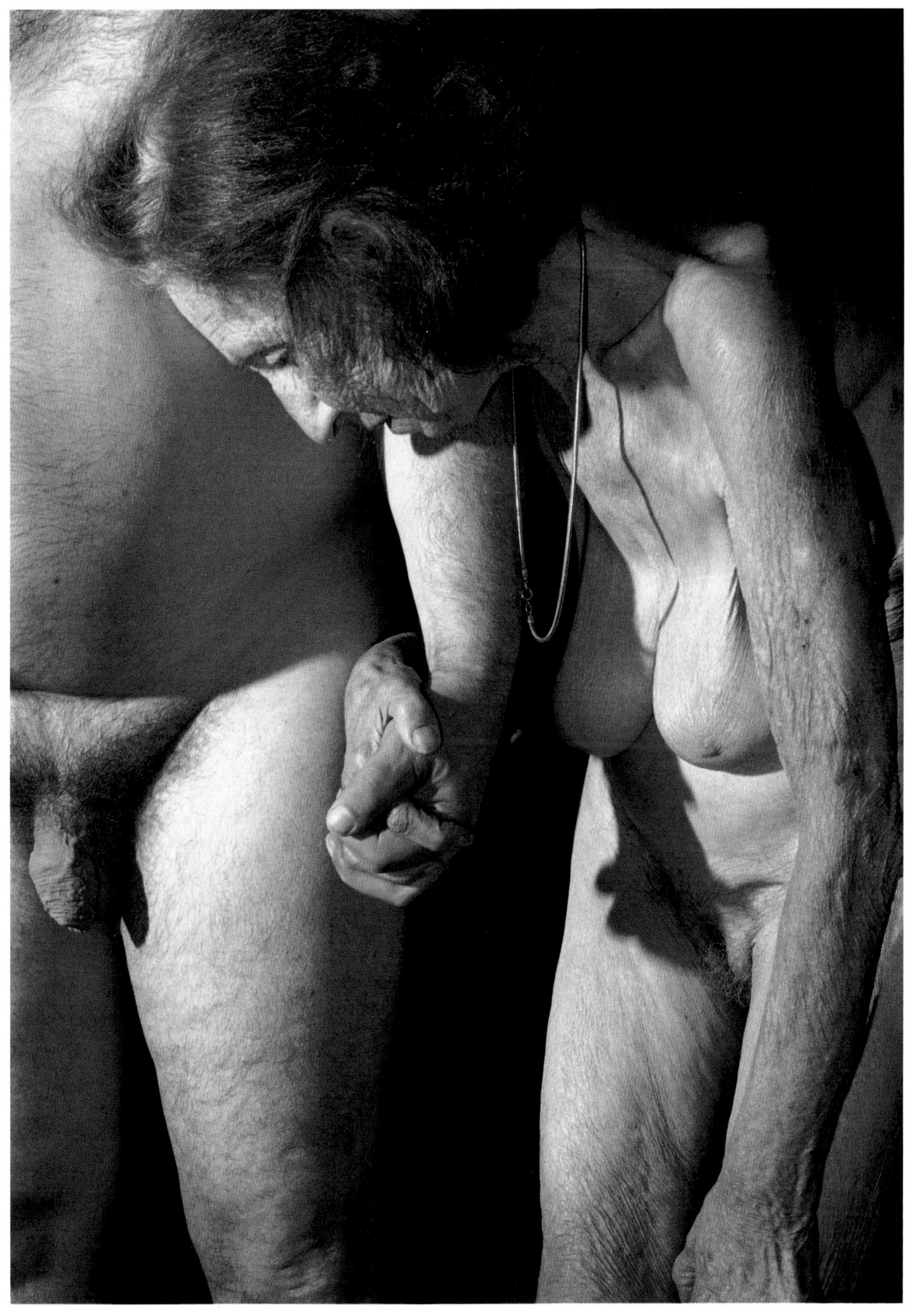



May 27, 1992

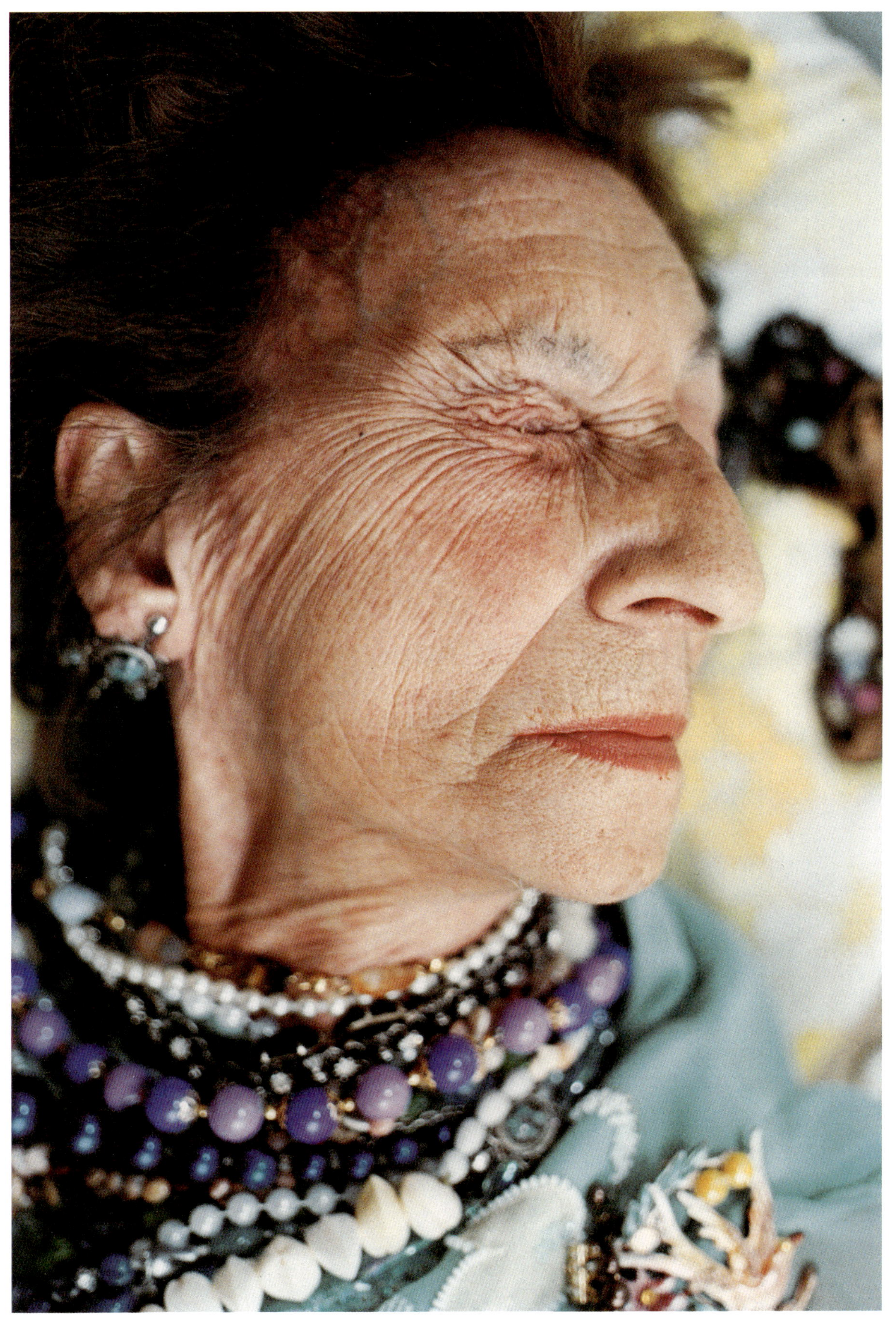



June 8, 1990

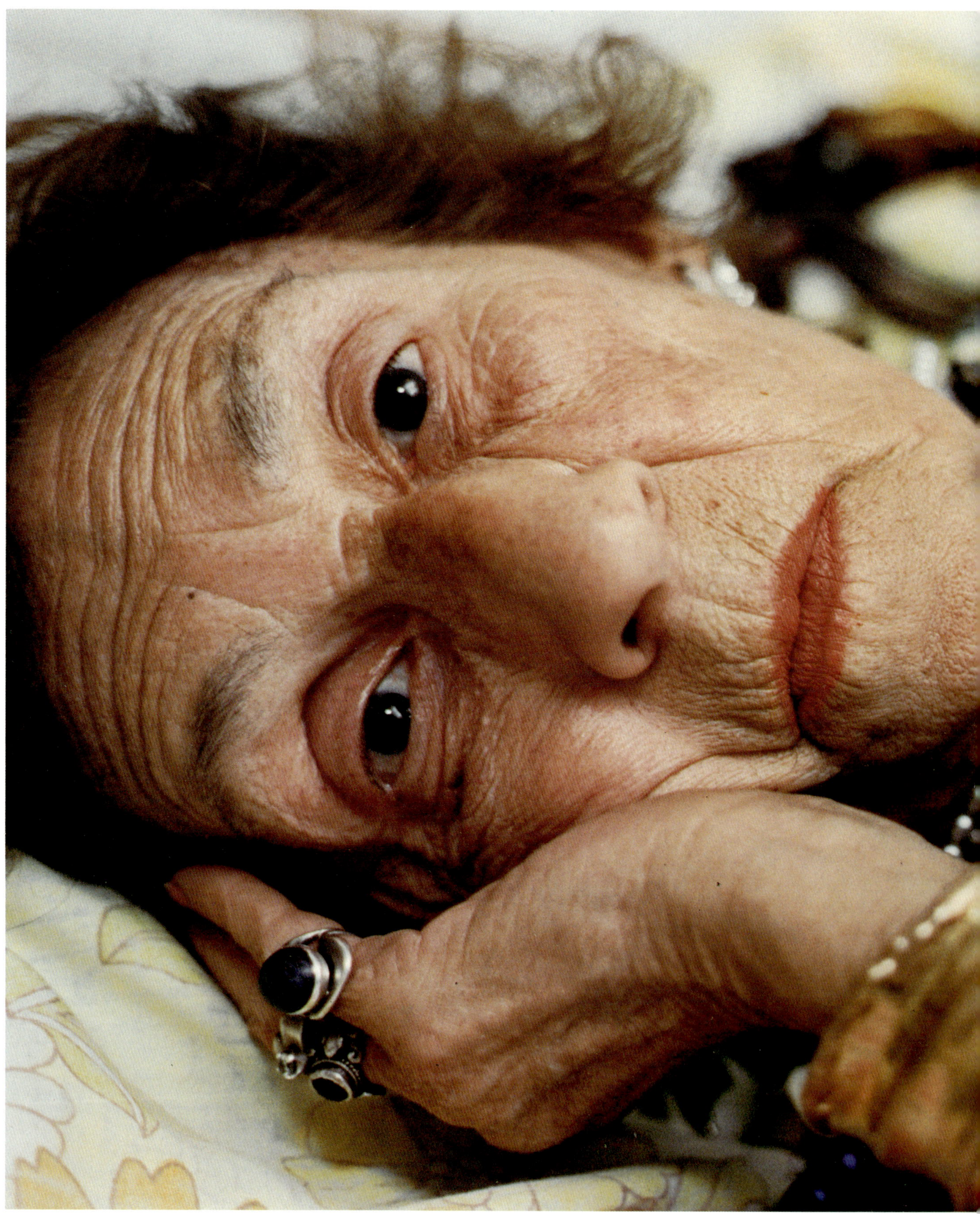

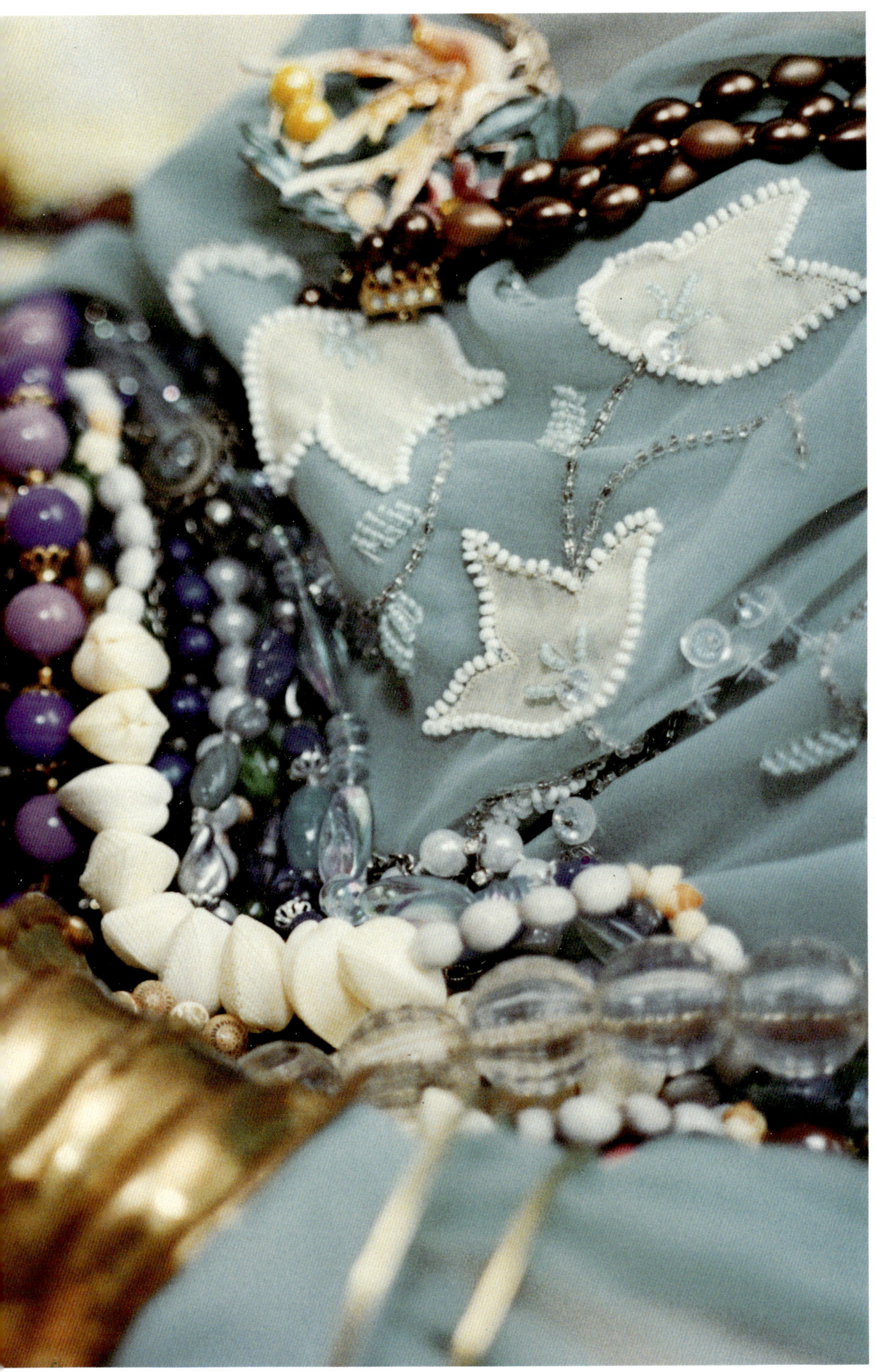

June 8, 1990

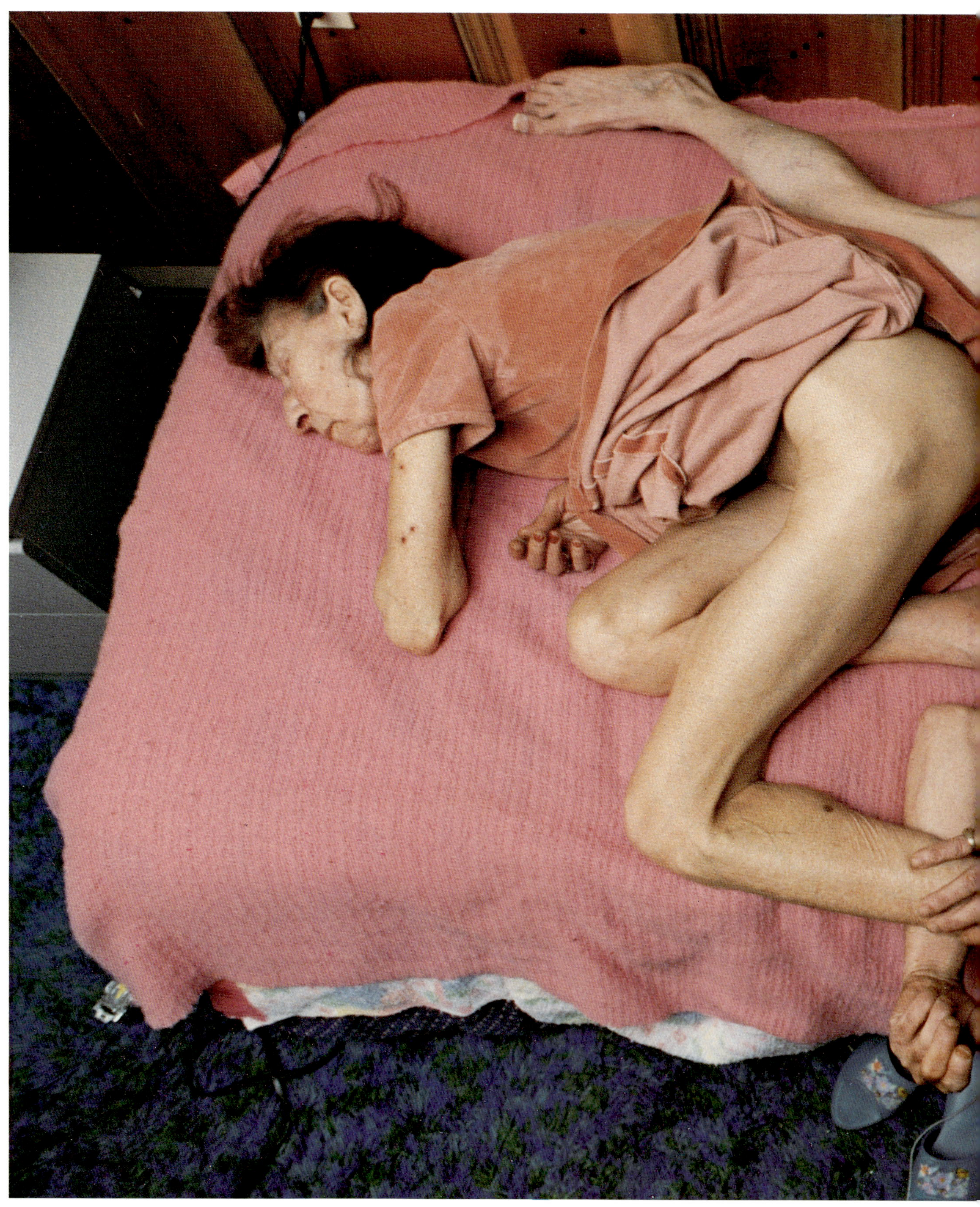

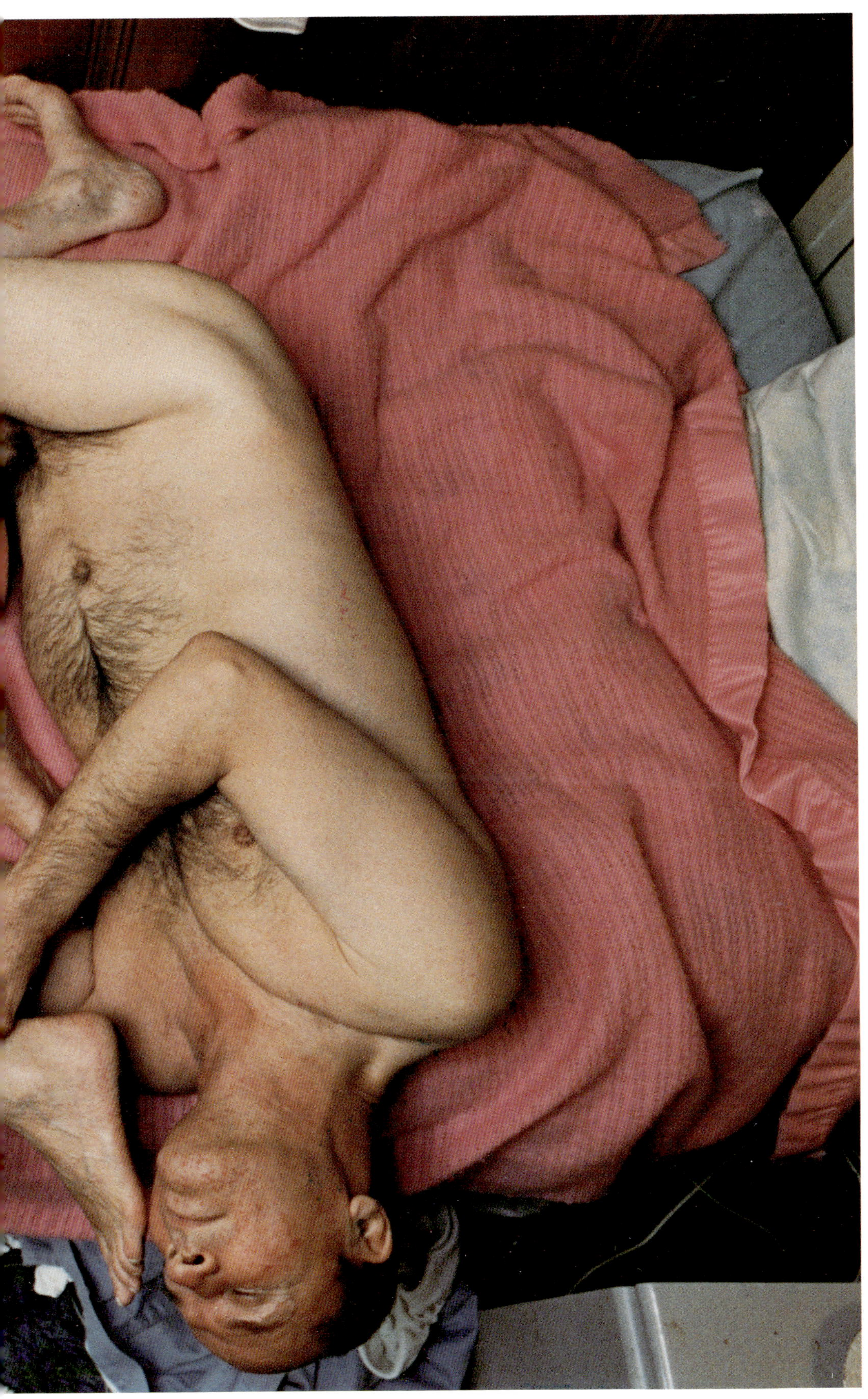

April 13, 1992

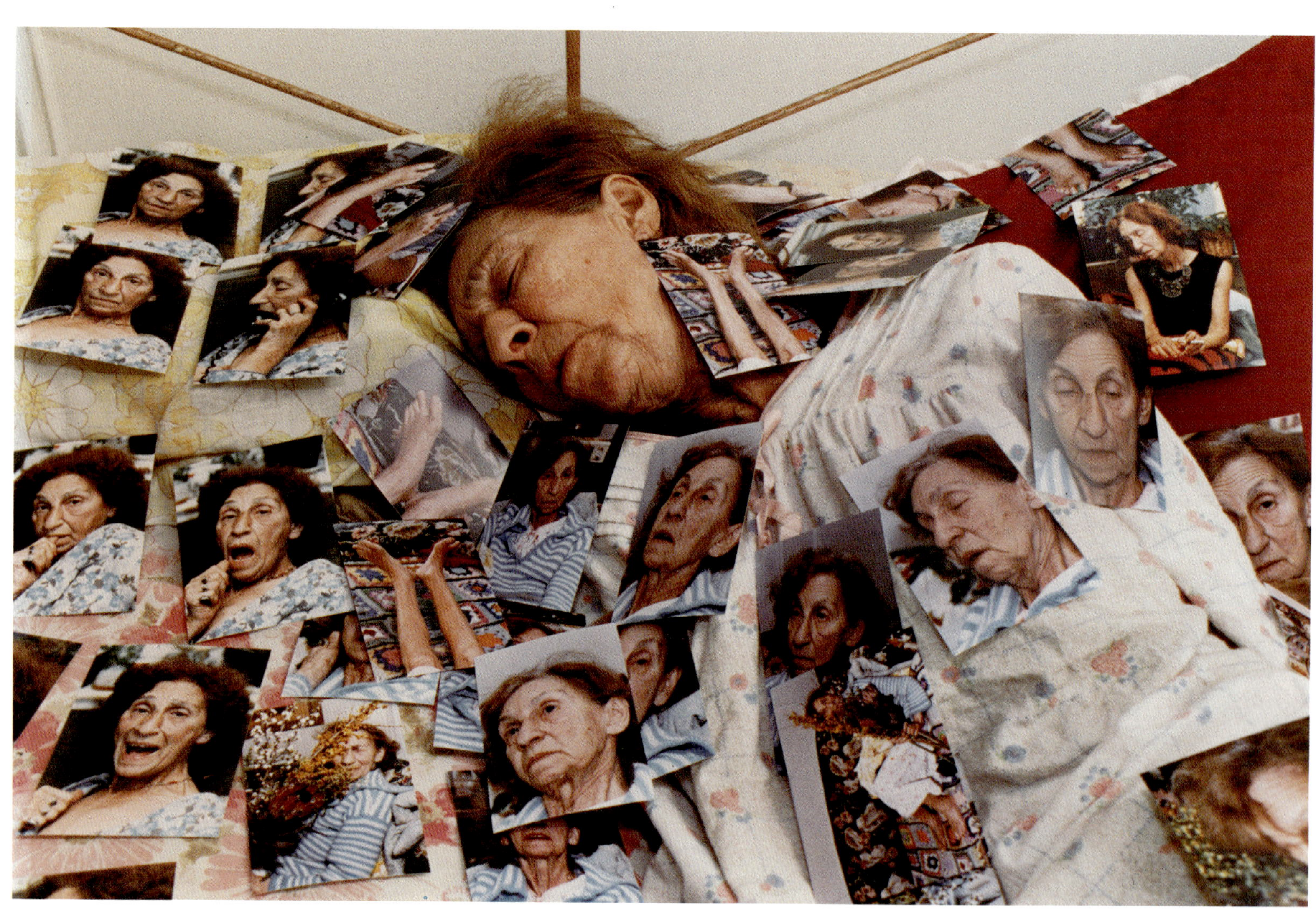

May 25, 1990

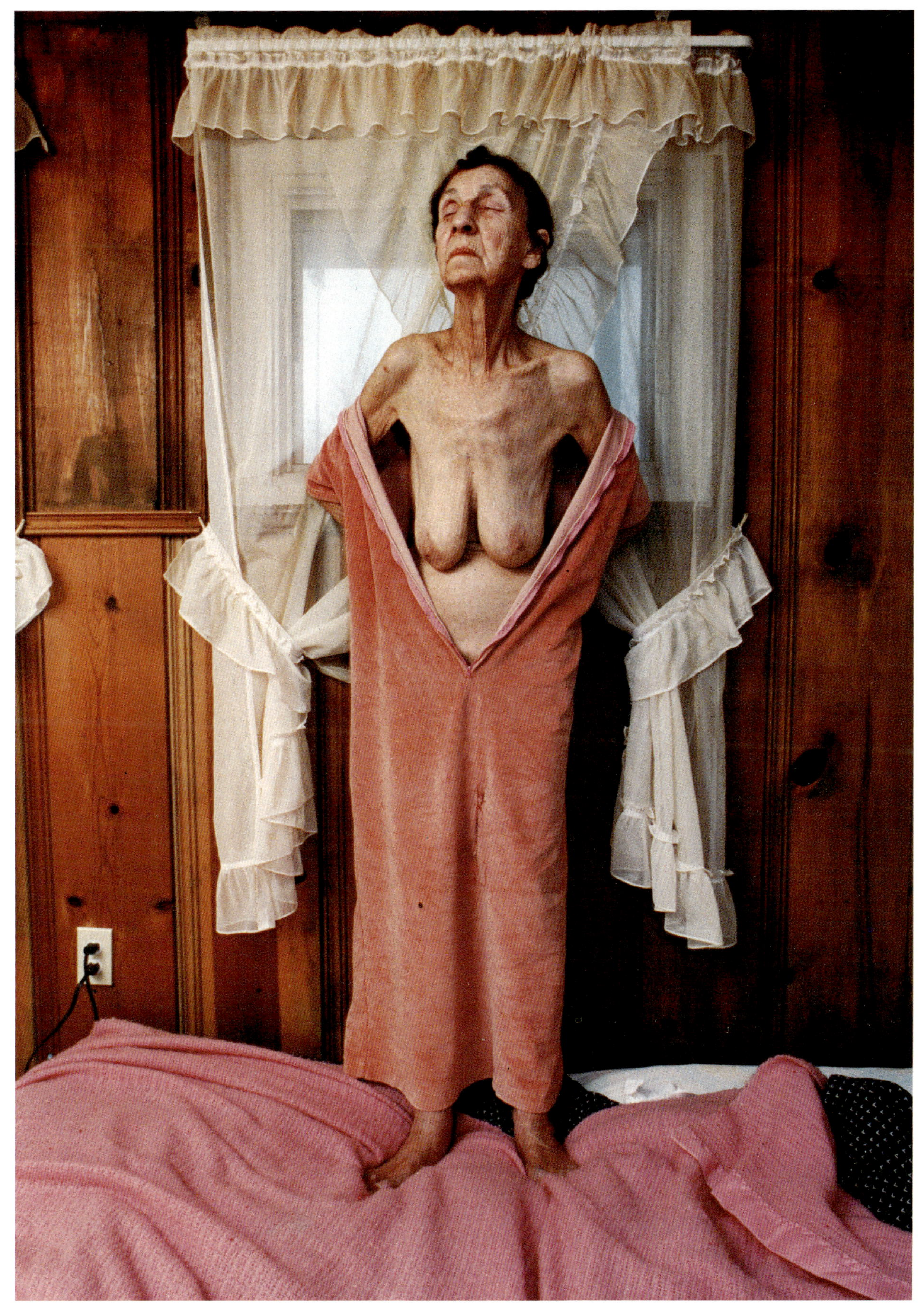



April 10, 1992

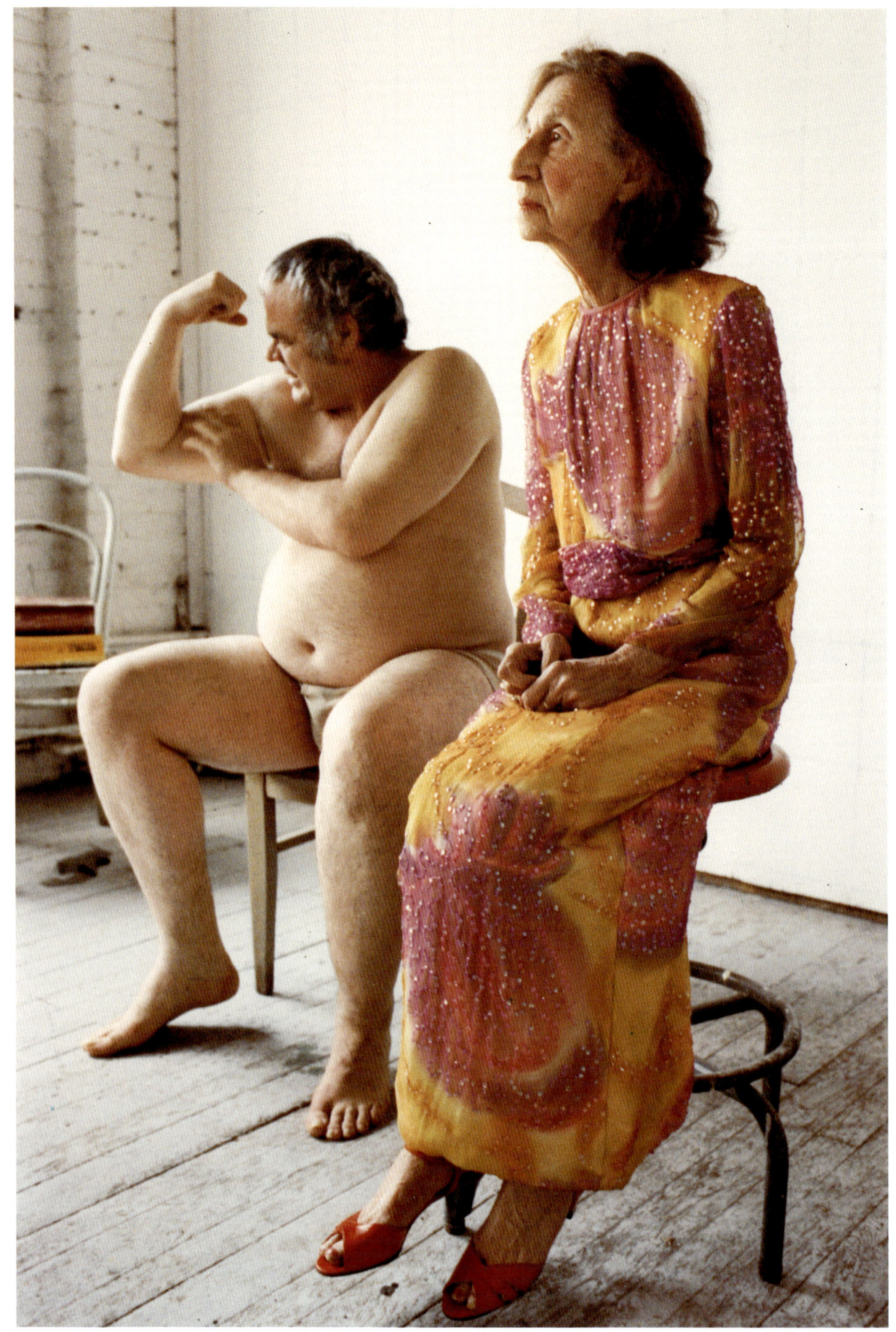



May 27, 1992

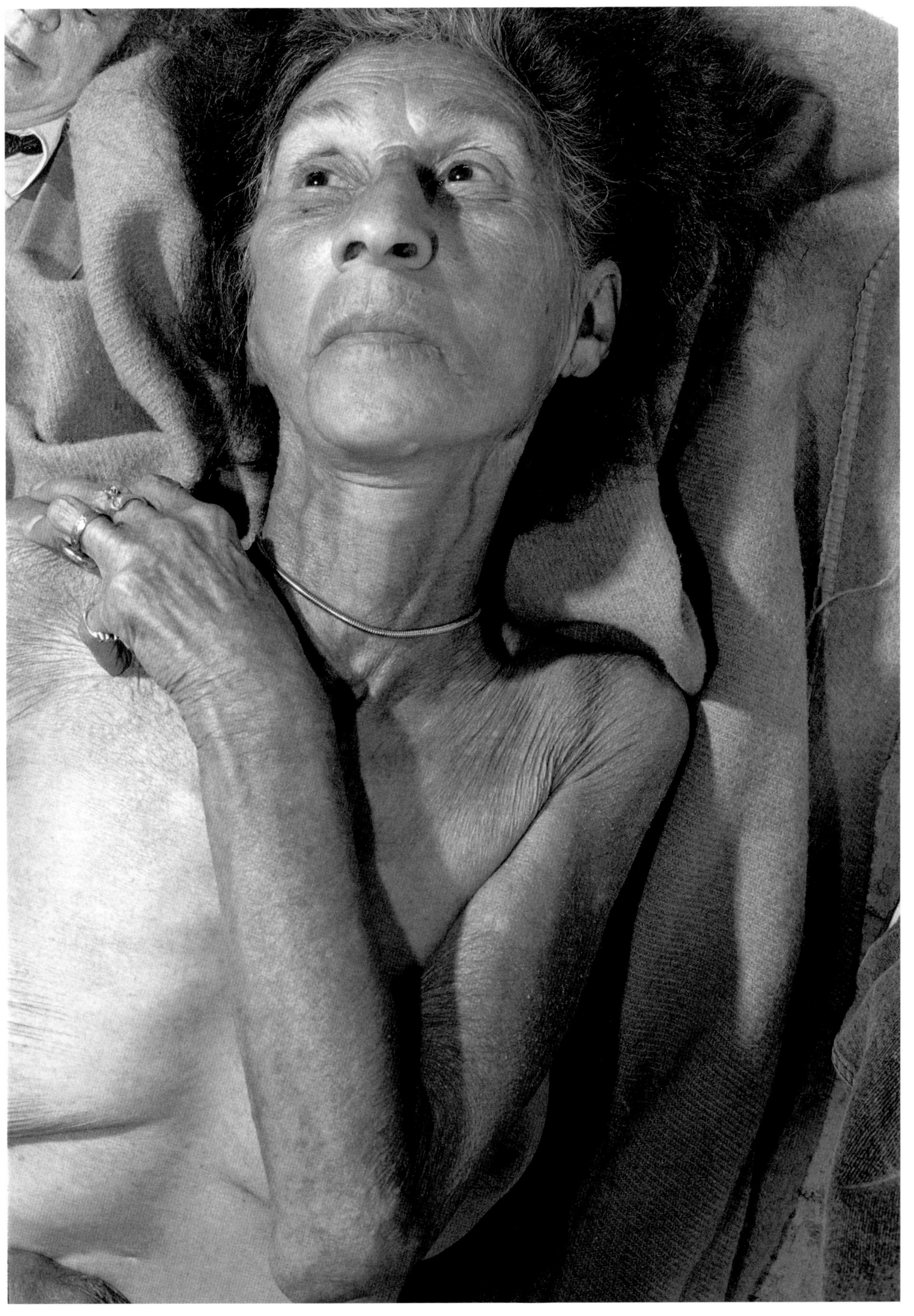



August 22, 1991

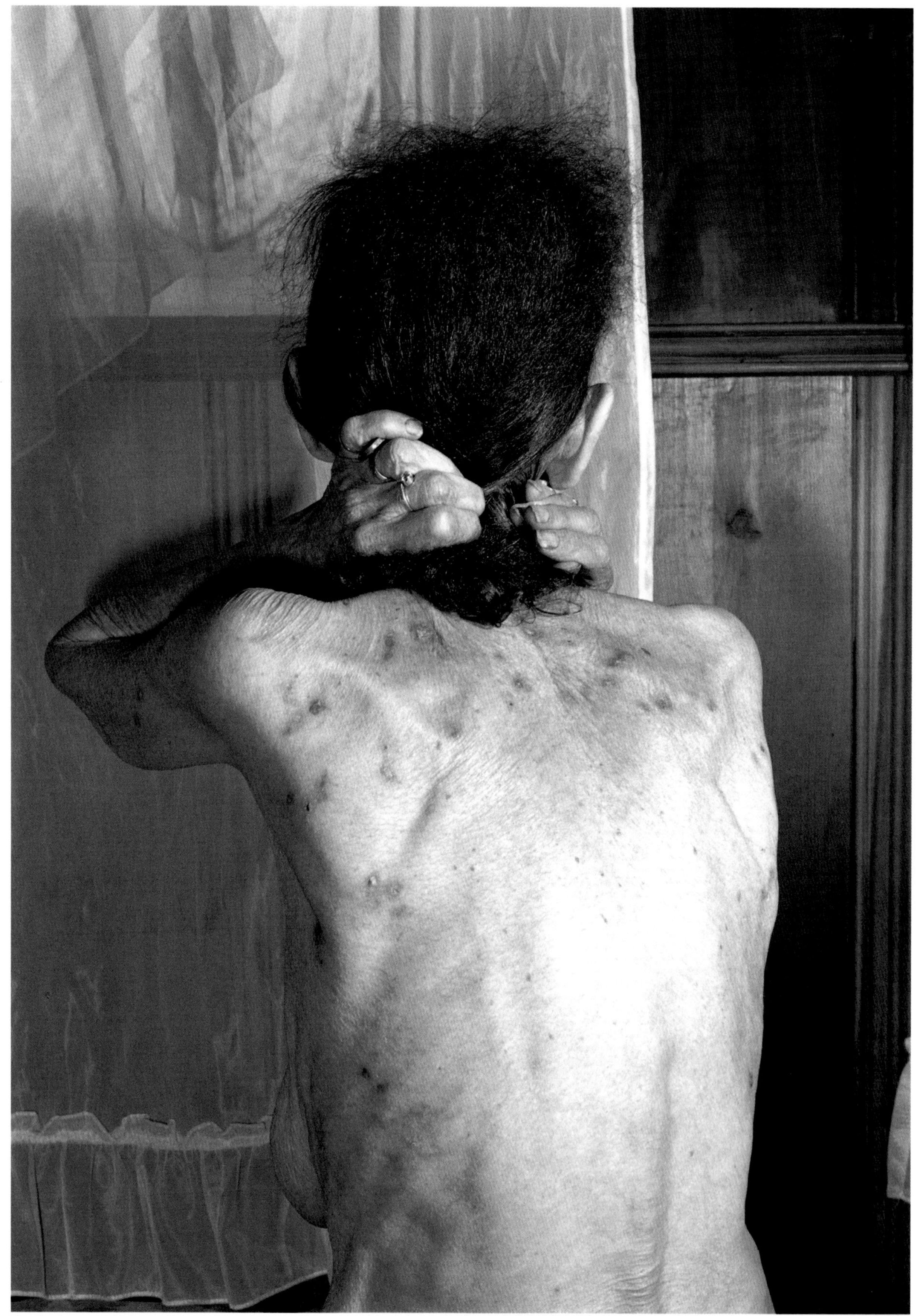



May 13, 1992

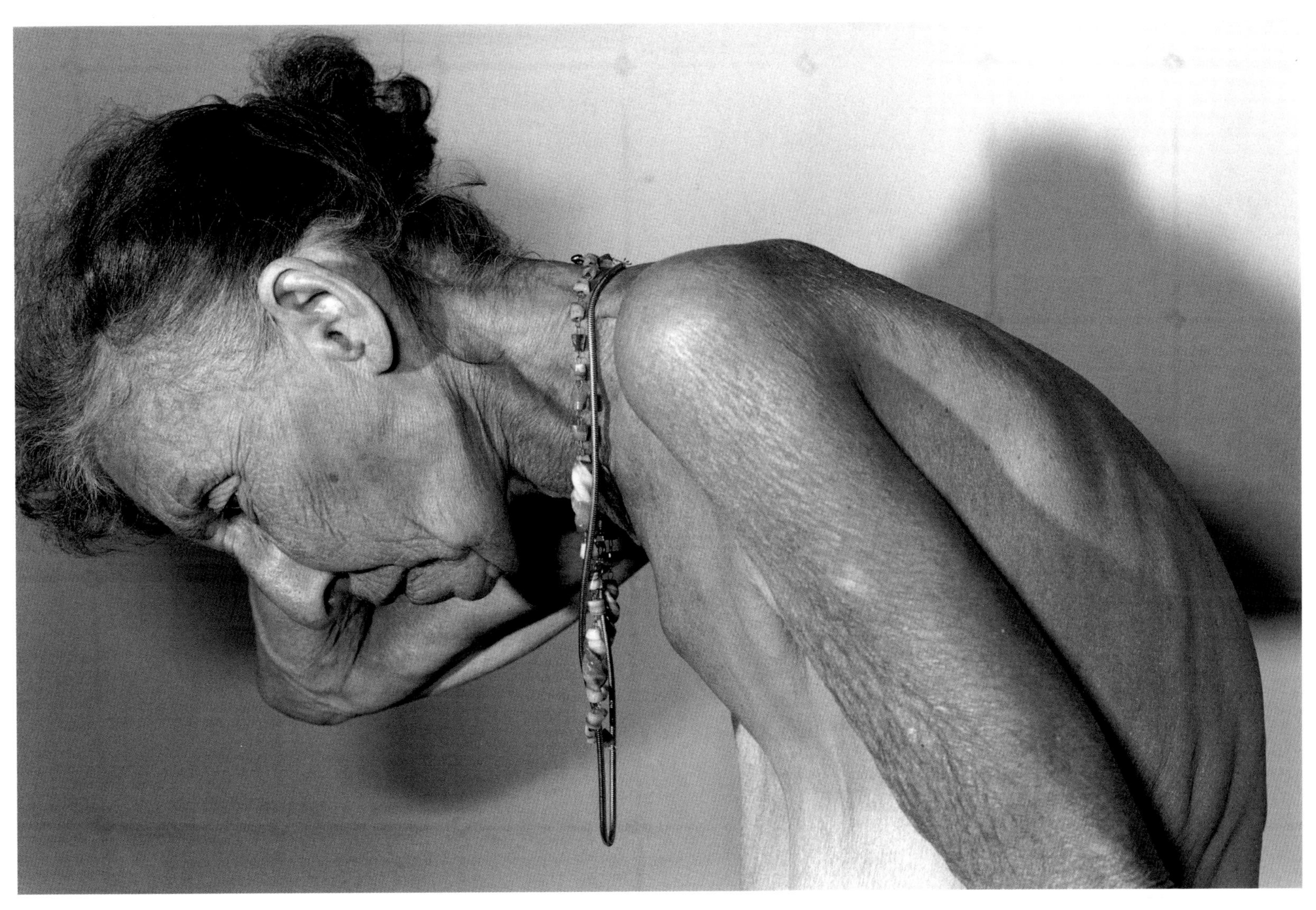

August 29, 1991

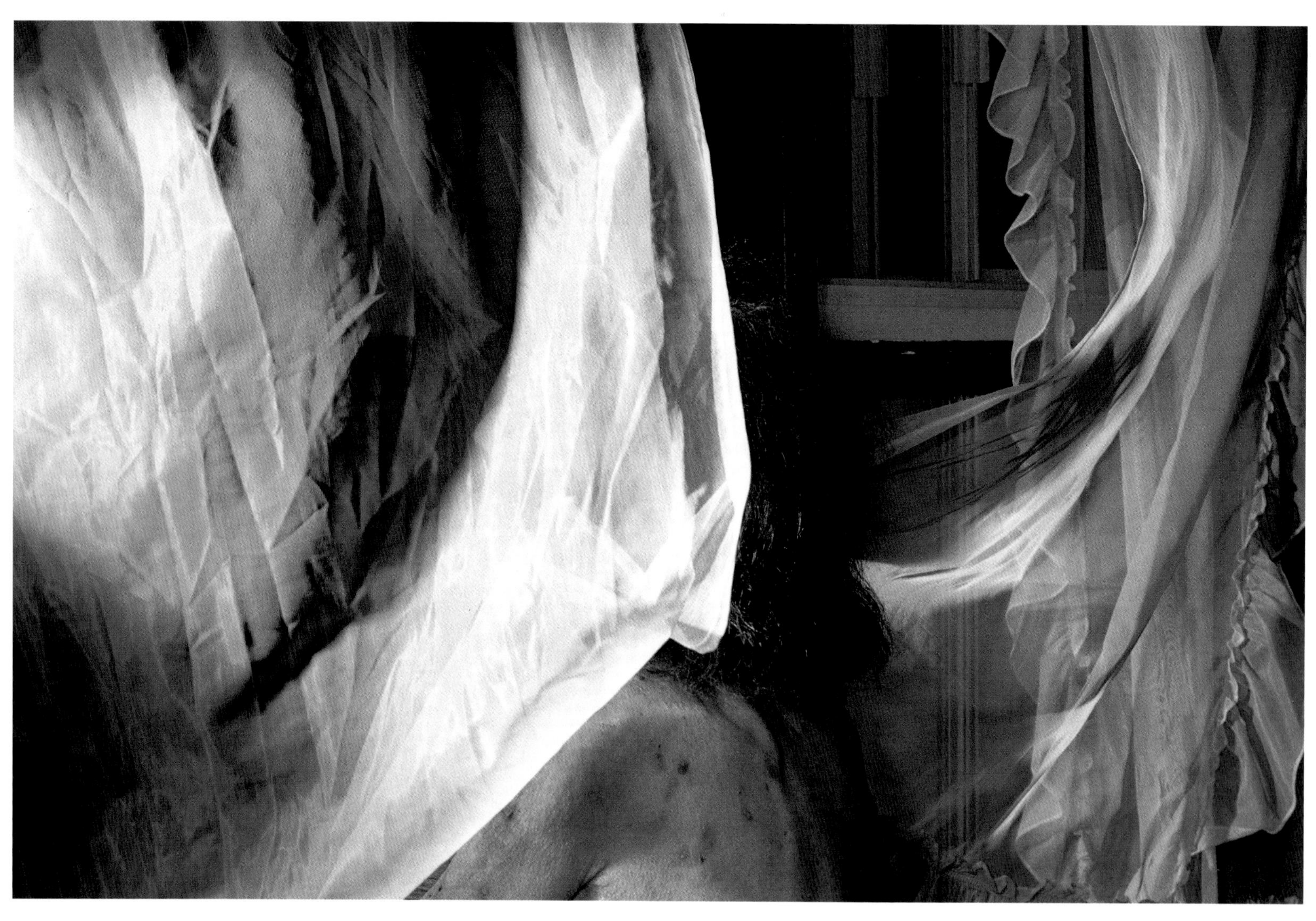

May 13, 1992

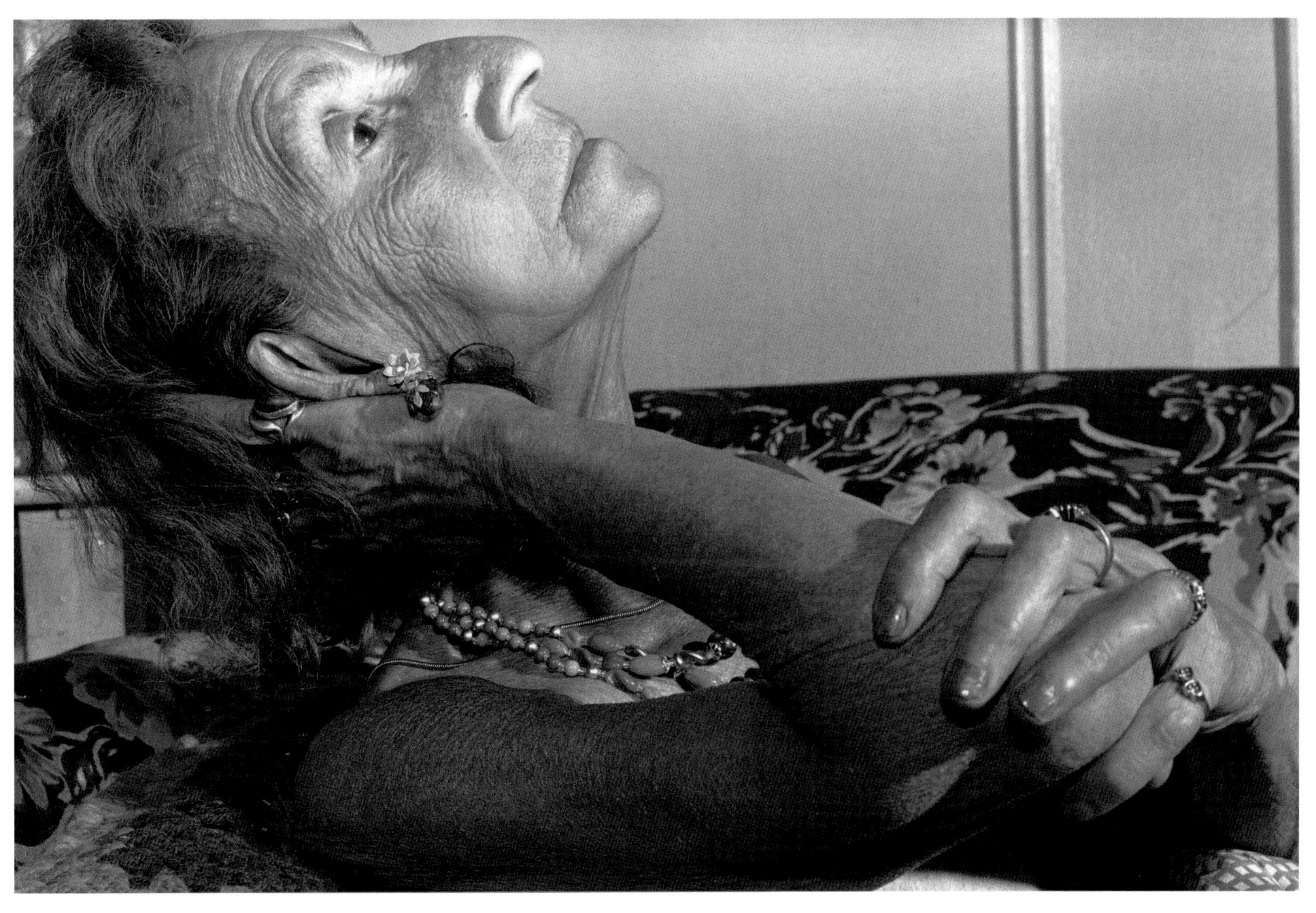

May 5, 1989

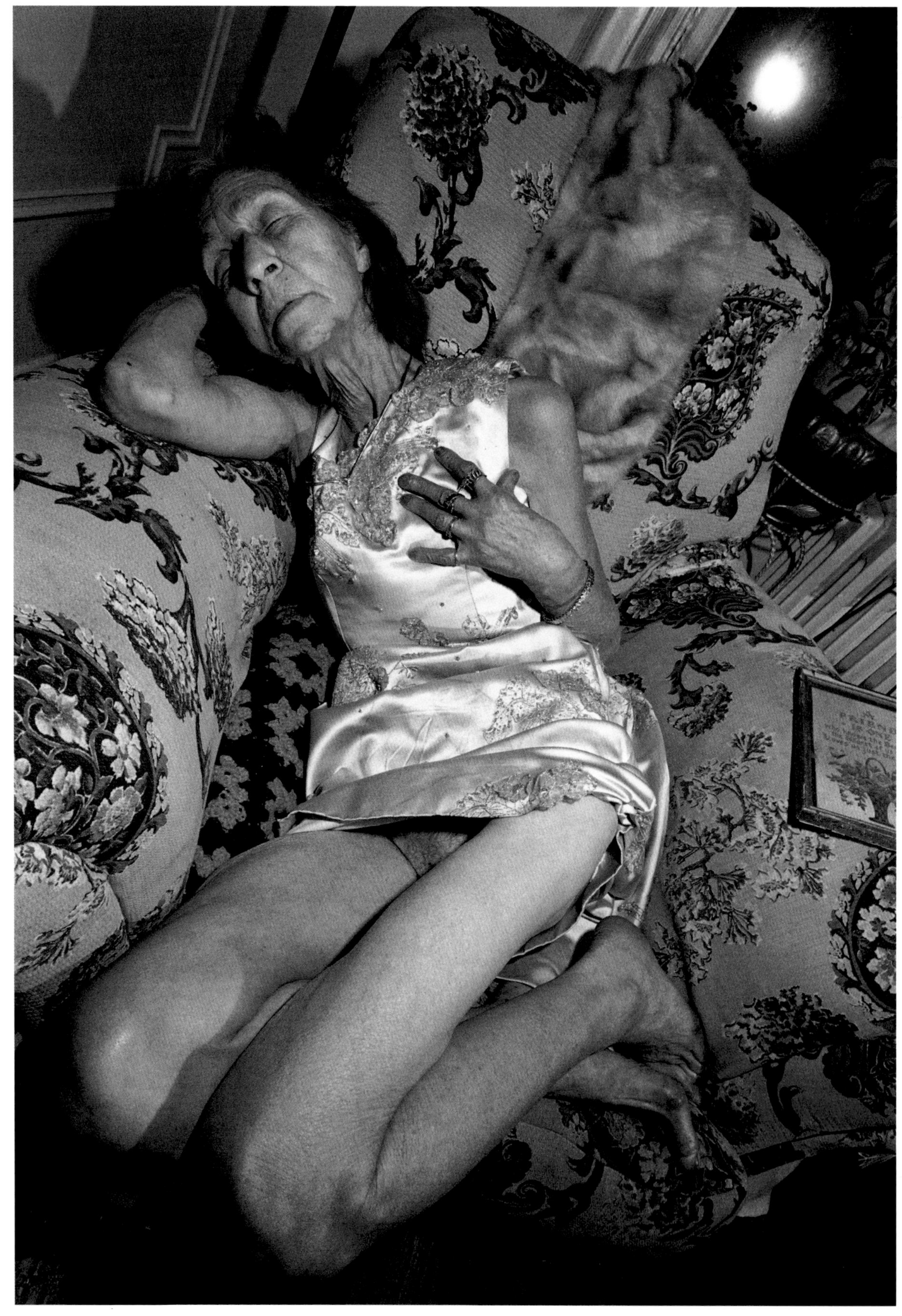



February 7, 1989

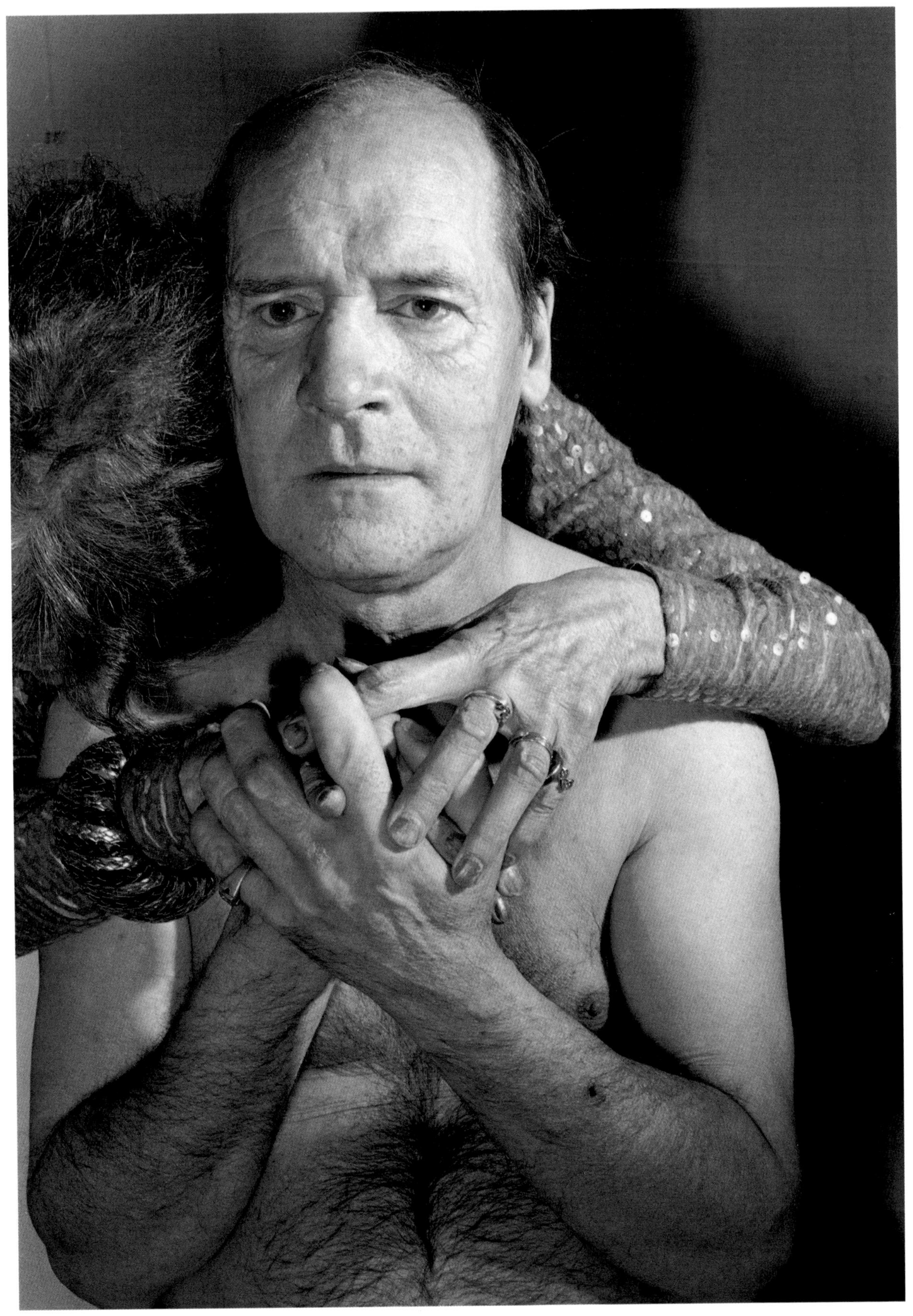



December 12, 1991

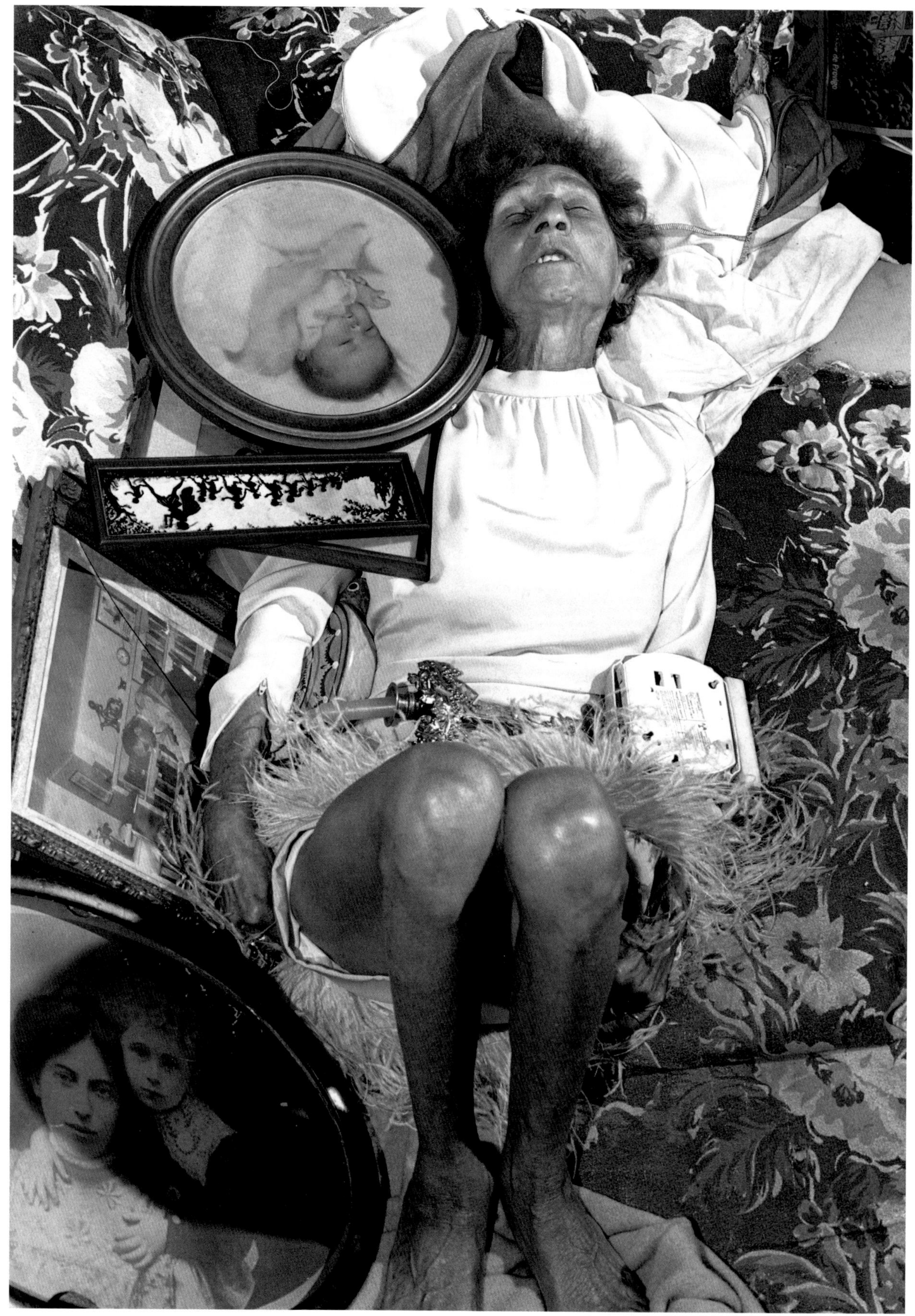



September 14, 1989

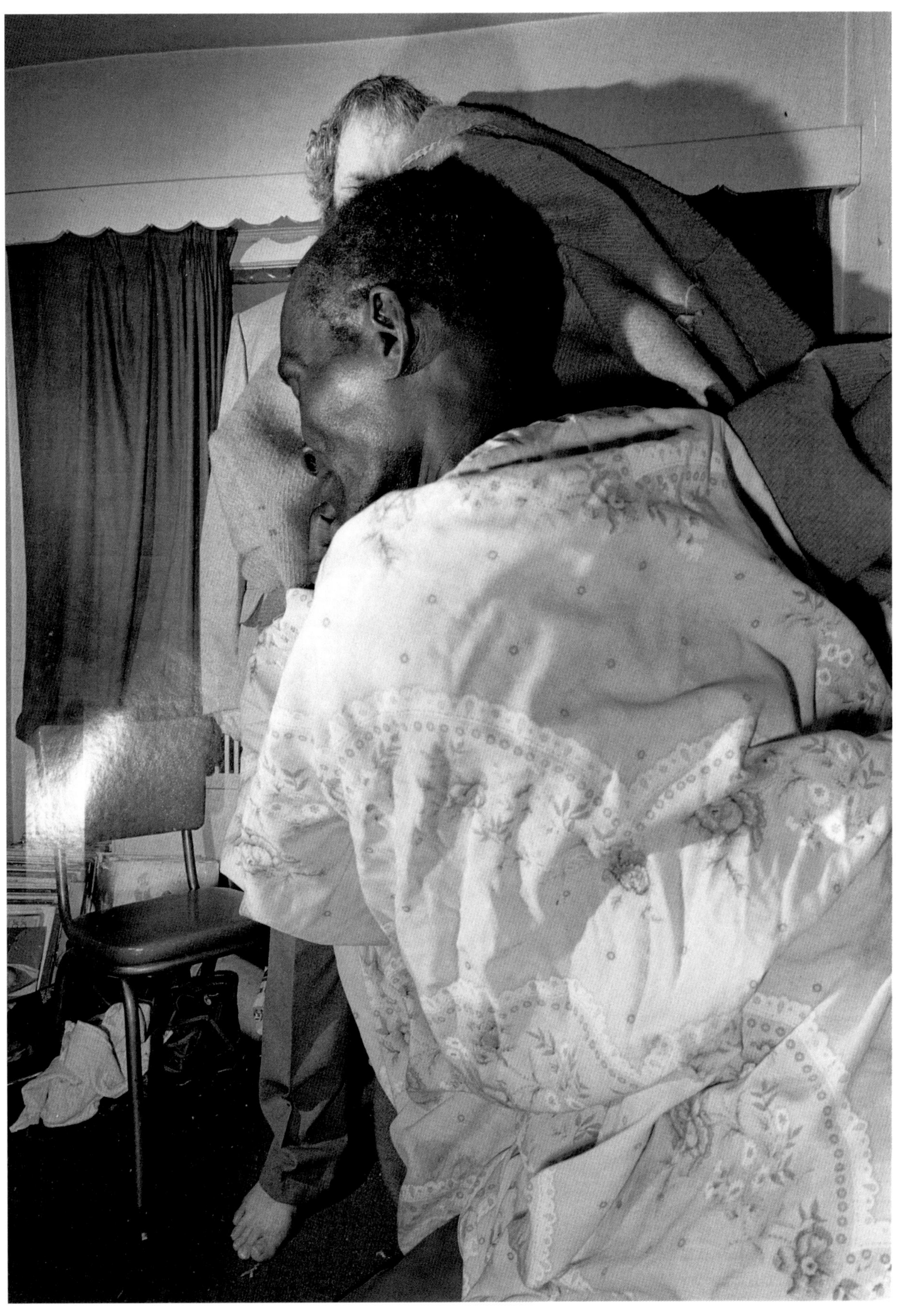

September 25, 1991

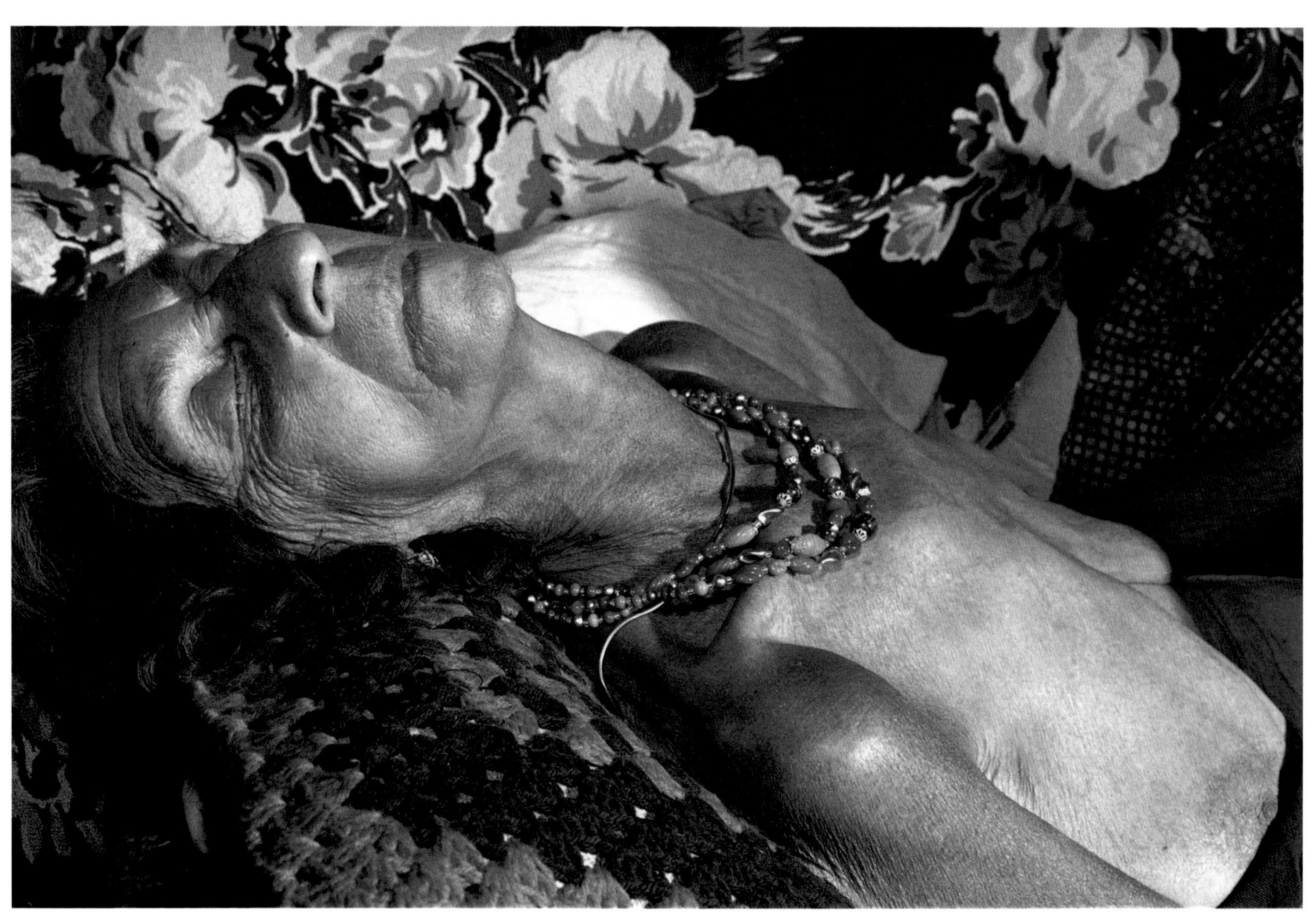

**May 5, 1989**

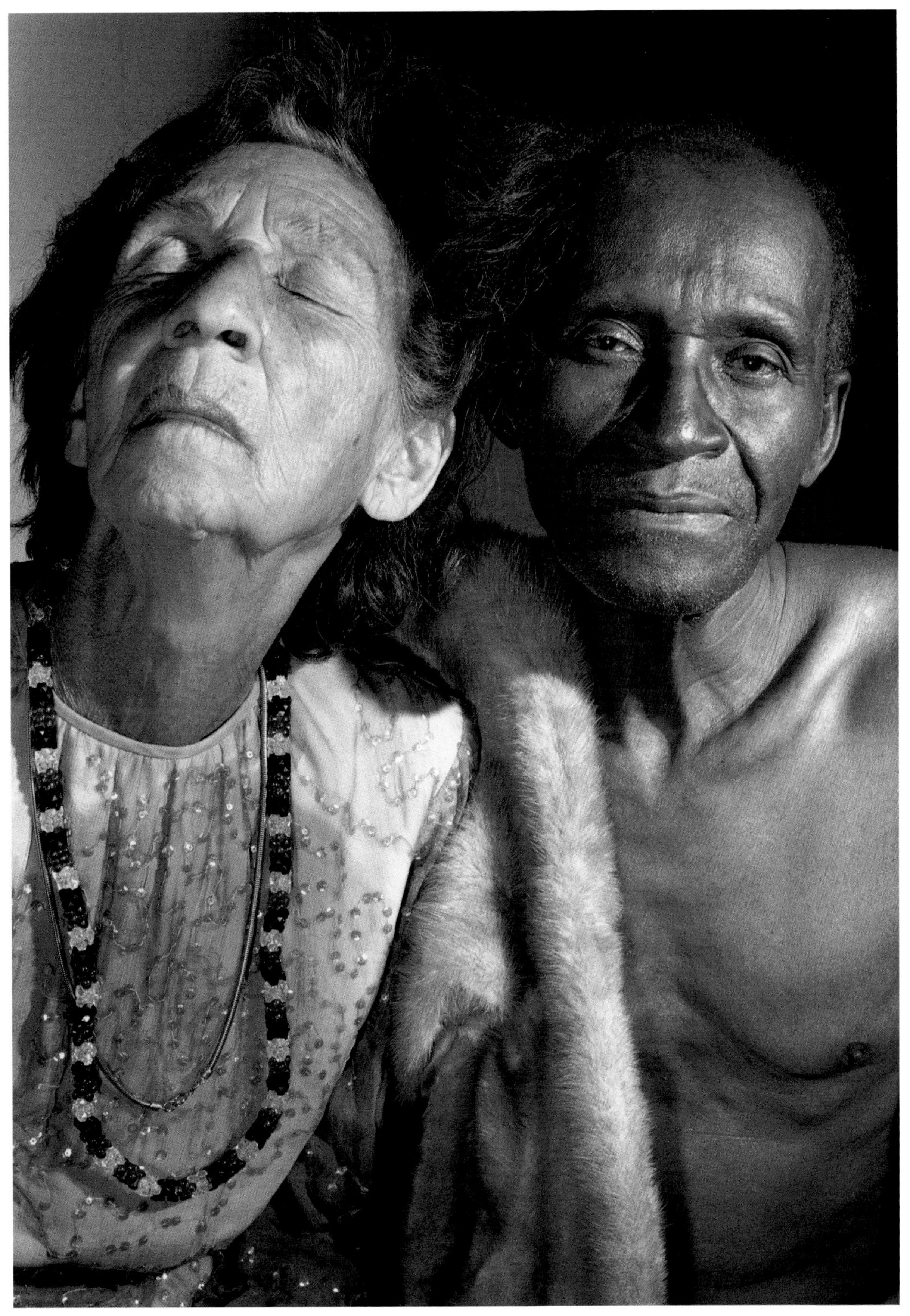



October 23, 1991

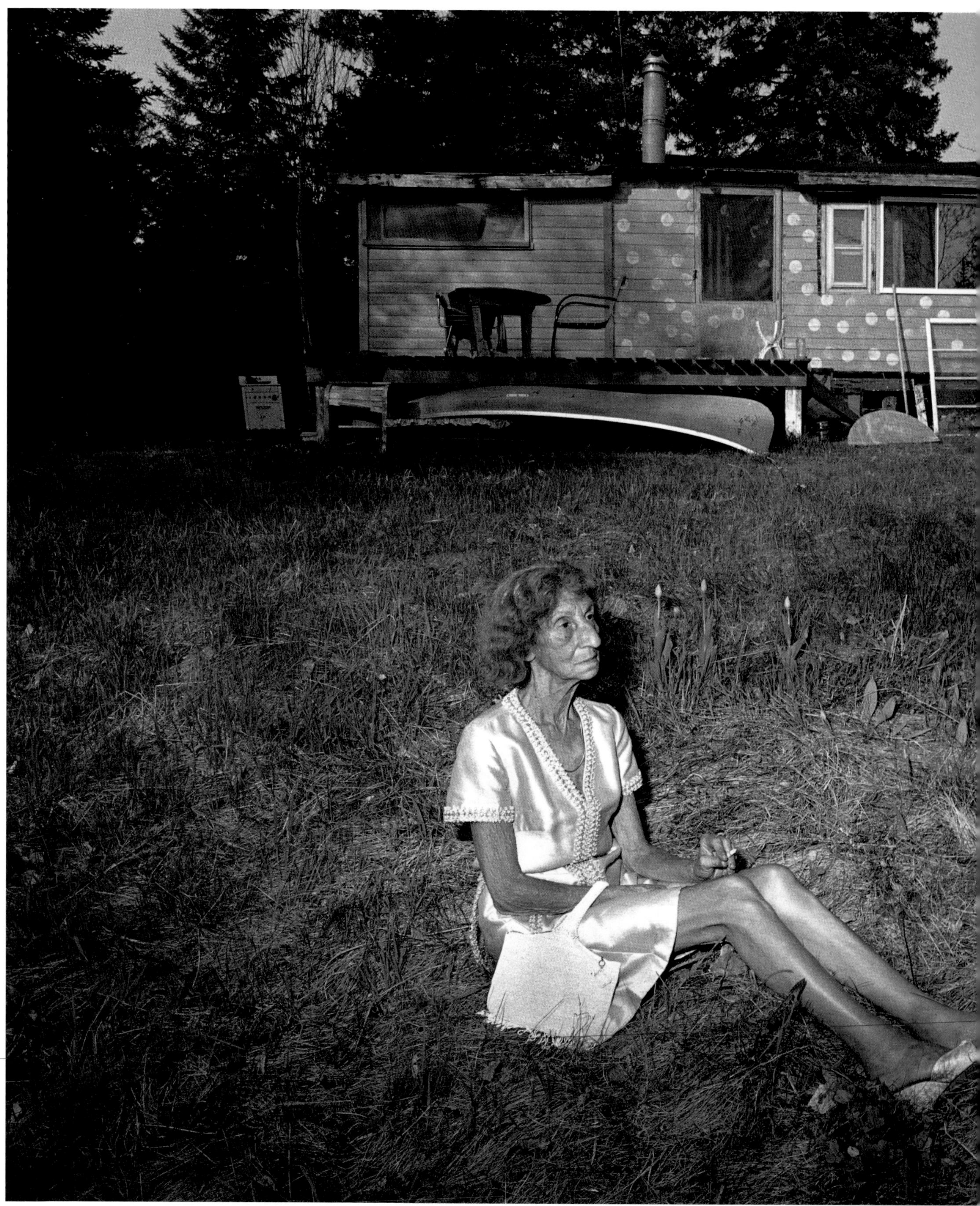

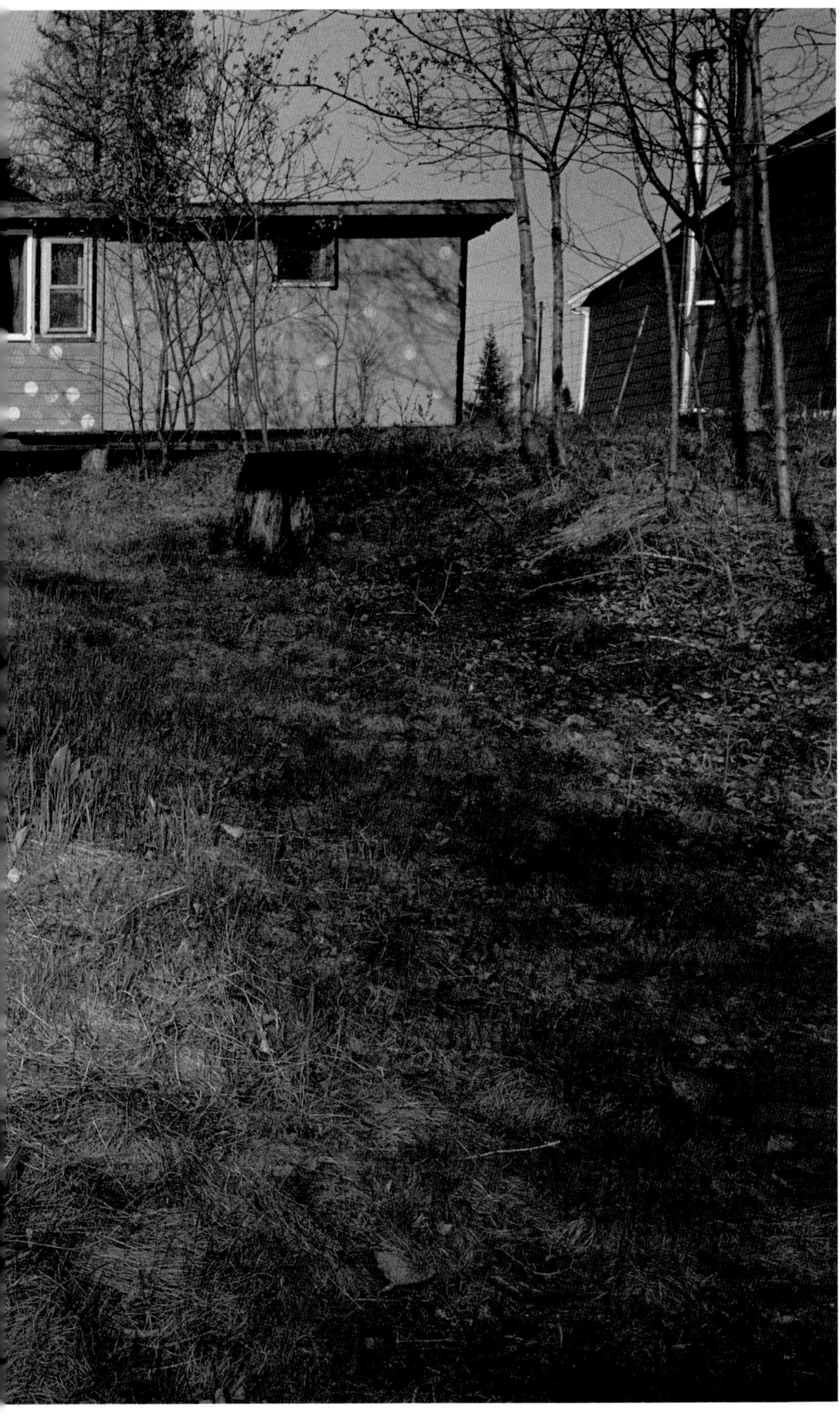

May 17, 1989

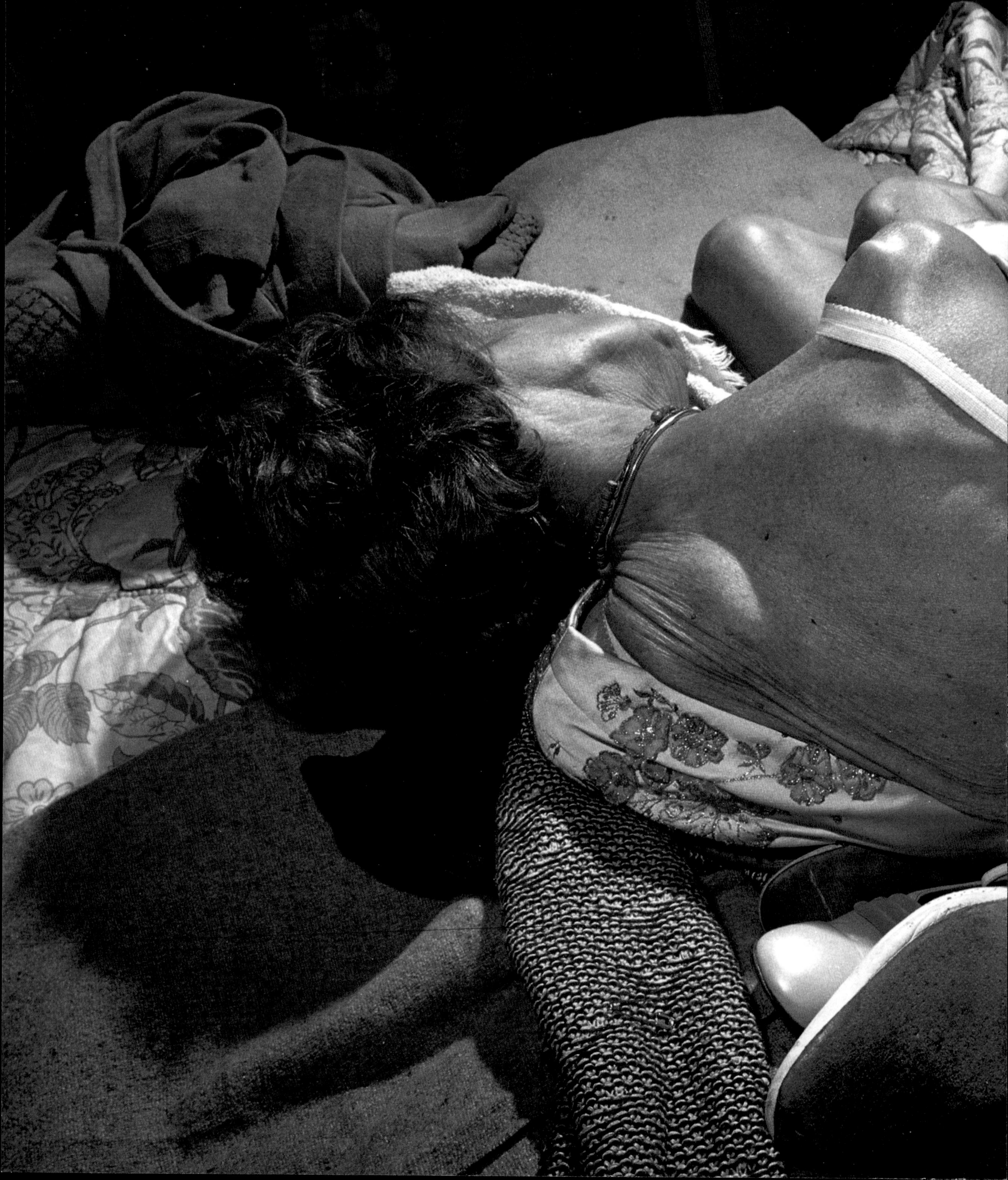

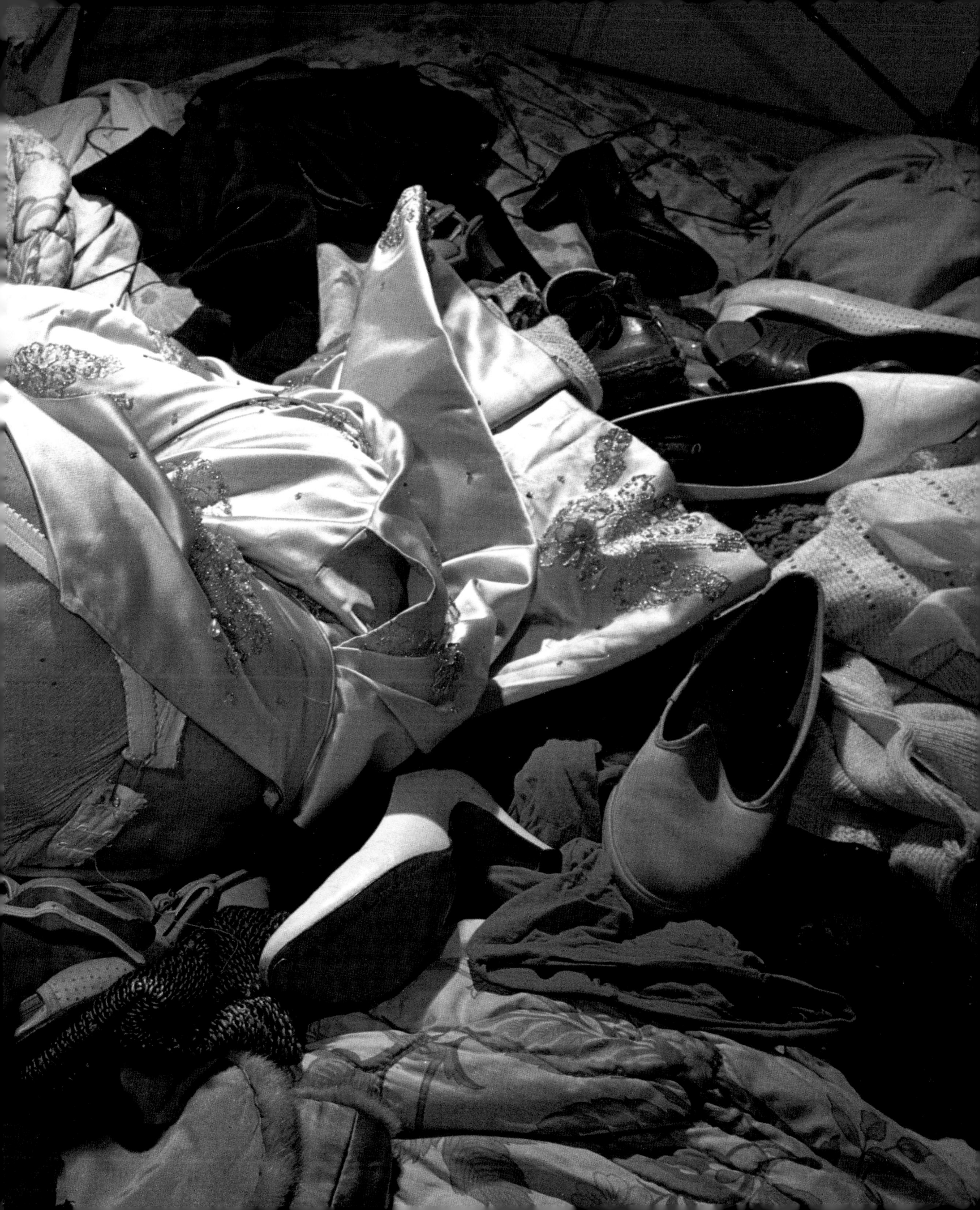

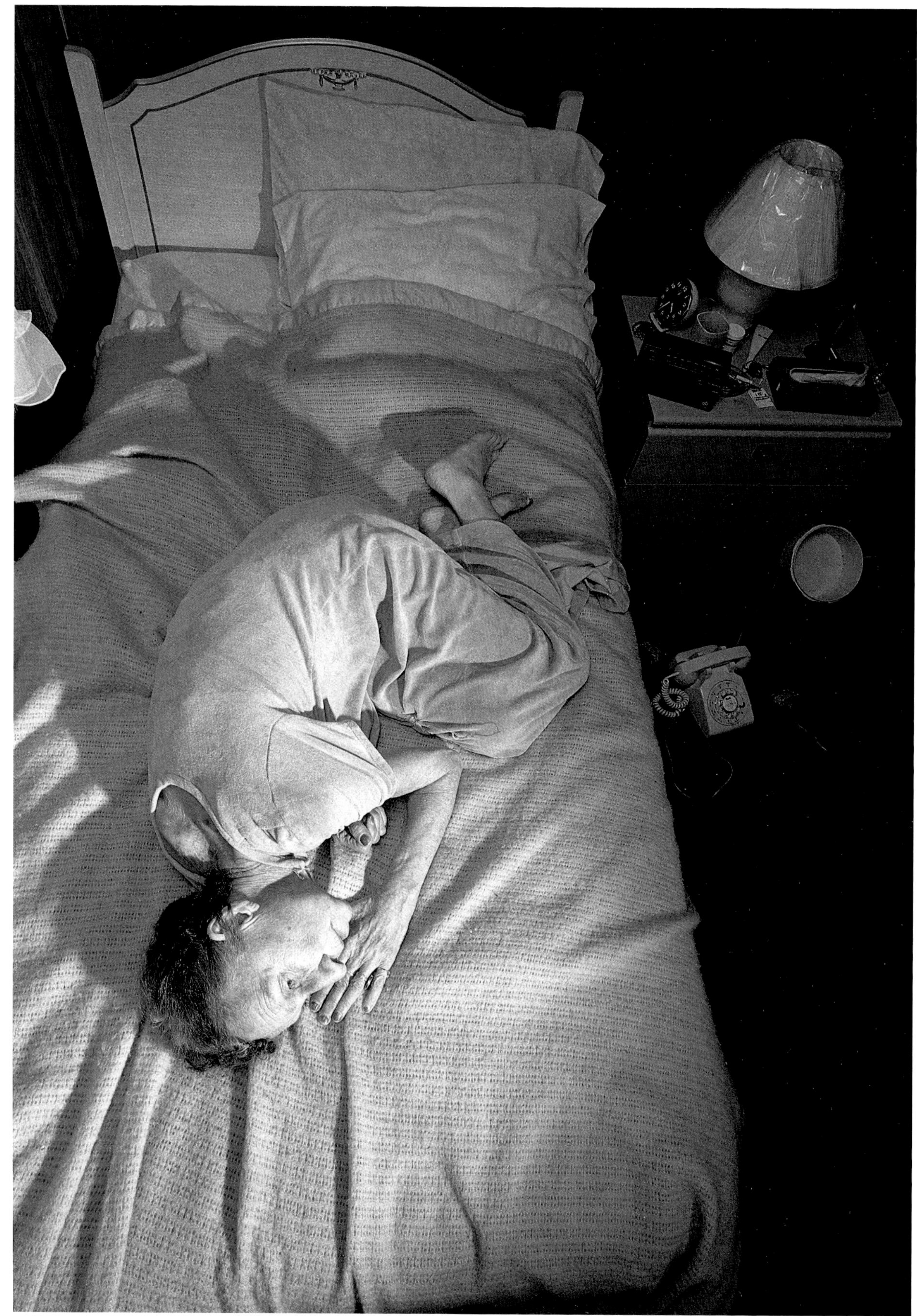



April 10, 1992

# *Appendix*

We have reprinted the following items for the benefit of readers who wish to know more about Nettie Harris. The first is an article ("Queen Sees Indians, Keeps Train Late") written by Nettie Harris herself for *The New York Times* in 1939. It is followed by the response printed in the same newspaper the next day. The last piece is her obituary from *The Gazette,* Montreal.

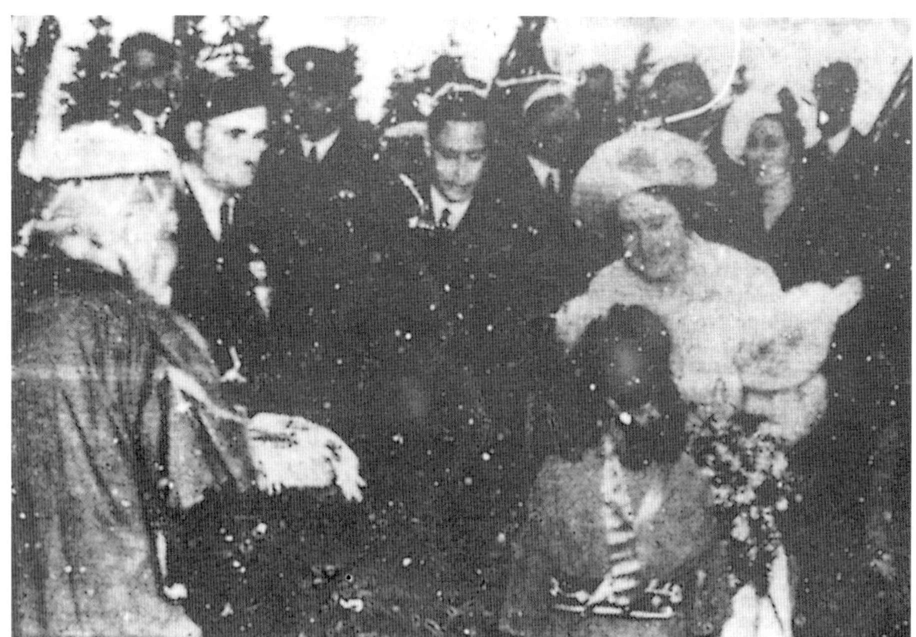

# QUEEN SEES INDIANS, KEEPS TRAIN LATE

## Delighted White River Elects a Mayor on the Spot to Act in Unexpected Visit

By **NETTIE NORMA MAGDER**
Special to THE NEW YORK TIMES.

WHITE RIVER, Ont., May 23.—The scene is the White River Railway Station, the coldest spot in Ontario. One hundred brown-skinned Indians with their wives and babies are there. One hundred and fifty school children from all sections of the wilderness are there. The 450 residents of White River are there, as are most of the residents of White River's sister railway town, Chapleau.

The temperature stands at 9 degrees above zero; there is half an inch of snow on the ground. The children hop from foot to foot trying to keep warm while they wave their flags.

The train is supposed to stop for twenty minutes for servicing. Speculation has been rife as to whether the King and Queen will step out on the observation platform and wave to the people of White River. A few of the committee on arrangements have dared to hope that the Queen will leave the train and get

**Continued on Page Twenty-seven**

# QUEEN HOLDS TRAIN TO GREET INDIANS

Continued From Page One

a little exercise on the boardwalk of the platform.

The people of White River have decorated their station with red, white and blue bunting, but there's no carpet on the depot boardwalk.

The royal train came streaming in, and this reporter stood on the station platform, hoping with the people of White River and Franz and Missanabie and Oba and Chapleau that the Queen would step out on the rear platform and wave.

### Queen Goes Among Crowd

Instead, she stepped down on the station platform and among the crowd, beckoning to King George to follow her. She stepped down that snowy boardwalk, and she wore no rubbers for she apparently didn't expect snow anywhere in Canada on May 23.

While her aides rushed fractically about, the Queen stepped down on the unpaved, muddy, cindery ground and talked to the people of White River.

One of the aides had rushed out and asked for the Mayor of White River.

"They are getting off here," he announced to the flustered railway men. "Quick, get your Mayor and welcome them!"

"Why, we'll try and find him," said W. Aiken of the welcoming committee.

He knew that there is no Mayor of White River, for it is not an organized municipality. Then and there one of the quickest elections ever to take place in the United States or Canada took place on the White River platform. George Freethy, a returned soldier, was elected Mayor of White River.

While the election was going on in a hasty consultation of the committee, the King and Queen were mingling freely with the awe-stricken and hushed people. The same aide came up to Mr. Aiken.

"For goodness' sakes, when is your Mayor coming," he asked. "Doesn't he know the King requires a welcome?"

"Here he is now. We found our Mayor," said Mr. Aiken, introducing Mr. Freethy.

In a gray suit and wearing a war veteran's beret, Mr. Freethy took over as Mayor. To him went the honor of escorting the King and Queen in and out among the citizens. Mr. Freethy rose to the occasion. He suggested to the sovereigns that if they required a little exercise they might walk to the end of the station platform.

### They Meet Engine Crew

"Why yes," said the Queen. "I haven't seen the engine that's drawing us yet. I'd love to see that."

She expressed a desire to meet the fireman and engineer of the train, and they were introduced to the royal pair. Walking back toward the car, the Queen spied an old Indian and his wife and stopped to talk. The squaw wore a checked dress, red bandana and mocassins. She carried a papoose in a cradle slung to her back.

"She asked me if I was born here, and if I liked to live here," the Indian, Michael Wissian, said later. "She asked me if the baby belonged to us and we told her no, that it was our grandson. My wife was standing beside me and does not understand English, only Indian. She asked my wife a few things, and I interpreted between my wife and the Queen. I feel very proud."

Eleven-year-old Pauline Adams then presented to the Queen a bouquet of May flowers arranged in a miniature canoe. Queen Elizabeth was so delighted that she asked to be introduced to the man who made the canoe, and so she met Herb McWatch, an Indian war veteran.

"She wanted to know how I made the canoe, and I told her it took three days, and that it was of birch bark," McWatch related. "Then she smiled at me and asked me what regiment I was in. When she smiled I felt funny all over."

The Queen talked to many of the school children. She singled out Hughetta Mulligan, 7, who told about it afterward.

"She asked me how old I am, and what class I'm in," Hughetta said.

The Queen stepped up to a school teacher, who is on crutches because he broke his leg in an accident about a month ago.

"Speaking to the Queen, ma'am," said the school teacher, "my wheels don't work so well," and she laughed, for she knew he was referring to his crutches.

### Indians Come From Distances

Some of the Indians came by canoe from 100 miles away to see the King and Queen. They had started for White River when no one was sure whether the royal train would even stop for servicing.

Michael Wissian had been trapping, and his son and daughter made a perilous canoe trip up forty miles of rapids to tell him the news. He immediately dropped his muskrat traps and got in the canoe with them.

Two other Indians paddled upstream all day yesterday to get here. Arriving, they found that the Bishop of Algoma was at Mowbray, an Indian village 100 miles west. They were torn between loyalty to their King and wish to see the Bishop. The King and Queen won when the Indians decided that their clothes were old and torn from the canoe trip, and in no condition for the Bishop of Algoma to see.

The royal train pulled out of White River eleven minutes late because the King and Queen were enjoying themselves. As the Queen boarded the train, the silence was broken by the cries of somebody's baby. "Poor little baby, I guess the crowds excite it," the Queen said, turning to the King.

The crowd found its voice and cheered until all were hoarse. A five-piece brass band struck up "God Save the King," and the frogs in the swamp back of the station took up a chorus.

Then every one went to the church supper and to the barn dance in Spadoni's Hall.

## REPORTER AT WHITE RIVER

White River, Ontario, burst upon our ken surprisingly Tuesday. The royal train had stopped there unexpectedly to be serviced and there were great doings. So from White River a lady, never before a correspondent of THE TIMES and unknown to anybody on it, telegraphed. Did THE TIMES want the story? It wanted it hard. The regular reporters were on the pilot train half an hour ahead of the royal train. We must depend upon Nettie Magder, the volunteer. The news room waited in hope, not unclouded by doubt. Would she be equal to the occasion or be a little flabbergasted by the sudden appearance of the royal visitors? Her dispatch turns up. Congratulations follow misgiving.

We see the Indians and their squaws and papooses. We almost feel the cold. Like the Queen, we have no rubbers, tramping through the mud and snow. The royal aide asking for the Mayor (possibly he expected that the little village had a Lord Mayor with robes and chains); the villagers with frontier readiness and humor electing a war veteran who shows perfect ease and tact; the Queen making herself at home with school children, Indians, everybody; the school teacher on crutches who tells the Queen that his "wheels don't work so well"; the canoeing Indians who persuade themselves that their clothes are too soiled to allow them to appear before the Bishop and so attend the royal show; the five-piece band that strikes up "God Save the King" as the train, eleven minutes late, leaves the station and the frogs make antiphone—the story is full, hearty, entire.

It was a great day for the King and Queen and all lucky enough to be there. And "then every one went to the church supper and to the barn dance in Spa[illegible]i's Hall." It is a grand yarn. As believers in the theory that reporters are born as well as made, we should like to hear that Nettie Magder was an amateur. We learn, however, that she is a free lance and a special correspondent of The Toronto Daily Star. She lives in Sudbury, 280 miles from White River.

OBITUARY

# Veteran newspaper, magazine writer also made name as model, actress

Nettie Magder Harris made a name for herself as a journalist, actress and model, but she will likely be remembered as "a person who couldn't be reinvented."

Mrs. Harris died Sunday morning at the age of 81.

Although in failing health, the past two weeks found her working on a video by director Bruno Carrière titled A Session with Nettie and planning to interview fellow residents of her nursing home for their monthly newsletter.

"She was waiting for a manual typewriter. She was blind in one eye and couldn't read a computer screen," but as a touch typist could still go to town, her son Leon Harris said yesterday.

Mrs. Harris, who was married to Ted Harris, the late editor of the defunct Montreal Herald, is survived by three children: Leon, Lewis Harris and Rosa Harris-Adler, all of whom are journalists.

In her late 60s, Mrs. Harris became interested in filmmaking and, in a bid to learn more about Quebec films, worked as a movie extra.

She came to know virtually everyone in the Canadian movie business, Montreal photographer Donigan Cumming said.

"She was very remarkable and people noticed her," he said.

Mrs. Harris worked as a model for Cumming in various projects, notably the Pretty Ribbons series that toured Canada and is part of the current Cent Jours d'Art Contemporain de Montréal.

"I never met anybody like Nettie and I don't think I will again," Cumming said.

"She was a person who can't be reinvented," her daughter-in-law Marian Scott said.

Family and friends attributed much of her character to her roots. Born the second-eldest in a family of 11 children, Mrs. Harris grew up in Sudbury, Ont., a mining town of few Jewish families.

She worked as a stringer for the Toronto Star during the 1930s and 1940s. She also sold freelance stories to other Canadian and U.S. papers.

At a time when most of the few female journalists wore white gloves and wrote about tea socials, Mrs. Harris had an exclusive story for the Toronto Star about the mysterious death of a tycoon.

Don Dodge died under questionable circumstances while fishing in northern Ontario during a period when he and his brothers were fighting for control of the Dodge empire, Mrs. Harris's family recalled yesterday.

Not only did Mrs. Harris get the story, she managed – by some admirable ploy or another – to tie up the telegraph lines, thereby ensuring her paper had a scoop.

Mrs. Harris met her husband at a Montreal city council meeting they both were covering. After her husband's death, she worked part time as a researcher for CTV and wrote for various newspapers and magazines.

Funeral services were held yesterday.

## Biography

Donigan Cumming is a photographic artist whose powerful use of the medium incorporates sound, video and installation. Major exhibitions of his work have been presented in numerous centres, including Vancouver, New York, Paris, Chicago, Boston, Montreal, Toronto, Berlin, Cologne, Amsterdam and Glasgow. Publications to date include *Reality and Motive in Documentary Photography* (1986), *The Stage* (1991) and *Diverting the Image* (1993). His work is represented in national museum collections of photography and contemporary art in Belgium, Britain, Canada, Denmark, France and the United States. Cumming has been a fellow of the National Endowment for the Arts (NEA) and the Guggenheim Foundation, and has received senior arts awards from the Canada Council and the Conseil des arts du Québec.

## Solo Exhibitions

**1996**

Musée de l'Elysée Lausanne, Lausanne, Switzerland

**1995**

Cumming, Donigan. *La Répétition,* FRAC Lorraine/Galerie Poirel, Nancy, France. Brochure (artist's statement)

*Donigan Cumming,* Galerie Pons, Paris

*Harry's Diary: Extracts from Pretty Ribbons,* Fotofeis '95, Tramway Gallery, Glasgow, Scotland

*La Répétition,* FRAC Lorraine/Galerie Poirel, Nancy, France

*Extracts from Pretty Ribbons,* (Alter) Ego Documents, De Praktijk Gallery and De Melkweg Gallery, Amsterdam, The Netherlands

**1994**

*Pretty Ribbons,* Les Rencontres Internationales de la Photographie, Arles, France. Catalogue

*Harry's Diary: Extracts from Pretty Ribbons,* Bravin Post Lee Gallery, New York

*Harry's Diary: Extracts from Pretty Ribbons,* Genereux Grunwald Gallery, Toronto, Ontario

**1993**

*Donigan Cumming: Diverting the Image,* Les cent jours d'art contemporain, Montreal, Quebec

*Donigan Cumming: Diverting the Image,* Art Gallery of Windsor, Windsor, Ontario. Catalogue

**1992**

*The Mirror, The Hammer and The Stage,* Photographic Resource Center, Boston, Massachusetts

**1991**

Glendon Gallery, York University, Toronto, Ontario

**1990**

*The Mirror, The Hammer and The Stage,* The Museum of Contemporary Photography, Chicago, Illinois

The Floating Gallery & Main/Access Gallery, Winnipeg, Manitoba

**1989**

XYZ Fotografie vzw, Gent, Belgium

**1988**

Musée de la Photographie, Charleroi, Belgium

Gallery Connexion & New Brunswick Craft School Gallery, Fredericton, New Brunswick

*Selections from work in progress for The Mirror, The Hammer and The Stage,* Grunwald & Watterson Gallery, Toronto, Ontario

Richard F. Brush Gallery, Canton, New York

**1987**

Université Laval, Quebec, Quebec

Photographers Gallery, Saskatoon, Saskatchewan

**1986**

*La Réalité et le Dessein dans la Photographie Documentaire,* Centre National de la Photographie, Paris, France. Exhibition produced by the Canadian Museum of Contemporary Photography. Catalogue

*Reality and Motive in Documentary Photography 1 & 2,* O. K. Harris, New York

*Reality and Motive in Documentary Photography 3,* 49th Parallel, New York

*Selections from Reality and Motive 1 & 2,* Grunwald Gallery, Toronto, Ontario

Blue Sky Gallery, Portland, Oregon

**1985**

Glengarry Historical Society, Cornwall, Ontario

Coburg Gallery, Vancouver, British Columbia

**1984**

University of Ottawa, Ottawa, Ontario

**1983**

*Selections from Reality and Motive 1,* The Photography Gallery, Toronto, Ontario

Bourget Gallery, Montreal, Quebec

**1978**

*Boxing,* Photo Progression, Montreal, Quebec

*Portraits of Men (as C. D. Battey),* Photo Progression, Montreal, Quebec

*Gardens (as Georgia Freeman),* Photo Progression, Montreal, Quebec

**1974**

*Hommage to John Marlowe (as John Marlowe),* Photo Progression, Montreal, Quebec

## Selected Group Exhibitions

**1995**

*Obsessions: From Wunderkammer to Cyberspace,* Foto Biennale Enschede, Rijksmuseum Twenthe, Enschede, The Netherlands. Catalogue

*The Dead,* National Museum of Photography, Film and Television, Bradford, England. Exhibition touring in Europe through 1997. Catalogue

*Collection célébration,* Centre international d'art contemporain, Montreal, Quebec

*Acte photographique, art contemporain,* Maison de la culture Frontenac, Montreal, Quebec

*The Body/Le Corps: Contemporary North American Art,* Lutz Teutloff Modern Art, Cologne, Germany

*Still Life, Portrait, Landscape,* Bravin Post Lee Gallery, New York

**1994**

*Animalia,* Galerie Pons, Paris

*The Body/Le Corps,* Kunsthalle Bielefeld, Bielefeld, Germany. Exhibition touring in Germany: Haus am Waldsee, Berlin. Catalogue

*Auction of Fine Art Photographs,* Photographic Resource Center, Boston, Massachusetts. Catalogue

**1993**

*Site Survey,* Canadian Museum of Contemporary Photography, Ottawa, Ontario

*Observing Traditions: Contemporary Photography 1975–1993,* National Gallery of Canada, Ottawa, Ontario

**1992**

*Women Photographed 1849–1988,* National Gallery of Canada, Ottawa, Ontario

Genereux Grunwald Gallery, Toronto, Ontario

*Real Stories: Revisions in Documentary and Narrative Photography,* Museet for Fotokunst, Odense, Denmark. Exhibition touring in Scandinavia and Europe: Norrköpings Konstmuseum, Norrköping, Sweden; Aineen Taidemuseo, Tornio, Finland; Fotomuseum Winterthur, Winterthur, Switzerland; Museum Folkwang, Essen, Germany. Catalogue

*Beau: a reflection on the nature of beauty in photography,* Canadian Museum of Contemporary Photography, Ottawa, Ontario. Exhibition travelling to Mois de la Photo à Paris, Centre culturel canadien, Paris. Catalogue

**1991**

*Découvertes,* Grand Palais, Paris

*Portraits, autoportrait et représentation(s),* Galerie Photogramme, Montreal, Quebec

**1990**

*Strip-Tease de l'intime,* Mois de la Photo à Paris, Galerie Urbi et Orbi, Paris. Catalogue Mois de la Photo à Paris

*Op-Positions: commitment and cultural identity in contemporary photography from Japan, Canada, Brazil, The Soviet Union and The Netherlands,* Fotografie Biënnale 2, Rotterdam, The Netherlands. Catalogue

*Public Exposures: One Decade,* Toronto Photographers Workshop, Toronto, Ontario. Catalogue

Grünwald Gallery, Toronto, Ontario

**1989**

*Culture Medium,* International Center of Photography, New York. Catalogue

*Faire image: penser la photographie,* Mirabile Visu; la photographie 150 ans après, Musée de la civilisation, Quebec, Quebec. Exhibition initiated by VU, touring in Quebec through 1992. Catalogue

*Zones Critiques,* Mois de la Photo à Montréal, Maison de la Culture Mercier, Montreal, Quebec. Catalogue

*What is Photography?,* Manes Center, Union of Czechoslovak Creative Artists, Prague, Czechoslovakia. Catalogue

Krakow Gallery, Polish Art Photographers Association, Krakow, Poland

*Interiors,* Concordia Art Gallery, Montreal, Quebec

*Power Plays: Contemporary Photography from Canada,* Stills Gallery, Edinburgh, Scotland. Exhibition touring in U.K.: Canada House, London, Great Britain; Fotogallery, Cardiff, Wales; Impressions Gallery, York, Great Britain; Posterngate Gallery, Hull, Great Britain; MacRobert Arts Centre, Stirling, Scotland; Duncan of Jordanstone College of Art, Dundee, Scotland; Eden Court Theatre, Inverness, Scotland. Catalogue

Artunion, Budapest, Hungary

**1988**

*Vivre Longtemps,* Musée de la civilisation, Quebec, Quebec. Exhibition touring in Quebec through 1991. Catalogue

Art Gallery of Ontario, Toronto, Ontario

Ogilvy (International Physicians for the Prevention of Nuclear War World Congress), Montreal, Quebec

Bányászati Museum, Sopron, Hungary

*Photographic Truth,* The Bruce Museum, Greenwich, Connecticut. Catalogue

**1987**

*Foto(con)tekst,* Perspektief Gallery, Rotterdam, The Netherlands

*The Working Artist,* A Space Gallery, Toronto, Ontario. Touring exhibition. Catalogue

*Un si grand âge…,* Centre National de la Photographie, Paris. Touring exhibition. Catalogue

*Photographs from the Permanent Collection,* Concordia Art Gallery, Montreal, Quebec

**1986**

*Photography: Suggestions and Facts,* Mandeville Gallery, La Jolla, California

*Art Support,* Galerie John Schweitzer, Montreal, Quebec

**1985**

*Contemporary Canadian Photography,* National Gallery of Canada, Ottawa, Ontario

*Portraits,* Galerie Articule, Montreal, Quebec

**1984**

*Contemporary Canadian Photography from the National Film Board,* Edmonton Art Gallery, Edmonton, Alberta

Photographers Gallery, Saskatoon, Saskatchewan

**1983**

Photo Union Gallery, Hamilton, Ontario

*Fait,* Galerie Articule, Montreal, Quebec

*Document: Aspects of Canadian Life,* The Photo Gallery, National Film Board, Ottawa, Ontario. Exhibition touring in Canada and United States through 1987: Winnipeg Art Gallery, Winnipeg, Manitoba, 1985; New Brunswick Craft School, Fredericton, New Brunswick, 1985; Dalhousie Art Gallery, Halifax, Nova Scotia, 1986; Art Gallery of Hamilton, Hamilton, Ontario, 1986; Watson Gallery, Houston, Texas, 1986; Musée du Québec, Quebec, 1987

## Lectures and Symposia

**1995**

Viewpoint Photography Gallery, Salford, England (artist lecture)

Galerie Poirel, Nancy, France (gallery talk)

Fotocafé, Amsterdam, The Netherlands (lecture, panellist)

Sint Joost Academy, Breda, The Netherlands (visiting artist lecture)

**1994**

Les Rencontres Internationales de la Photographie, Arles, France (artist lecture)

University of Guelph, Ontario (gallery talk at Genereux Grunwald Gallery, Toronto, Ontario)

**1993**

Saidye Bronfman Center, Montreal, Quebec (visiting artist lecture)

Les cent jours d'art contemporain, Montreal, Quebec (gallery talk)

Art Gallery of Windsor, Windsor, Ontario (gallery talk)

Concordia University, Department of Fine Arts, Montreal, Quebec: 1993, 1990, 1989, 1988, 1984 (visiting artist lecture)

**1992**

Photographic Resource Center at Boston University, Boston, Massachusetts (gallery talk)

**1991**

University of Florida, Department of Fine Arts, Gainesville, Florida (visiting artist, lecture)

**1990**

*Debate on Issues in Contemporary Photography,* presented by The Floating Gallery and Main/Access Gallery, Winnipeg, Manitoba (lecture, panellist)

*Op-Positions: Commitment and Cultural Identity in Contemporary Photography from Brazil, Canada, Japan, The Soviet Union and The Netherlands,* Symposium, Erasmus University, Fotografie Biënnale 2, Rotterdam, The Netherlands (lecture)

*Words of Vision Series,* The Museum of Contemporary Photography Columbia College Chicago, Chicago, Illinois (lecture, gallery talk)

**1989**

*Photography in Canada and Scotland,* open forum discussion, Stills, The Scottish Photography Group Gallery, Edinburgh, Scotland (panellist)

XYZ Fotografie vzw, Gent, Belgium (two-day workshop)

**1984**

University of Ottawa, Department of Fine Arts, Ottawa, Ontario (visiting artist lecture)

## Collections

Art Gallery of Windsor, Windsor, Ontario

Bibliothèque Nationale, Paris

Canada Council Art Bank, Ottawa, Ontario

Canadian Museum of Contemporary Photography, Ottawa, Ontario

Fond nationale d'art contemporain (FNAC), Paris

Leonard and Bina Ellen Art Gallery, Concordia University, Montreal, Quebec

Maison Européenne de la Photographie, Paris

Musée de la Photographie, Charleroi, Belgium

Museet For Fotokunst, Odense, Denmark

National Gallery of Canada, Ottawa, Ontario

National Museum of American Art, Washington, D.C.

National Museum of Photography, Film and Television, Bradford, England

The Museum of Fine Arts, Houston, Texas

Winnipeg Art Gallery, Winnipeg, Manitoba

## Major Awards

**1988, 1993, 1995**
Ministère des Affaires culturelles, Quebec, Grant "A"

**1990, 1991, 1993**
Canada Council, Arts Grant "A"

**1984**
John Simon Guggenheim Memorial Foundation Fellowship, New York

**1980**
Photographers' Fellowship, National Endowment for the Arts, Washington, D.C.

## Education

**1985**
M.F.A. (Master of Fine Arts), Concordia University, Montreal, Quebec

**1978**
B.Sc. (Bachelor of Science), Florida State University, Tallahassee, Florida

## Books

**1994**
Lavoie, Vincent. *Dictionnaire mondial de la photographie.* Paris: Larousse, p. 160.

**1992**
Roegiers, Patrick. "Autobiographie au Québec" in: *L'Œil multiple.* Paris: Editions La Manufacture, pp. 245–248.

**1991**
Cumming, Donigan. *The Stage.* Montreal: Maquam Press.

Marcus, Greil. "The Last Breakfast" in: *Dead Elvis.* New York: Doubleday, p. 79.

**1990**
Bogardi, Georges. "In Camera: The Photography of Donigan Cumming" in: *Thirteen Essays on Photography.* Ottawa: Canadian Museum of Contemporary Photography, pp. 66–78.

Bogardi, Georges. "Dans l'intimité: les photographies de Donigan Cumming" in: *Treize essais sur la photographie.* Ottawa: Musée canadien de la photographie contemporaine, pp. 72–86.

Cumming, Donigan. "Statement: Donigan Cumming" in: *The Position of contemporary photography within the media, the art world and historiography,* p. 6. Collection of texts in Dutch and English printed for a symposium held on August 30 & 31, during the Fotografie Biënnale 2, Rotterdam, 1990.

Herst, Deanna. "Introductie Donigan Cumming" in: *The Position of contemporary photography within the media, the art world and historiography,* p. 6.

**1988**
Canadian Museum of Contemporary Photography. Travelling exhibitions catalogue. Ottawa: Canadian Museum of Contemporary Photography.

**1984**
National Film Board. Travelling exhibitions catalogue. Ottawa: National Film Board of Canada.

Contemporary Canadian Photography from the Collection of the National Film Board. National Film Board of Canada Still Photography Division. Edmonton: Hurtig Publishers, p. 162.

## Catalogues

**1993**
*Donigan Cumming: Diverting the Image.* Windsor: Art Gallery of Windsor. Accompanied by a compact disc: "Donigan Cumming: Installation Soundtracks 1986–1993", 76:02 min.

**1986**
*Reality and Motive in Documentary Photography.* Ottawa: Canadian Museum of Contemporary Photography.

## Texts in Catalogues

**1995**
Cousineau, Penny. "Post-post" in: *L'éternel et l'éphémère.* Le Mois de la Photo à Montréal. Montreal: Vox Populi, pp. 14–22.

Williams, Val. "Secret Places" in: *The Dead.* Bradford: The National Museum of Photography, Film and Television, pp. 9–17.

"Donigan Cumming" in: *Fotofeis '95.* International Festival of Photography in Scotland, October 5 – November 5, pp. 36–37.

**1994**
Herzog, Hans-Michael. "The Body/Le Corps" and "Donigan Cumming" in: *The Body/Le Corps.* Kilchberg/Zurich: Edition Stemmle and Kunsthalle Bielefeld, Bielefeld, pp. 7–15 and 16–19.

"Donigan Cumming" in: *L'Officiel des Rencontres.* Arles: 25ème Rencontres Internationales de la Photographie, July 5 – August 15, p. 11.

**1993**
Gingras, Nicole. "Disquieting Poses" in: *Donigan Cumming: Diverting the Image.* Windsor: Art Gallery of Windsor, pp. 32–50.

Roegiers, Patrick. "A Descent into the Hell of Donigan Cumming" in: *Donigan Cumming: Diverting the Image.* Windsor: Art Gallery of Windsor, pp. 53–61. Reprinted in L'Œil complice as "Une descente aux enfers". Paris: Editions Marval, pp. 101–109.

Roegiers, Patrick. "La singularité est-elle indécente?: A propos de Diane Arbus et Donigan Cumming" in: *La photographie inquiète de ses marges.* Actes du Colloque, March 14 & 15, 1992. Le Triangle Rennes: Centre Culturel Triangle, pp. 31–38.

**1992**

Langford, Martha. (Afterword in English and French) in: *Beau: a reflection on the nature of beauty in photography.* Canadian Museum of Contemporary Photography.

Lundström, Jan-Erik. "Real Stories" in: *Real Stories.* Odense: Museet for Fotokunst, pp. 2–10; 66. Reprinted in Danish and English: "Virkelige Historier Real Stories". Catalogue, vol. 4, no. 4, June, pp. 4–18.

**1990**

Brilliant, Richard. "Portraits: A Recurrent Genre in World Art" in: *Likeness and Beyond: Portraits from Africa and the World.* New York: The Center for African Art, pp. 11–29.

Buchanan, Hamish and Levitt, Nina. "On Mapping a Decade" in: *Public Exposures: One Decade of Contemporary Canadian Photography, 1980–1990.* Toronto: Toronto Photographers Workshop, pp. 47–53.

Wollheim, Peter. "A Short History of Documentary Photography" in: *Public Exposures: One Decade of Contemporary Canadian Photography, 1980–1990.* Toronto: Toronto Photographers Workshop, pp. 21–26.

**1989**

Langford, Martha. "An Interview with Martha Langford" in: *Le Mois de la Photo à Montréal.* Montreal: Vox Populi, pp. 118–119; 202.

Powell, Rob. (Introduction) in: *Power Plays: Contemporary Photography from Canada.* Edinburgh: Stills Gallery, pp. 3–5.

Stainback, Charles. *Culture Medium.* New York: International Center of Photography.

**1986**

Bogardi, Georges. *Donigan Cumming: Reality and Motive in Documentary Photography, Part 3.* Exhibition brochure, New York: 49th Parallel.

Graham, Robert. "Documentary and the Powers of Description" in: *Reality and Motive in Documentary Photography.* Ottawa: Canadian Museum of Contemporary Photography, pp. 6–13.

Langford, Martha. "Donigan Cumming: Crossing Photography's Chalk Lines" in: *Reality and Motive in Documentary.* Ottawa: Canadian Museum of Contemporary Photography, pp. 14–36.

**1983**

Barbour, David. *Document: Aspects of Canadian Life.* Exhibition brochure, Ottawa: National Film Board of Canada.

## Selected Articles in Periodicals

**1995**

Boecker, Susanne. "Klare Form für das Chaos der Gefühle" in: *Kölner Stadt-Anzeiger,* Cologne, no. 80, April 4, p. 21.

Chapuis, Frédérique. "La vieille dame modèle" in: *Télérama,* Paris, no. 2364, May 3, p. 32.

D. R. "Nancy censure la photo de Nettie, affiche d'exposition" in: *Libération. Le Magazine,* Paris, April 21, p. 42.

Laurence, Robin. "Singing the Body Eclectic" in: *Border Crossings,* Winnipeg, vol. 14, no. 2, April, pp. 62–65.

McConaughy, Claire. "Still-Life Portrait Landscape" in: *Flash Art,* May–June, p. 70.

Menu, Frédéric. "La répétition choc de Donigan Cumming" in: *L'Est Républicain Nancy-Meurthe-et-Moselle,* April 19, p. 1.

Schroeder, Annette. "Blick auf den alten Körper" in: *Kölnische Rundschau,* Cologne, no. 81, April 5.

Schwartz, Ineke. "Openhartig, analytisch, aangrijpend en dicht-bij-huis" in: *de Volkskrant,* February 6.

Steenbergen, Renée. "Verrassende ego-documenten van filmers en fotografen" in: *NRC Handelsblad,* February 4, p. 7.

**1994**

"Etat des lieux avant la fermeture" in: *Le Provencal,* August 10.

Baqué, Dominique. "Réflexions sur l'irregardable" in: *Le Monde,* Paris, June 30, Arts & Spectacles, p. 2.

Baqué, Dominique. "Variations pour monochromes blancs" in: *art press,* no. 195, October, p. 72.

Bellavance, Guy. "Donigan Cumming: Centre international d'art contemporain de Montréal" in: *Parachute,* no. 73, January/February/March, pp. 42–44.

Chapuis, Frédérique. "La féria des images" in: *Télérama,* Paris, no. 2325, August 3, pp. 26–27.

Cron, Marie-Michèle. "La fonction sociale du photographe" in: *ETC Montréal,* Montreal, no. 25, February 15–May 15, pp. 35–38.

Debraine, Luc. "En Arles, la photographie met au défi le regard du spectateur" in: *Le Nouveau Quotidien,* July 12.

E. F. "Arles rénove ses murs mais pas ses structures" in: *Le Journal des Arts,* Paris, no. 6, September, p. 16.

Gingras, Nicole. "Donigan Cumming: Le Journal de Harry" in: *CV Photo,* Montreal, Summer, p. 19. English Translation, p. 26.

Kurzhals, Frank G. "Die Meta-Erotik: Ausstellung in Bielefeld kündet vom neuen Körperbewußtsein" in: *Hannoversche Allgemeine Zeitung,* Hanover, September 28.

Lepik, Andres. "Körper-Bilder: Kanadische Photographie in Berlin" in: *Neue Zürcher Zeitung,* Zurich, November 12, p. 31.

Morose, Edward. "The Social Art of Conscience" in: *Blackflash,* Saskatoon, vol. 12, no. 2, Summer, pp. 4–6; 17–18.

Ramspacher, Marie-Sophie. "Donigan Cumming: le troisième sexe" in: *Université jeune journaliste magazine,* July, p. 5.

Strecker, Manfred. "Stadtwerke plakatieren in Bus und Bahn nicht: Körperkunst eckt an" in: *Neue Westfälische,* Bielefeld, July 29.

Tessmar-Pfohl, Catherine. "Lieber nur halbe Plakate bestellen" in: *Frankfurter Allgemeine Zeitung,* Frankfurt (Main), September 30, no. 228, p. 43.

Tremblay, Odile. "De Glenn Gould à Rascar Capac: Séance avec Nettie" in: *Le Devoir,* Montreal, February 8.

**1993**

Aquin, Stéphane. "Un monde sans pitié" in: *Voir,* Montreal, vol. 7, no. 38, August 19–25, p. 21.

Baillargeon, Stéphane. "Cent jours sans installations" in: *Le Devoir,* Montreal, July 29, p. C14.

Bissonnette, Lise. "Méditation en catacombes" in: *Le Devoir,* Montreal, vol. 84, no. 188, August 16.

Campeau, Sylvain. "Diverting the Image/Donigan Cumming/Détournements de l'image" in: *Parachute,* no. 71, July/August/September.

Cron, Marie-Michèle. "Au pays des anti-héros" in: *Le Devoir,* Montreal, September 11 & 12, p. C14.

Cron, Marie-Michèle. "Les coups de foudre absolus" in: *Le Devoir,* Montreal, December 31, p. C10.

Duncan, Ann. "Arresting Images" in: *The Gazette,* Montreal, August 7, p. G2.

Jones, Owen. "A New Wrinkle to Art" in: *The Windsor Star,* February 19, p. B1.

Laurence, Robin. "Docu-Dismantler" in: *Border Crossings,* Winnipeg, vol. 12, no. 1, February, pp. 58–59.

Legrand, Jean-Pierre. "La mise à nu: travestissement et dévoilement" in: *Vie des Arts,* Montreal, vol. 28, no. 152, Fall, pp. 28–33.

Lepage, Jocelyne. "Sexe, femmes et horreur" in: *La Presse,* Montreal, August 7, pp. D1–D2.

Mayrand, Céline. "Parcours d'ici et d'ailleurs" in: *Parcours Arts Visuel,* no. 11, Fall, p. 61.

Quine, Dany. "Sous le signe de la provocation" in: *Le Soleil,* Quebec, August 7, p. G7.

Roegiers, Patrick. "Donigan Cumming ethnologue iconoclaste" in: *art press,* no. 176, January, pp. 38–41. English Translation, pp. E21–E23.

Skene, Cameron. "100 days of sodom" in: *Hour,* Montreal, vol. 1, no. 27, August 5–11, p. 18.

Vaillancourt, Julie. "Cumming le provocateur" in: *MTL,* Montreal, Summer, pp. 39–40.

**1992**

"The Mirror, The Hammer and The Stage" in: *PRC Newsletter,* Photographic Resource Center, Boston, vol. 16, no. 6, September.

Baele, Nancy. "A snapshot of Canadian imagination" in: *The Ottawa Citizen,* Ottawa, May 11, p. B10. Reprinted in: *The Gazette,* Montreal: "Canada's photo collection finds a home: Ottawa railway tunnel has been transformed into elegant museum", May 16, p. J1.

Coleman, A. D. "Up Canada Way: Mois de la Photo à Montréal" in: *European Photography,* vol. 13, no. 49, issue 1, Winter, pp. 9–11.

Wise, Kelly. "Pumping up the drama" in: *The Boston Globe,* Boston, September 22, p. 35.

**1991**

Bauret, Gabriel. "Joseph Koudelka, Prix HCB" in: *Photographies Magazine,* no. 34, Summer, pp. 30–31.

Byrnes, Terry. "Stage Fright" in: *Photo Life,* vol. 16, no. 9, November, pp. 6–7.

Ellis, Scott. "Lines of Photographic History" in: *Border Crossings,* Winnipeg, vol. 10, no. 1, January, pp. 50–52.

Enright, Robert. "Dressing Up, Dressing Down" in: *Border Crossings,* Winnipeg, vol. 10, no. 1, January, p. 5.

Enright, Robert. "Pretty Ribbons: Photographs by Donigan Cumming" in: *Border Crossings,* Winnipeg, vol. 10, no. 1, January, pp. 25–33.

Hodgert, John. "The Many Faces of Vulnerability" (letter to the editor) in: *Border Crossings,* Winnipeg, vol. 10, no. 2, April, pp. 65–66.

Lawrence, P. Scott. "Photos give underclass a voice" in: *The Gazette,* Montreal, November 16, p. K2.

Lundström, Jan-Erik. "Fotografie Biënnale 2, Rotterdam: Op-Positions" in: *Perspektief,* no. 40, January, pp. 67–70. Text in English and Dutch.

Thijsen, Mirelle. "Op-Positions: Rotterdam's Second Biennial" in: *European Photography,* no. 45, vol. 12, January/February/March, pp. 13–15.

Wolfe, Morris. "Subject's voice strangely missing from 'collaboration'" in: *The Globe and Mail,* Toronto, February 28, p. A10.

**1990**

Byrnes, Terry. "Taking Photography to Pieces" in: *Photo Life,* vol. 15, no. 2, March, pp. 2–18.

Campeau, Sylvain. "Espaces révélateurs: là, au travers, hors de là et retour" in: *Parachute,* no. 57, January/February/March, pp. 52–56.

Campeau, Sylvain. "L'absolument réel de la photographie" in: *ETC Montréal,* Montreal, no. 11, Spring/Summer, pp. 45–47.

Cuvelier, Pascaline. "Strip Thèse" in: *Libération,* Paris, November 26, pp. 42–43.

Davis, Tony. "Photography explores how lens can lie" in: *Winnipeg Free Press,* Winnipeg, October 15, p. 18.

Foerstner, Abigail. "Exhibits explore documentary art from four perspectives" in: *Chicago Tribune,* Chicago, February 16, Section 7, pp. 61–62.

Hlynsky, David. "Public Exposures: One Decade Mapping the Photo Ghetto" in: *Views,* vol. 7, no. 2, May, pp. 7–8.

McIlroy, Randal. "Photo images produce skepticism" in: *Winnipeg Free Press,* Winnipeg, October 20, p. 32.

Roegiers, Patrick. "Impasse et modernité du reportage – A Rotterdam, la 2e Biennale repose sur une exposition au concept original et provocant" in: *Le Monde,* Paris, September 7, p. 13. Reprinted in: *L'Œil multiple,* Paris, Editions La Manufacture, 1992, pp. 241–244.

Steketee, Hans. "Kijk, dit zijn alleen maar vlekken op het celluloid" in: *NRC Handelsblad,* September 6.

Vroege, Bas. "Mois de la Photo à Montréal" in: *Perspektief,* no. 38, May, p. 66. Text in Dutch and English.

**1989**

"'Culture Medium' On View Photography Center" in: *East Side Express,* New York, July 27, p. 15.

"Photography" in: *The New Yorker,* New York, August 28, p. 12.

Aletti. "Culture Medium" in: *The Village Voice,* New York, August, p. 47.

Berman, Arthur. "Images of the Brave New World" in: *TNT,* London, issue 294, April, p. 36.

Coleman, A. D. "Show at International Center Turns the News Into a Snooze" in: *The New York Observer,* New York, August, p. 17.

Dessureault, Pierre. "Quelques images de la collection du Musée canadien de la photographie contemporaine" in: *Summum,* Sainte-Foy, vol. 2, no. 3, April/May, pp. 14–19.

Gosselin, Gaétan. "Tactics and Strategies: The Question of Politics in Current Quebec Photography" in: *Blackflash,* Saskatoon, vol. 7, no. 4, pp. 3–9.

Grundberg, Andy. "Two Shows: One Works, the Other Bogs Down" in: *The New York Times,* New York, August 13, pp. 33–36.

Lipson, Karin. "Focusing in on Reality" in: *Newsday,* Long Island, July 21, pp. 18–20.

Henry, Claire. "Power Plays: Contemporary photography from Canada" in: *The Glasgow Herald,* Glasgow, February 3.

Macdonald, Murdo. "Disturbing challenges to documentary photography" in: *The Scotsman,* Edinburgh, January 17, p. 19.

Paquette, Annie. "Donigan Cumming at The Shooting Party" in: *ETC Montréal,* Montreal, no. 10, Winter, p. 57.

Sochor, Nicole. "Power in its many different faces" in: *Western Mail,* Cardiff, May 16.

Walther, Annie. "A Montréal: La Photographie Canadienne Contemporaine" in: *Photographies Magazine,* no. 17, November, pp. 33–34.

**1988**

"Donigan Cumming: Le mépris des frontières artificielles" in: *Photographie Ouverte* (newsletter: Musée de la Photographie Charleroi), Charleroi, no. 62, November/December, pp. 2–4.

"Au Musée de la Photographie de Charleroi, jusqu'au 31 décembre: Donigan Cumming: La Réalité et le Dessein dans la Photographie Documentaire" (communiqué), in: *La Wallonie,* Liège, December 2.

Bioncolli, Amy. "Odd Folks Focus of Exhibit" in: *Watertown Daily Times,* Watertown, January 6.

Bioncolli, Amy. "Photo Exhibit 'Shock Art'" in: *Watertown Daily Times,* Watertown, January 17.

Bogardi, Georges. "Donigan Cumming" in: *XYZ Fotografie vzw* (newsletter), Gent, first year, no. 3, December 1988/January 1989. Text in Dutch.

Eelbode, Erik in: *DE WITTE RAAF,* Gent, no. 15, November, p. 4. Text in Dutch.

Gibbs, Michael. "Documentary in a New Context" in: *Perspektief,* no. 31/32, April, pp. 46–56. Text in Dutch and English.

Gillemon, Daniele. "Donigan Cumming, photographe: le procès du 'naturel'" in: *Le Soir,* Brussels, November 24.

Hlynsky, David. "Donigan Cumming" in: *Views,* Photographers Workshop, Toronto, vol. 5, no. 1, May 19, p. 4.

Koch, Terry. "Exhibit at SLU Questions Photographic 'Reality'" in: *Watertown Daily Times,* Watertown, February 3.

Meuris, Jacques. "Les gens, le monde et le photographe" in: *La Libre Belgique,* Brussels, December 9, p. 20.

Sabat, Christina. "Visual Arts in Review" in: *The Daily Gleaner,* Fredericton, April 16, p. 11.

Sabat, Christina. "Cumming Photo Exhibit Elicits Strong Response" in: *The Daily Gleaner,* Fredericton, April 21.

Stevens, Fiona. "Documentary Photography Exhibit Opens at Brush Gallery" in: *The Hill News,* Canton, vol. 88, no. 1, February 12, p. 13.

**1987**

Baillargeon, Richard. "Le regard limitrophe de Donigan Cumming" in: *Photo Séléction,* July/August, pp. 39 & 54.

Boone, Danielle. "Photosocio" in: *Révolution,* Paris, no. 364, February 20/26, p. 49.

Bourcier, Noël. "Donigan Cumming: Palais de Tokyo (C.N.P.)" in: *art press,* no. 112, March, p. 80.

Burton, Randy. "Documentary Mode Re-examined" in: *Blackflash,* Saskatoon, vol. 5, no. 4, Summer, pp. 12–13.

L'Hostis, Nane. "Donigan Cumming" in: *Télérama,* Paris, January 14.

Mitchell, Michael. "Identifying Portraiture" in: *Photo Communiqué,* vol. 9, no. 3, Fall, p. 11.

Robertson, Sheila. "Ugly, exploitive photos offer warped perspective" in: *Star-Phoenix,* Saskatoon, August 29.

Roegiers, Patrick. "Donigan Cumming au Palais de Tokyo: l'insolite quotidien" in: *Le Monde,* Paris, January 7, p. 12. Reprinted in: *Les Cahiers de la Photographie,* L'Œil vivant, Paris, no. 21, 1988, pp. 101–102; partially reprinted in: *Vox Populi,* Le Mois de la Photo à Montréal, Montreal, 1989, p. 106.

Roegiers, Patrick. "Un si grand tort" in: *Le Monde,* Paris, April 15, p. 26.

Wollheim, Peter. "Cumming/Golberg/Woodman: Beyond Semiotics" in: *Photo Communiqué,* vol. 9, no. 2, Summer, pp. 9–21.

**1986**

Auf Der Maur, Nick. "Photographer of gloss fascinated by ordinary" in: *The Gazette,* Montreal, June 4, p. A2.

Bogardi, Georges. "The Dark Visions of Donigan Cumming" in: *Canadian Art,* vol. 3, no. 1, Spring, pp. 70–73.

Corbeil, Carole. "Exploring art's potential to refuse its viewers the privilege of control" in: *The Globe and Mail,* Toronto, May 29, p. E6.

Gagnon, Monika. "Abuse of the Title" in: *C Magazine,* no. 11, September, pp. 38–39.

Grundberg, Andy. "A New Breed Puts its Own Stamp on the Medium" in: *The New York Times,* New York, December 28, pp. 27–28.

Lugo, Mark-Elliot. "Photography: Suggestions and Facts" in: *The Tribune,* San Diego, October 10.

McDonald, Robert. "At the Galleries" in: *Los Angeles Times,* Los Angeles, October 24, pp. 17–18.

O'Reilly. "Donigan Cumming" in: *The Village Voice,* New York, June 17, p. 73.

Orsini, Françoise. "Donigan Cumming: Centre National de la Photographie Palais de Tokyo, Paris" in: *Des Arts,* Rennes, no. 5, Winter 1986/1987, p. 137.

**1985**

Johnson, Eve. "How the Poor Folk Live – an Unkind View" in: *The Vancouver Sun,* Vancouver, January 25, p. F1.

Wallace, Keith. "Donigan Cumming Photographs" in: *Issue,* Vancouver, vol. 2, no. 4, March/April, p. 36.

**1984**

Graham, Robert. "Donigan Cumming: Undoing Documentary" in: *Parachute,* no. 34, March/April/May, pp. 19–24.

Gutsche, Clara. "Open Parody, Hidden Agenda: Donigan Cumming" in: *Vanguard,* vol. 13, no. 4, May, pp. 21–25.

**1983**

St. Gelais, Thérèse. "Brian Collins, Donigan Cumming, Robert Ouellet" in: *Vanguard,* vol. 12, no. 9, November, pp. 43–44.

Wollheim, Peter. "Document: Aspects of Canadian Life" in: *Vanguard,* vol. 12, no. 7, September, pp. 42–43.

## Photography Reproduction

**1995**

Cumming, Donigan. "March 10, 1984", from the series Reality and Motive in Documentary Photography in: *International Center of Photography, Twenty Years 1974–1994,* p. 90.

Cumming, Donigan. "May 27, 1992"; "April 10, 1992", from the series Pretty Ribbons in: *Perspektief,* no. 49, Spring, pp. 26–27.

**1994**

Cumming, Donigan. "April 27, 1991", from the series Pretty Ribbons in: *Magazine Grec,* September, p. 42.

Cumming, Donigan. "Harry's Diary", from the series Pretty Ribbons in: *CV Photo,* Montreal, Summer, pp. 18–27.

Cumming, Donigan. "May 27, 1992", from the series Pretty Ribbons in: *Auction Catalogue of Fine Photographs Photographic Resource Center,* Boston, May, illustration no. 48.

Cumming, Donigan. "May 25, 1990", from the series Pretty Ribbons in: *Border Crossings,* Winnipeg, vol. 13, no. 2, April, p. 48.

**1993**

Cumming, Donigan. "April 27, 1991"; "August 24, 1989"; "May 31, 1989", from the series Pretty Ribbons in: *ViceVersa,* Montreal, no. 43, November/December, pp. 47–49.

Cumming, Donigan. "May 17, 1989", from the series Pretty Ribbons in: *Mirror,* Montreal, August 5–12, p. 12.

Cumming, Donigan. "April 27, 1991", from the series Pretty Ribbons in: *International Contract,* Toronto, vol. 2, no. 5, April/May, p. 58.

**1991**

Cumming, Donigan. "May 24, 1989", from the series Pretty Ribbons in: *La recherche photographique,* Paris, no. 11, December, pp. 112–113.

Cumming, Donigan. "March 15, 1988", from the series The Mirror, The Hammer and The Stage in: *Views: The Journal of Photography in New England,* vol. 12, no. 12, Spring, p. 22.

Cumming, Donigan. "December 24, 1982", from the series Reality and Motive in Documentary Photography in: *City & Country Home,* Toronto, vol. 10, no. 10, December, p. 87.

Cumming, Donigan. "August 30, 1989"; "February 7, 1989"; "April 11, 1990"; "May 24, 1989"; "August 24, 1989"; "June 4, 1985"; "May 25, 1990"; "June 8, 1990", from the series Pretty Ribbons in: *Border Crossings,* Winnipeg, vol. 10, no. 1, January, pp. 26–33.

**1989**

Cumming, Donigan. "November 16, 1986", from the series The Mirror, The Hammer and The Stage in: *Creative Camera,* May, p. 6.

**1985**

Cumming, Donigan. "November 18, 1984"; "March 20, 1984"; "June 5, 1984", from the series Reality and Motive in Documentary Photography in: *Artforum,* vol. 23, no. 5, February, pp. 66–68.

## Other Media

**1996**

*Photography in the 1990s* (CD-ROM publication). Dayton: Wright State University, February.

**1995**

*A Prayer For Nettie* (video). Montreal: Donigan Cumming. 1 cassette, 33 min., ½ in.

**1993**

Lehmann, Henry. "Daybreak" (review of *Donigan Cumming: Diverting the Image* at the Les cent jours d'art contemporain). Montreal: CBC Radio, August 18.

Cumming, Donigan. "Saturday Spotlight" (interview with Anne Dowson). Montreal: CBC Radio, July 31.

Cumming, Donigan. "Home Run" (interview with Maura Kealey). Montreal: CBC Radio, July 21.

*A Session With Nettie* (video). Montreal: Bruno Carrière, Les films de la cinétrie inc.. 1 cassette, 56:25 min., ½ in. (Séance avec Nettie, V.O. anglaise – S.-T. français).

Cumming, Donigan. "Stereo Morning" (interview with Bob Steele). Toronto: CBC Radio, February 2.

Enright, Robert. "Arts Tonight" (review of *Donigan Cumming: Diverting the Image* at the Windsor Art Gallery). Toronto: CBC Radio, March 10.

**1991**

*To See and be Seen: Contemporary Portraits* (video). Ottawa: Canadian Museum of Contemporary Photography. 1 cassette, 25 min., ½ in. (for educational purposes).

**1990**

Cumming, Donigan. "Arts Tonight" (interview with Robert Enright). Toronto: CBC Radio, October 24.

**1988**

*Fotofest '88* (video disk). Houston: Fotofest.

Translation from the German by John S. Southard
Editorial direction by Mirjam Ghisleni-Stemmle
Art direction and typography by Peter Renn, Teufen, Switzerland
Photolithography by Colorlito Rigogliosi S.r.l., Milan, Italy
Printed and bound by A.G.M. S.p.A., Arese (Milan), Italy

ISBN 3-905514-82-6 English Edition
ISBN 3-905514-81-8 German Edition